MW00811532

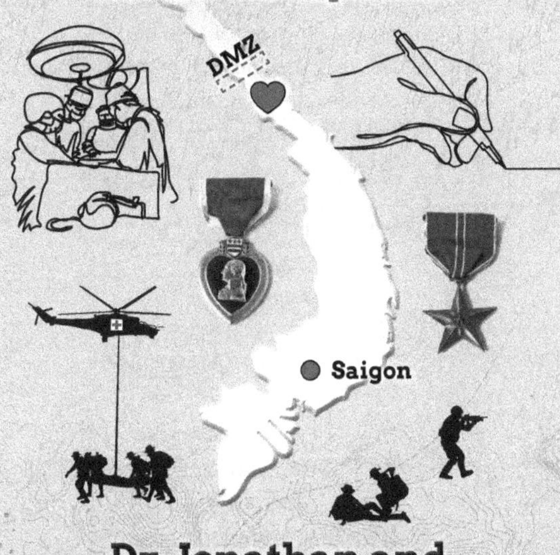
LETTERS FROM
THE HEART
A Young Army Doctor's 1969
Vietnam War Experience
DMZ
Saigon
Dr. Jonathan and
Sherrie Benumof

LETTERS FROM THE HEART

A Young Army Doctor's 1969 Vietnam War Experience

Dr. Jonathan and Sherrie Benumof

ISBN 978-1-953120-20-5

Printed in U.S.A.

First U.S. Edition: March 2021

Published by
Park Place Publications
Pacific Grove, California
www.parkplacepublications.com

We dedicate this book
to one another
and to our family ~

Benjamin, Kimberley, Sarah, Jeff,
Maile, Taylor, Brooke, Kai, Mikaela

TABLE OF CONTENTS

PART I:

Authors' Commentary

On the Important Issues, Events, Thoughts and Feelings Expressed in the Letters

HOW THIS BOOK CAME TO BE

Indicative of Sherrie's loving and caring nature, Sherrie saved all 282 letters Jon wrote her from Vietnam in a little storage box. Wherever Jon and Sherrie went after Jon's return home to the USA in January of 1970, for the next 50 years, the little storage box went with us. Jon and Sherrie went sequentially to the Army Hospital (Fort Rucker, Alabama) to serve out the remainder of Jon's 2-year tour of Army duty, then to Columbia-Presbyterian Medical Center in New York City for 2 years to finish his anesthesia training and finally to University of California San Diego Medical Center for the next 47 years.

During our 47 years in San Diego we lived in a condominium for 2 years, an older single family home for 2 years, and in a relatively new single-family home for 43 years. We moved from San Diego to Rancho Mission Viejo, California in 2019. The little storage box containing the letters always went with us (really with Sherrie, because they were special to her) and neither of us had ever read the 282 letters again, since they were written by Jon in 1969 (51 years earlier).

Then one day in early 2020, when our friends (Larry and Arlene) were visiting us in our new home in Rancho Mission Viejo, Jon stumbled across the little storage box for the letters, asked Sherrie what was in there, and she replied, "the old letters that you wrote me from Vietnam." Jon replied "Really?" and grabbed one, read the first 2 sentences out loud ("Today started with a Bang. We were attacked."). With that opening sentence, interest in reading the letters was captured right then and there and Sherrie and I decided to read all 282 letters. So, for the next 60 days we sat outside and read 4-5 letters a day to each other. After digesting what was in the letters, we thought our immediate family (2 children, 2 children-in-law, 5 grandchildren) would appreciate getting a copy of all the letters. To make the collection of letters presentable we decided to publish the letters in a self-published book format. As we (really Sherrie) began typing the 282 letters, Jon thought some commentary/explanation would be helpful to the reader to see and understand the big picture on various themes and stories that ran throughout the letters. As the commentary grew, so did the idea that the commentary was well complimenting the letters and that the commentary and the letters together made for a "real" book and that this "real" book might be of interest to readers outside of our family. We hope that this proves to be the case.

1966, Jon in his third year of medical school, wearing his medical student jacket.

WHO WAS JONATHAN BENUMOF IN 1969?

I was born in 1942 in New York City, was raised in New York City, attended New York City public schools, earned a BS degree at the City College of New York (1959-1963), and then an MD degree at the USC School of Medicine (1963-1967). In 1966, in my junior year of medical school, I started dating and fell in love with Sherrie. I did my medical internship at the Los Angeles County General Hospital (July 1967 - July 1968). Sherrie and I married in July of 1968.

At the end of my internship (July 1968) I could not decide what medical sub-specialty to go into, so I did not enter any medical sub-specialty residency program. Because I was not a conscientious objector to the war in Vietnam and had not selected a residency program, I was required by the national draft that was in place at the time to enter the armed services (U.S. Army) and I did so in July of 1968. In August of 1968, as a new Captain, I had 3 weeks of basic training at Fort Sam Houston (in San Antonio, Texas). Because I had agreed to become an On-the-Job-Trainee (OJT) in anesthesia (thinking that anesthesia might be a

Jon standing in front of the massive Los Angeles County General Hospital where he completed his medical school clinical education and his medical internship year (from 1967-1968).

specialty I might enter after my 2-year commitment to the Army), I started training to be an Anesthesiologist at Ireland Army Hospital at Fort Knox, Kentucky in September of 1968.

Much to my naive surprise, in November of 1968, I received orders to go to Vietnam. I therefore had 3 months of training to be an Anesthesiologist.

THE NORMAL RESIDENCY TRAINING PROGRAM TO BE AN ANESTHESIOLOGIST, IN 1968, WAS 24 MONTHS.

Consequently, I was going to Vietnam to take care of critically injured and dying soldiers with approximately 10% of the training that a fully trained Anesthesiologist would have been required to have to go into standard anesthesia practice on civilians in the USA.

When I left for Vietnam, in early January 1969, I was neither for nor against the war. I was well aware of the intense, fiercely heated debate going on, in the USA, as to whether the war in Vietnam was justified. I did not know who was right and who was wrong. I was in the Army simply because I felt I had no other choice. I was heading to Vietnam, in January of 1969, because MD anesthesia providers were badly needed there. Because I was still basically very much a student-in-training, I was scared and insecure about my medical capability when I went to Vietnam. As you will see from my letters to Sherrie, my overarching goal and all I wanted to do was stay alive, take care of the soldiers properly, return home to Sherrie, start a family with Sherrie, finish my medical education and then start my medical career. In terms of the intensity of the fighting in Vietnam, I was sent to the worst place (just below the DMZ) at the worst time (the 1969 TET offensive by North Vietnam against South Vietnam). I often had to work very hard for long durations in inherently dangerous conditions. Thus, despite my own initial low expectations of what I could do medically prior to going to Vietnam, it turned out that because of what I had to do (namely, a lot of hard, 100% effort, good work under difficult conditions), I received a Bronze Star and a Purple Heart (see following pages and Comment Section 4: 10/14/69; L-215: bolded entry).

THE UNITED STATES OF AMERICA

TO ALL WHO SHALL SEE THESE PRESENTS, GREETING:

THIS IS TO CERTIFY THAT
THE PRESIDENT OF THE UNITED STATES OF AMERICA
AUTHORIZED BY EXECUTIVE ORDER, 24 AUGUST 1962
HAS AWARDED

THE BRONZE STAR MEDAL

TO

CAPTAIN JONATHAN BENUMOF, MEDICAL CORPS, UNITED STATES ARMY

FOR
MERITORIOUS ACHIEVEMENT
IN GROUND OPERATIONS AGAINST HOSTILE FORCES
DURING THE PERIOD JANUARY 1969 TO JANUARY 1970 IN THE REPUBLIC OF VIETNAM

GIVEN UNDER MY HAND IN THE CITY OF WASHINGTON
THIS 5TH DAY OF JANUARY 1970

David E. Thomas
DAVID E. THOMAS
BRIGADIER GENERAL, MC
COMMANDING GENERAL
44TH MEDICAL BRIGADE

Stanley R. Resor
SECRETARY OF THE ARMY

The Bronze Star Medal was awarded for Jon's exemplary medical care under difficult and dangerous conditions as the Anesthesiologist for his MASH Unit's Hospital in Vietnam (from January 1969 to January 1970).

Citation

BY DIRECTION OF THE PRESIDENT

THE BRONZE STAR MEDAL

IS PRESENTED TO

CAPTAIN JONATHAN BENUMOF, MEDICAL CORPS,
UNITED STATES ARMY

who distinguished himself by outstandingly meritorious service in connection with military operations against a hostile force in the Republic of Vietnam. During the period

JANUARY 1969 TO JANUARY 1970

he consistently manifested exemplary professionalism and initiative in obtaining outstanding results. His rapid assessment and solution of numerous problems inherent in a combat environment greatly enhanced the allied effectiveness against a determined and aggressive enemy. Despite many adversities, he invariably performed his duties in a resolute and efficient manner. Energetically applying his sound judgment and extensive knowledge, he has contributed materially to the successful accomplishment of the United States mission in the Republic of Vietnam. His loyalty, diligence and devotion to duty were in keeping with the highest traditions of the military service and reflect great credit upon himself and the United States Army.

The Bronze Star Medal Citation describes Jon's outstanding professionalism, dedication, performance, and initiative during the year he served in the Army in Vietnam (January 1969 to January 1970).

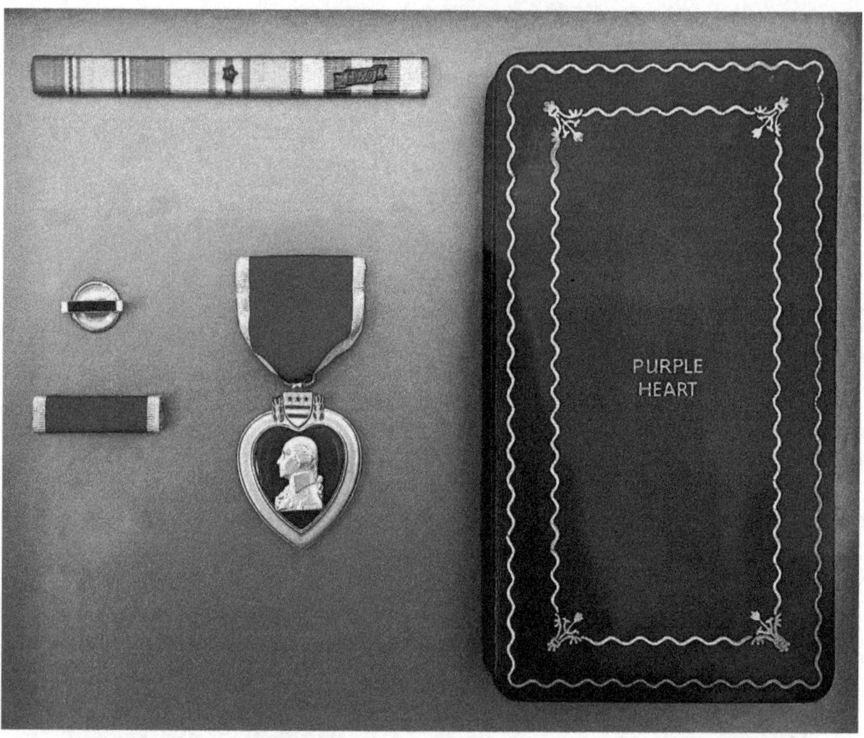

The Purple Heart was given to Jon as a result of him receiving a head injury when his MASH Unit's Hospital Operating Room was impacted by a blast from an incoming rocket (Vietnam 1969).

1966, Sherrie sitting on a wall just outside her nursing school dormitory.

WHO WAS SHERRIE BENUMOF IN 1969?

I was born in 1944 in Austin, Texas and lived with my family in Texas, Oklahoma, Louisiana, Alaska and California. In 1962, I graduated from Excelsior Union High School in Norwalk, California. In high school I had decided that I wanted to become a nurse, so I applied to the Los Angeles County General Hospital (LACGH) School of Nursing. The Nursing School's admissions were at full capacity for the Fall semester of 1962, so I was accepted for the Fall semester of 1963. During that year, following my high school graduation (Summer of 1962–Fall of 1963), I obtained a full-time clerical position in a gas and electric utilities office. There, the Management staff offered me an increase in pay and responsibility if I would continue my employment with them rather than leave for Nursing School.

1966, Sherrie with her mother, Jerry, at her Los Angeles County General Hospital School of Nursing graduation.

Because I was determined to become a nurse, I left the utilities company position (after one year) to begin my Registered Nurse (RN) Diploma Program at LACGH. My 3 years in the RN program were filled with many new friendships, adventures, experiences and opportunities. It was in my third year of Nursing School (January 1966) that I met Jon who was in his Junior year at the University of Southern California (USC) School of Medicine. He saw me working as a student nurse on the Diabetic Unit, at LACGH, and approached me to ask where he could get some Diabetic education pamphlets for the patient he was seeing. I politely told him where the pamphlets were and quickly got back to my patients. Over the next few weeks, he approached me 2 to 3 more times to ask me to go out with him. I declined the first 2 times and then relented the third time when he very humorously said that I had to eat at some point in time and he knew of a great pizza restaurant near the hospital.

Jon's persistence, good looks, dynamic personality, intelligence and great humor swept me off my feet and over the next few months I fell madly in love with him. We had so much fun going to the beach, to music venues (such as "The Ice House" in Pasadena and "Whiskey-a-Go-Go" in Hollywood), to Palm Springs and Las Vegas, going to parties, hanging out with friends, attending USC football games, going horseback riding and eating out at our favorite pizza restaurant near the hospital.

During the 2 1/2 years that we dated, I graduated from Nursing School in June 1966 and went on to work as an RN (at LACGH) in Pediatrics and the Renal Dialysis/Kidney Transplant Specialty Unit. Jon graduated from Medical School, in June 1967, and immediately started his 1-year rotating Internship at LACGH. It was in the latter part of his Internship year when he became aware that he was going to have to go into the Army.

We knew that we loved one another, and Jon didn't want to leave me behind, so he asked me to marry him and we very quickly and cost efficiently planned our wedding. Even though we had limited time, and a limited budget, we planned a very lovely wedding (and reception) with about 40-50 guests. Jon's parents (from New York City) and Jon's sister and niece (from Northern California) were able to attend. In addition, my parents and sister were able to attend. Both sets of our parents were remarkable in their love, for us, as I had recently converted to Judaism (my parents were Southern Baptists). Jon's parents were so welcoming, and loving, to me as a newly converted Jew. And, my parents loved Jon so very much (as they did me) that they were accepting of my decision to change religions. We married, in a Reform Jewish Synagogue, a week after Jon's Internship ended. Luckily, we had time to take a wonderful week-long honeymoon in beautiful Lake Tahoe, Nevada. It was great to have that time together before Jon's Army obligation was to begin.

Two weeks later, we were headed to San Antonio, Texas where Jon received his Army induction training. When that training was completed, we then headed directly to his first Army assignment which was at Fort Knox, Kentucky. It was here that Jon received 3 months of

Anesthesiology On-the-Job-Training (OJT) by a new Army officer MD (Anesthesiologist) who had just completed his 2 years of Anesthesiology Residency. All too soon, Jon then received notification that he was going to be sent to Vietnam for a year. This was very nerve wracking, for both of us, because he had only received 3 months of Anesthesiology training and the uncertainty of him going to a war zone was extremely unsettling.

We decided that I would return to live in Los Angeles, for the year that Jon would be in Vietnam, and I would return to my previous RN job at LACGH in the Renal Dialysis/Kidney Transplant Specialty Unit. When it was time for Jon to leave for Vietnam, from the San Francisco area, it was heart wrenching for both of us. We made our tearful good-byes to one another and I headed back to the hotel before driving back to Los Angeles the next morning. When I got back to the hotel, I received a call from Jon that his flight had been cancelled and he wasn't leaving until the next day, so I returned to get him. We were so glad to have another few hours together, but we dreaded another tearful goodbye the next day. Jon told me to be sure to get in contact with the Army, as soon as possible, should there be any kind of critical medical emergency regarding me or his parents while he was in Vietnam. I assured him that I would, but of course we were both hoping that none of the 3 of us would have a health crisis while he was gone for the year.

SPECIAL THEMES AND STORIES THAT RUN THROUGHOUT ALL THE LETTERS

It is very possible that the uninitiated reader passing through Jon's 282 letters to Sherrie might miss or have a blurry vision or view of some special important big pictures/stories that run throughout all the letters. The reasons why these big pictures or stories might be out of focus or missed are: (1) the pieces of the big picture or stories are widely dispersed throughout all of the letters and therefore not emphasized or concentrated in any particular letter or place within a given letter; (2) the important matters/issues may simply be expressed in just a phrase or one sentence within a long letter and be easily overlooked; and (3) the reader may simply fail to understand or recognize some words have special big picture/story meaning. **If the reader sees/understands the big picture/story, we think the individual pieces of the picture, that are dispersed throughout the 282 letters, will be more meaningful to the reader when they come across the individual pieces.** The special big picture/stories that we think should be called out to the reader before the reader gets to the actual letters are:

1. Feelings and thoughts during Jon's travel from the USA to, and upon arrival at, his MASH Unit, the "18th Surgical Hospital", in the Fire Base "Camp Evans" just below (south of) the demilitarized zone (DMZ).
2. Jon's love for Sherrie and desire to return home to Sherrie (because this is the overarching message of all the Letters, this big picture/story deserves special emphasis).
3. The danger and physical discomfort Jon experienced during his year in Vietnam.
4. The intermittently occurring very long hours of non-stop work of saving lives.

5. Jon's growing despair and negative feelings about the loss of young men in the prime of their lives.
6. What Jon did between working on the injured soldiers.
7. Drinking alcohol and alcoholism.
8. No "Welcome Home." No "Thank You for Your Service" from the public.

Some of these big picture/story matters (see #s 3, 4, 5, 7, 8) have great importance since Jon came home an alcoholic with post-traumatic stress disorder (PTSD). Equally important, but simply to be noted here (see Jon's and Sherrie's post-Vietnam War autobiographies following the 282 letters), Jon was able to eventually and very successfully enter Recovery from Alcoholism through Alcoholics Anonymous (AA). His PTSD is well compartmentalized and is expressed, with an outpouring of great sadness, when the subject of young soldiers dying in war comes up (for example, visiting the Vietnam War Memorial).

COMMENT SECTION 1

Feelings and Thoughts During Jon's Travel From the USA to, and Upon Arrival at, His Mash Unit, the "18th Surgical Hospital" in the Fire Base "Camp Evans"

Traveling to Vietnam and then on to my MASH Unit was a very negative experience. In short, it took a very long time (5 days) to go to a place I did not want to go to. I had "never been so lonely" (see Letters #1 and #2, hereafter referred to as L-1, L-2, etc.) and I "felt so alone" (see L-1) during these travels. I was leaving a known world for an unknown world and war. When I walked off my large jet transport plane from the USA in the Bien Hoa Airport, Vietnam, wearing my starched Captain's khaki uniform, complete with Captain's bars and officer's cap, I saw a sea of mud-caked men (waiting for a flight home to the USA) staring silently at us (me) with weary gaunt eyes and a smirk on their faces saying 'you (me) are assholes'. I said to myself a little "Whoa", "What is that about?" and I added to my list of feelings about going to a war more confusion, uncertainty and less confidence.

I then had to travel from Bien Hoa, in the relatively safe southern part of South Vietnam, northward to my MASH Unit in the relatively unsafe most northern part of South Vietnam by a series of helicopter flights. From the relatively low flying helicopters I could see the war was on full force. **"I saw bombs go off all over the country"** (see L-3). When I got to the 18th Surgical Hospital, I realized I would have to perform as a fully trained and functioning Anesthesiologist, and be Chief of the Anesthesia Department with only 10% of the training a fully trained Anesthesiologist has to have: the life and death of our soldiers would be in my hands and I was **"on my own"** (see L-5) and because of that **"I was so scared"** (see L-5) that I might fail to fulfill this tremendous responsibility. I later learned (see L-104) that I was "the only OJT in

Vietnam in charge of a department and responsible for all the anesthesia here" (18th Surgical Hospital).

Feeling alone, inadequate and scared makes for a very negative 'getting there' experience. BUT those feelings went away quickly as soon as I began to save some lives. By the end of my third month, in Vietnam, I stated to Sherrie on 3/31/69 (L-70) "I know now I can do this job and do it well." By the end of my year, in Vietnam, I ended up with a Bronze Star for my good work as a Doctor.

COMMENT SECTION 2

Jon's Love for Sherrie and Desire to Return Home

In January of 1969, when Jon went to the Vietnam war, Sherrie and Jon were newlyweds of only 6 months. Jon loved Sherrie very much and she was by far Jon's most important connection to the outside world, namely the non-war world. In L-115 Jon wrote "She was the most cherished thing in my life." In contrast, the war world was a "hell hole" (L-20). Jon felt extremely "isolated" in his Vietnam War environment (L-18) and "the pain of the isolation was intense" (L-88) and outside of Sherrie, the non-war world was "meaningless" (L-18 and L-88). I never think of the real world much (e.g. the flight to the moon was "either unknown or of little interest to us" (L-148) because "we felt too far removed" (L-148) and therefore Jon told Sherrie "don't send any news of the outside world to me" (L-18). "I felt that I was here (in the war), I would always be here, and that the real world did not exist" (L-199). When I did not get a letter from Sherrie it seemed like I would "never get back to Sherrie in the non-war world" (L-18). I felt that "my life depends solely on your {Sherrie's} letters", "I'm dying" when I did not get one (L-29). "I can't describe how important those letters were to me" (that Sherrie wrote). Although 10's and 10's of letters expressed great joy and happiness when I received a letter from Sherrie, in L-199 I described in detail how I felt when I got a letter from Sherrie: "A feeling and sensation of peace descended upon me. Suddenly the real world was there, a future, a bright happy future was there. My life has meaning. I have something to live for! Yes, I can love. I feel at peace again. Something is lifting me up and that something is you" (L-199).

My goal was to stay alive and get back to Sherrie and "my love for Sherrie lifted me up to look forward to a future" (L-24) with Sherrie. I saw myself "in terms" of "living" for Sherrie (L-40), "the thought of returning" to Sherrie "kept me going" (L-71). "I knew deep down that my feeling of love for you is what will get me through" (L-156). The goal of getting back to Sherrie kept me functioning normally, "made everything mean something to me" (L-32) and without Sherrie "I'd be lost" (L-32). I "existed" to get back to her (L-33). "I must get back to you" (L-181).

Writing my letters to Sherrie was my escape from the war and when I could be "alone" with her (L-25 and L-147) even when I was flat on my stomach, with gun, helmet and flak jacket on, in a bunker, with 8 rockets hitting our fire base (L-25).

Every single letter of the 282 letters expressed great love for Sherrie in one way or another, either in the salutation, body of the letter, or in the sign off. Most of the letters expressed this love for Sherrie in multiple parts of the letter.

A. Love Expressed in the Salutation of The Letters

Every single one of the 282 letters began with a very loving salutation. In the beginning of my year in Vietnam (1/69 - 1/70), the vast majority of the first 49 letters began with the salutation "Dearest Sherrie". Then, I distinctly remember I felt I needed to be more creative and for the rest of the letters, in order for them to be more loving/interesting/enjoyable to read, I began trying to make the salutations different from one another. For just a very few of the very many examples, I began the letters with "Hi Sweetheart", "Every Beat of my Heart is for you", "Sherrie Sweet Darling", "Dearest/Adorable/Sweet/Precious/Beloved Darling", "Dearest Wife", "Pudding Dumpling" (can you believe that one?), "Honeydew", "Pumpkin Head", "a Million Kisses". There were many more permutations of words and adjectives that were used throughout the letters. The reader should get the idea from just this small sampling of quotes from the early letters that I was expressing much love in the salutation, trying to make the salutations a little more interesting, creative and sometimes a little more humorous (i.e. "Honeydew", "Pumpkin Head") and was just another way of saying to Sherrie "I Love You."

1969, Jon in Vietnam, with a sad face, holding a picture of Sherrie made by a Vietnamese artist. The artist made the picture from photos (of Sherrie) that Jon gave him. The artwork was not very good, so it wasn't saved.

Another photo of Jon looking lonely as he views the artwork of Sherrie, by a Vietnamese artist.

B. Love Expressed in the Body of the Letters

In many of the letters, Jon explicitly stated his love for Sherrie in the body of the letter and these expressions of love ranged from a sentence to a paragraph; most were serious and some were humorous (see below). Here are just a very few of the very many examples (short version) of expression of love, said over and over in the body of the letter. "I love you/miss you very much/great deal", "I was thinking of how wonderful and giving you have been", "I'm so thankful for having you", "I dream of you all the time", "You have done wonders for me", "You are very beautiful inside and outside", "I could not find much meaning or happiness in life without you", "Think of you and look at your picture all the time", "You are the most wonderful person in the whole world", "Everyday my love for you grows larger", "I know that you will be a wonderful wife", "You are already", "Part of loving you is wanting to have children, with you, which I do very much". "I got a very loving letter from you today. And my thirsty longing heart just literally drank up every word. I need so much more. I need you. I want to be back with you very badly."

Some statements of Jon's love for Sherrie were humorous. In L-64, I made the Beef Stew Analogy: "Tonight we had beef stew (canned). I love that stuff. But I love you much more Pumpkin." In L-66, I made the Heat, Bugs, Viet Cong Analogy: "Who is going to get me first? The Heat? The Bugs? The Viet Cong? The answer is......of course you are."

C. Love Expressed in the Sign Offs of the Letters

Virtually every single letter ended with a very loving sign off. Here again I distinctly remember trying to vary the statement of my love for Sherrie in the sign off so that it would be a little more interesting, enjoyable and comforting to read. A few of the more common sign offs were: "All my love and thoughts/devotion/hopes" and "I love you very much/a great deal/deeply/with all my heart and soul." Mixed in frequently were: "Thinking of you constantly/all the time", "Miss you very much", "Goodnight Sweetheart", "Only Yours Forever", "You are the sun of my life", "How I wish I could be back with you", "You are beautiful inside and outside." There were many more, with every conceivable combination of loving words put together, but we think the reader gets the idea (from this small sampling of sign offs) that the sign off was just another (and final) way of saying to Sherrie "I love you."

Jon, in Vietnam, missing Sherrie. Jon built his desk and the multi-shelf clothing container at his left shoulder. The desk and clothing container can be found in Figure 2 (in the area labeled personal area).

COMMENT SECTION 3
The Danger and Physical Discomfort Jon Experienced During His Year in Vietnam

The danger and physical discomfort Jon experienced during his year in Vietnam can be broken down into four categories, namely, (A) and (B) From rockets and attacks on the perimeter of the fire base; (C) From the monsoon rains; (D) From the heat of the day following the monsoon rain season; (E) Other conditions and diseases.

A. General Thoughts on the Danger Jon was in from Rockets and Attacks on the Perimeter of the Fire Base

Several general understandings need to be clearly stated before calling out/highlighting the specific instances of danger as revealed by the letters.

First, an important necessity in writing to Sherrie about the events of the war and the dangers of the war to Jon, was to be truthful in the letters, to a degree, but not scare Sherrie and cause her to worry too much. As such, my 282 letters to Sherrie should be viewed as understatements, to a degree, of the real danger. In fact, Jon/I was nearly killed in the war, for which I received a Purple Heart. One important example of my understating actual events, in my letters to Sherrie, was the actual event/injury that led to my being awarded a Purple Heart. The actual event is described in the legend to Figure 1 with the definition of "XI". A rocket hit an operating room (O.R.) that I was in, which caused a significant scalp laceration, which caused significant blood loss, which caused me to be ordered to go to the ICU for the rest of that day and night. What I said to Sherrie on 10/5/1969 (L-207) was that "I have a tremendous lump on my head because 2 nights ago, we took 2 incoming rockets and I banged my head hitting the floor."

Second, the intensity of the fighting between the US forces against the North Vietnam Regulars and Viet Cong varied in a

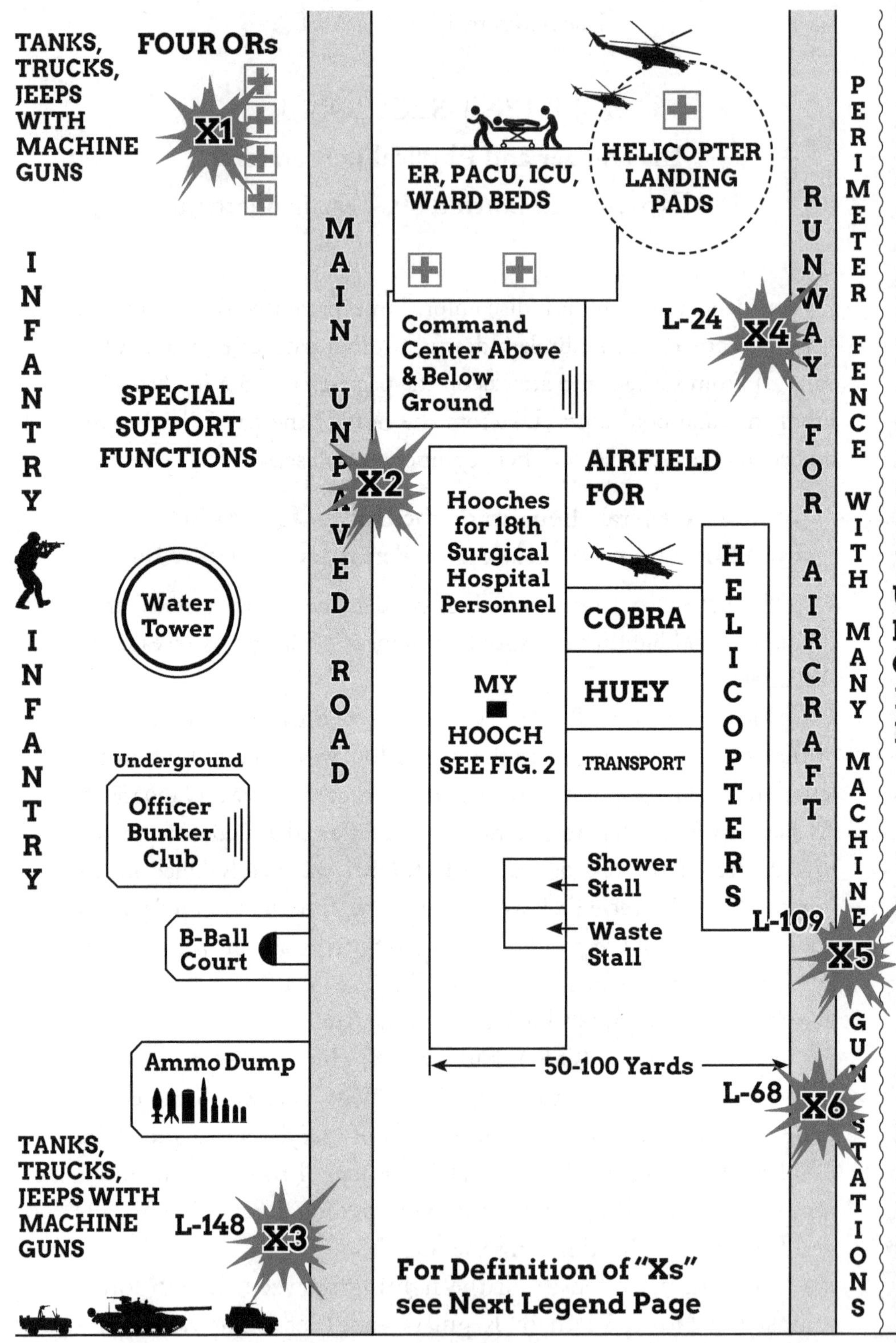

FIGURE 1: Schematic Diagram of Camp Evans Fire Base and where Rockets (X1-6) landed

LEGENDS
For Figure 1

X1 = Place where a rocket hit the OR I was in. The rocket caused me to be knocked to the floor which caused me to have a significant scalp laceration which caused me significant blood loss which caused me to be admitted to the ICU for the night for observation. The injury due to combat with the enemy resulted in my getting a Purple Heart.

X2 = Place where a rocket hit the road behind me just as I went over a crest in the road. I was on the downside of the crest and the shrapnel from the blast flew up the crest and just missed hitting my back and the back of my head. This close call (X2), from which I had no injury, was a much closer call to death than X1.

X3 = See L-148. A grenade hit our ammunition dump (storage area) and set off several more explosions. I was not close enough to get hit by shrapnel but the noise from all the explosions was deafening. Five of "our people", "all infantry soldiers", were killed." "We could not save any of the 5". "Very sad thing." "When it happened, every gunship and dust off ship was in the air. The ammo dump was firing things in every direction. Everybody was flat on their stomachs. We thought we were being over run."

X4 = See L-24. Rocket caused everyone to hit the floor, but I could not because I was in the process of intubating a patient with a tracheal tube and could not stop. The patient was under general anesthesia and was paralyzed. If I stopped the intubating process, the patient would have died.

X5 = See L-109. "I can see the fighting from here" (my hooch). "Rockets and machine guns".

X6 = See L-68. "Dead Viet Cong on the barbed wire perimeter fence."

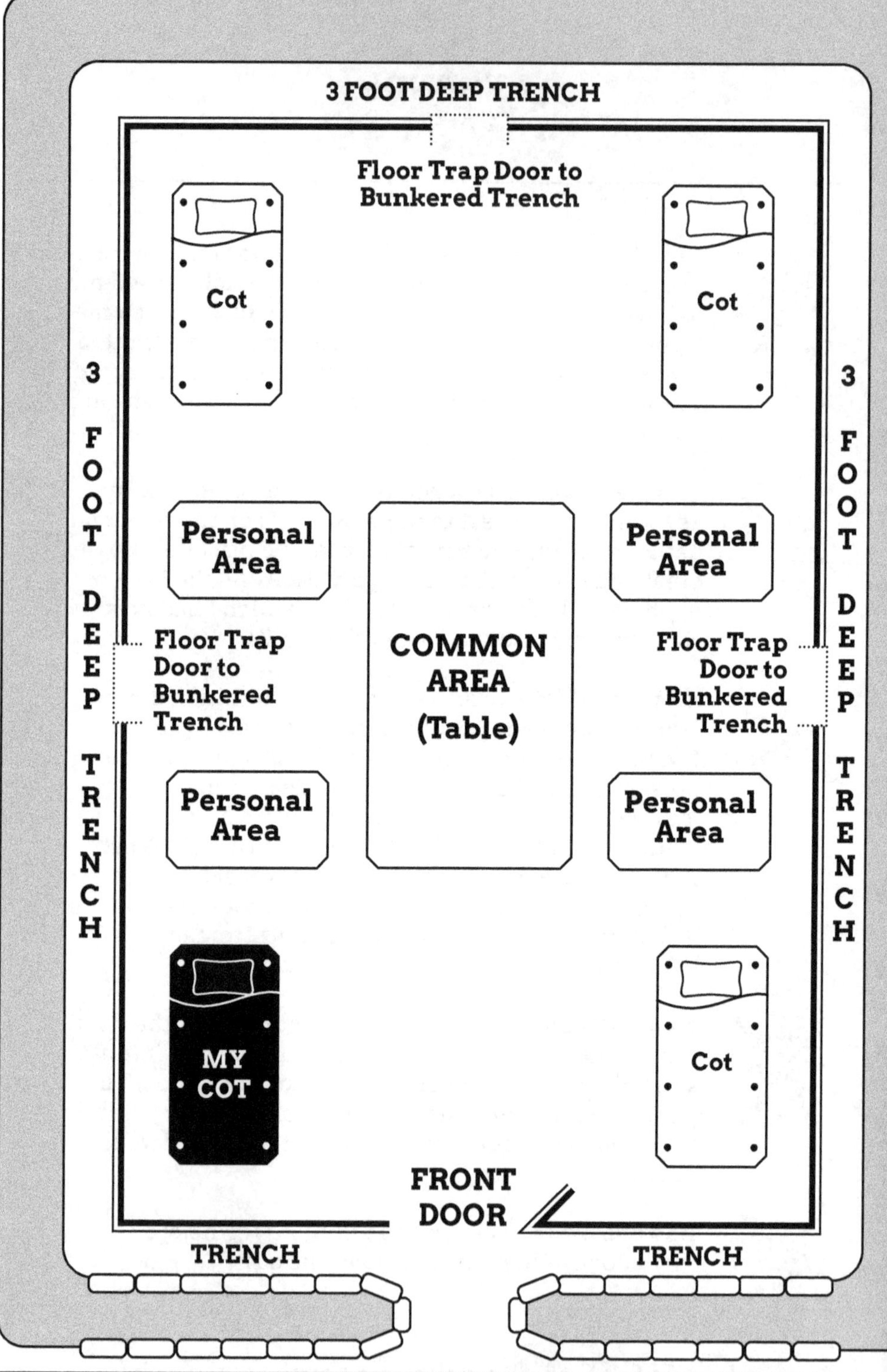

FIGURE 2:
Diagram of My Hooch

specific pattern in 1969. January 1969 to March 1969 were largely pre-1969 massive TET offensive days. There was considerable, significant, moderately intense fighting going on all the time, all over South Vietnam in early 1969. But, this fighting, was not nearly as extensive and intense as the fighting was from March 1969 to July 1969 when the North Vietnamese forces launched what was called the TET offensive. The TET offensive was massive involving hundreds of thousands of soldiers and involved most of South Vietnam. The fighting was most intense and fierce in the very northern part of South Vietnam, just below the demilitarized zone (DMZ), which is where my MASH Unit was. The reason North Vietnam launched the TET offensive in March of 1969 was because March coincided with the start of the monsoon season (officially began February 15th). The monsoon season meant endless days of relentless rain, which meant good "cover" for the North Vietnamese forces on the ground.

The 1969 TET offensive was successful for the North Vietnamese (the US was essentially defeated by the 1969 TET offensive) and therefore it was the beginning of the end for the United States in Vietnam. As the wounded soldiers came into my care, in 1969, they knew we were losing and therefore I knew we were losing. Unfortunately, the war dragged on until 1975 and many more thousands of lives were lost.

Third, many of my letters describe in-coming rockets to the Camp Evans Fire Base, within which was my 18th Surgical MASH Unit. It would be helpful to the reader to understand/visualize the anatomy and geometry of the Fire Base and where I was and where the operating rooms (really 12-foot by 12-foot refrigerated boxes) were within this fire base (see Figure 1). For example, some letters describe in-coming rockets while I was in the operating room taking care of anesthetized patients who I could not leave. Indeed, one of those rockets hit the operating room I was in at the time (Xl in Figure 1), which led to my receiving a Purple Heart. Figure 1

(X2) shows where a rocket hit a dirt road that goes through Camp Evans. I was running on that road (from rockets) to the officers' underground bunker (see Figure 1). I had just gotten over a crest in that road and I was on the downside of the crest in the road, when a rocket hit the upside of the road to the crest. I was shielded, from the shrapnel coming up the road from the rocket blast, by the crest in the road. I felt the shrapnel whiz past my back and the back of my head. Close call, but no harm done to me or anyone else.

Fourth, many of my letters describe in-coming rockets while I was in my hooch. A hooch is a four-sided large room/hut made of plywood walls which contained four beds (in the four corners of the room) with a common central area (Figure 2). Many of my letters describe a great effort, by me and my hooch mates, to build a very strong bunker around our hooch (the quality of your hooch bunker could determine whether you lived or died). Figure 2 is a diagram of the inside of the hooch and the surrounding bunkered trench. When the alarm sirens went off, sending out the alarm that there were in-coming rockets and we were in the hooch, we were required to grab our helmets, flak jackets and guns, dive through the trap doors on the floor of each side wall of the hooch and roll into the 3-foot deep trench that surrounded each hooch. The trench had a 3-4 foot tall sandbag bunkered wall on all 4 sides of the hooch and the trench at the back of the hooch also had a sandbagged roof. The trench, plus the sandbag wall, constituted the bunker. The sandbagged roof, at the back of the hooch, also occasionally served as a sundeck to put lounge chairs on and relax in the sun outside. Getting hit by rockets when I was in my hooch and diving into the bunker is well described in L-110: "Well now I know what the 'Star Spangled Banner' is all about." "Man, were we ever hit and hit hard. Just after writing you last night (about midnight), all hell broke loose. We took 20 rockets in rapid succession (over a half hour). I was in the bunker before the crash of the first had ended."

1969–Jon (second from right) with other doctors from two of the doctor hooches. They are standing in front of sandbags that they manually filled. The sandbags were used to bunker the hooches and surrounding trenches (see Figure 2).

1969–The front door of Jon's hooch and the 4-foot tall sand-bagged front wall (see Figure 2). Immediately behind the sandbagged front wall was the surrounding trench (see Figure 2). The "Playboy" logo is painted on the front door. A monsoon rain drainage ditch, with walking plank over it, is in front of the hooch.

1969–Jon, in O.R. clothes, standing in front of the door to his hooch.

1969–Jon (second from right), with his three hooch-mates, standing in front of the sand-bagged bunkered wall of their hooch.

On this occasion, I was ordered to leave the bunker and go to the operating room. "Right in the middle of the rockets, I was asked to come to the operating room. So, I ran my ass off with helmet, gun and flak jacket to the operating room. On the way I saw a sight most people will never ever see and I hope that I never see again. With the crash of the landing rounds (shells) and the blinding of the flash as they hit, I saw Viet Cong out in the fields to the North and East of us (coming at us)." See Figure 1.

"Our machine guns were tearing the hell out of them. The sky was completely studded with helicopter gunships pouring rockets in on them. Flares were all over the sky. It was like a daydream. Sirens were screaming out red alert constantly." The reader should, also, see L-68: "Dead Viet Cong being picked off the barbed wire fence right on our perimeter." See Figure 1.

1969–Jon inside his hooch.

Fifth, how did I feel about the fact that I could die in this war? L-110 well describes how I felt about dying. "I don't feel afraid of dying. I think the worst part of dying is the fear of dying. I don't fear death. I don't know why, but I just don't. Maybe it is because it is inconceivable to me and I don't think it will happen. Sherrie, you know that it is fear that makes any situation painful. If I was worried or filled with anxiety, then you could be reasonably also. But, I'm not so you shouldn't. I don't think Camp Evans could ever be overrun by Viet Cong. I really mean it. If a rocket falls on my head, I can't do anything about it. And, neither can you or any General. It could happen at any time and place here. That is the only way I could get it. There is nothing anybody can do about it, so don't worry. Things to worry about are things like getting killed on the freeway. That is something you can do something about. Drive more carefully, take a different route, etc. OK? Do you understand me?" In L-160, I said the same thing. "It is like I told you, before, the only way I'm going to get it is if a rocket comes down on my head", which nearly did happen (see X1 and X2 in Figure 1). "You can die a thousand deaths if you are afraid and worry too much before anything has happened. This goes for you too. Be brave."

Sixth, in order to better anticipate when I would be called to work on/save soldiers I learned to recognize the sounds of war: i.e. the difference between rockets (enemy relatively far away) and mortar fire (enemy relatively close), the difference between in-coming and out-going rockets, machine gun fire on the perimeter (see Figure 1) and the difference between the different helicopters (Cobra gunships vs Huey Med-Evacs vs Transport), bombers and regular planes.

Seventh, and finally, it should be understood that any time our soldiers engaged the enemy in any sort of battle, casualties increased and that meant I was going to work a lot more (see next Comment Section 4: Long hours/days of non-stop work for me on patients). Many of my letters refer to the realization that increased in-coming rockets and increased fighting always meant increased casualties and much hard work for me.

B. Specific Instances of Danger Due to Rockets and Attacks on the Perimeter of the Fire Base

When I first arrived in Vietnam, in the middle of January 1969, the monsoon season and the TET offensive had not yet arrived. My early letters to Sherrie detail the anticipation and expectation that the TET offensive was coming and that both sides were preparing physically and mentally for this major battle and the start of rockets coming into my fire base. Even when I first arrived in Da Nang, going from the Bien Hoa Airport to the 18th Surgical Hospital in Camp Evans, "everyone seemed to be bracing for the TET offensive" (L-6). The next day I was helicoptered 60 miles more north to the 18th Surgical Hospital and I found everyone to be "quietly waiting for the TET offensive" (L-8). "The artillery was busy and flares were in the sky all night" (L-8). The Viet Cong were "tunneling in" and "we were putting bunkers around our hooches" (L-10) (See Figure 2) and we worked "building up the bunkers for days" (L-19). In late January 1969, it "seemed like the Viet Cong activity was increasing and more Viet Cong were being seen every day" (L-12) and on 1/30/69 we "took rockets" and "spent about 4 hours in bunkers with guns on" (L-14). I was told that "the incoming rockets will be a nightly occurrence and I will become an old pro at shitting in my pants" (L-14). "Our own casualties were increasing", "we were catching more Viet Cong" and the "Amateur Generals" (our regular soldiers) "think all this was the starting of the TET offensive." On 1/31/69, the 18th Surgical Hospital had "long meetings on how best to deal with the TET offensive and be efficient" (L-15). By February rockets came in and we were in the bunkers regularly. It seemed the Viet Cong "could hit us when they wanted to" (L-16) and "rockets came in from the north, south, east and west...all over the perimeter" of the fire base (L-22). When the rockets started coming in regularly, you could see "the tension in everyone that their presence made" in contrast to the lack of tension in everyone when it was quiet for 2 days (L-21). To summarize, from the point of view of when the TET offensive began (late February-early March 1969) and where it took place (where I was), I basically arrived at the worst place at the worst time.

The magnitude of the danger of in-coming rockets and attacks on the perimeter of the fire base, as well as other perceived dangers (in terms of frequency of occurrence and degree of severity) can best be appreciated by seeing the list, in one place, of the many specific instances of these dangers as I related them to Sherrie in my letters to her. By sequential date of actual occurrence, and the associated number of the Letter, here are the actual quotes from each Letter:

2/10/69 (L-24): "While I was in the process of intubating a Vietnamese soldier" (means patient was paralyzed and could not breathe on his own) "2 big rockets came in, everybody hit the floor, but I could not because I had to get the tube in. I was so scared."

2/11/69 (L-25): "8 in-coming rockets. Flat on stomach in the bunker."

2/13/69 (L-27): Sometimes there was "so much shooting going on at night and flares being put up" "a flashlight was unnecessary."

2/15/69 (L-29): A captured North Vietnamese Regular tells us "his battalion is on its way to attack us (Camp Evans)" (see L-68) below; Camp Evans was attacked 3/27/69).

2/22/69 (L-35): The fire base generator was hit, so "we have no lights."

3/1/69 (L-42): We took incoming rockets this morning "because a two-star General was near where the rockets landed."

3/10/69 (L-52): Very occasionally I needed to go to the Post Office to send a package to Sherrie. "I dare not walk there" because the path leads close to the perimeter (see Figure 1) where there is "dense jungle foliage" that "could conceal Viet Cong." I would wait for a "protected" jeep which had a manned machine gun in the back to take me.

3/18/69 (L-58): A "big fight just broke out", just outside the perimeter (See Figure 1). The noise from the guns made "our whole hooch shake."

3/22/69 (L-62): "My area is a very hot war zone", "Fighting is intense", "Everybody could use a break."

3/27/69 (L-68): "Last night was a big horror show." "Couldn't sleep, too hot", "Guns constantly going off', "Sky filled with choppers", "Our own Camp Evans under attack", "4 AM called to the Emergency Room", "tremendous number of casualties", "I myself ran 3 ORs all day", "Dawn came and the Viet Cong were being picked off our perimeter barbed wire fence", "Gotten in so close", "Fighting had been very intense."

The months of June and July were relatively quiet regarding in-coming rockets and attacks.

8/6/69 (L-157): "Last night our perimeter was attacked" (50-100 yards from my hooch). "Another 4th of July with rockets going off everywhere." "Quite a show." The more rockets, the more danger.

8/12/69 (L-160): "I was seeing a patient on the ward." Then "Boom, Boom, Boom" (rockets very close). "Had to put the patients on the floor even with their breathing tubes, intravenous lines, gastric and urinary tubes, wound drains, etc."

8/16/69 (L-163): "Tonight we are on a red emergency alert for a ground attack, but this is nothing new. We've had such alerts before. Everybody has to wear helmets, flak jackets, carry weapons and give passwords around the hospital and hooches. Feel shaky, spooky."

9/4/69 (L-179): "We got 16 Dead-on-Arrival soldiers yesterday and today. Sherrie, I am telling you, this war is bad. Things come down out of the sky, from nowhere, and blow your head off. Most of them have no chance to escape. No chance. They get it on the first rocket. The second and third rockets don't get you because you have a few seconds to hit the bunker."

9/6/69 (L-181): "There's lots of shooting, cases, alerts, issuing guns, etc."

10/25/69 (L-225): "We all know about President Nixon's unilateral cease fire, but you can't tell anything has changed here. Everything goes on as usual. There are fights on the perimeter, howitzers shooting all night (etc. etc.). The war won't be over, for any of us, until we go home."

11/13/69 (L-232): I wrote Sherrie "A massacre took place at Quang Tri last night." "We took 30 dead and 70 injured." When we move "I will be extremely careful. I'm not going outside of my hooch, ever, without a gun, flak jacket and steel helmet on. I think I'll quit running."

11/16/69 (L-235): Two days before my MASH Unit moved to Quang Tri, I wrote Sherrie "We go the day after. It will have to be by jeep. We will be heavily armed. I'll have a steel helmet and flak jacket on. I'll try to go with as many people as possible. We'll have gunships in the air over us, most of the way, and a minesweeper in front of us."

11/17/69 (L-236): The day before my MASH Unit moved to Quang Tri, I wrote Sherrie "Tomorrow I go to Quang Tri and I will literally be riding shotgun. I'll shoot anything that moves." Perhaps this was just bravado. But, it turns out I thought I saw something in the bushes and I did shoot (see next day/next letter immediately below). There is no question that moving a MASH Unit, in a long convoy of vehicles over contested territory, was an inherently dangerous mission. Everyone was nervous about taking rockets, and a frontal ground attack, while we were moving in a convoy to Quang Tri.

11/18/69 (L-237): I wrote Sherrie "Today was quite a day. I'm totally exhausted, but alive and well in Quang Tri. Moved, today, under extremely difficult conditions. It poured rain all day long, bridges washed away and detours had to be made. I fired my first real bullets today. I saw something moving in the brush, off the road, and let 'it' have it. I didn't stop to find out what it was." At the time this occurred, our right flank (shotgun side of jeep) was not being covered by any real soldiers. We were bare, exposed on that side, in contested territory and admittedly nervous.

C. Physical Discomfort Jon Was in Due to the Weather: Constant Rain and Constantly Being Wet

Here again this discomfort is best appreciated by simply listing, in one place, how frequent, for how long and how much it rained as revealed in my letters to Sherrie. During the monsoon season (February-April 1969) it was constantly raining, I was constantly wet, and I was often cold. Although the monsoon season was not supposed to officially start until 2/15/69 (L-10), the monsoon rains actually started on 1/31/69 (L-15).

2/1/69 (L-16): "Absolutely everything is wet", "Impossible to get dry", "raining for 3 days", "will rain for weeks."

2/2/69 (L-17): "Still raining", "Getting chilly."

2/4/69 (L-18): "Expected to rain for a month." "It has become cold (50 degrees F)." "Wear scrub suit+ 2 pairs of fatigues + a field jacket."

2/6/69 (L-20): "It hasn't stopped raining for a minute", "It is driving me crazy."

2/7/69 (L-21): "Still raining steadily and it is cold", "Become cold...... and I wear a tee shirt, scrub suit, 2 pairs of fatigues and poncho when I am not in the OR."

2/8/69 (L-22): "Rain let up for the first time."

2/27/69 (L-40): "Pouring rain again for 3 days."

3/5/69 (L-46): "The rain never stops." "I think this is where Noah built his ark." "Out of the last 30 days, it rained 25 days."

3/9/69 (L-50): "It just seems to rain harder and harder. It hasn't stopped now for 2 weeks and everything is wet."

3/13/69 (L-54): "Still raining steadily."

3/15/69 (L-56): "First day it didn't rain for several weeks."

3/16/69 (L-57): "Rained all day (seemingly harder than ever)."

3/18/69 (L-58): Regarding the monsoon rains: "You have to see it, or be in one, to believe it could rain so much."

3/19/69 (L-59): "Today was beautiful", "Monsoon season behind us?"

4/5/69 (L-75): Rain had not ended. "Last night I was very scared. I thought the world was coming to an end. It rained so hard, I can't describe it to you. Each drop seemed like the size of a grape. Wind was howling. Shutters banging."

Then, it began to warm up, becoming incredibly hot for a few months (see Section D immediately below) and then there was another period of relentless rain.

9/9/69 (L-184): "Rained 4 days in a row."

10/5/69 (L-207): "Today it just rained and rained. This makes the sixth day in a row and everything is wet, everything. It rains so much here that when it is just a mist and drizzling, I don't really consider it rain."

10/7/69 (L-208): In one of the 6 days referred to in L-207 immediately above, "it rained 22 inches in one day! Near that today."

10/12/69 (L-213): "Rain, rain every day."

D. Physical Discomfort Jon Was in Due to Weather: Extremely Hot Temperature

By early 4/69, the monsoon rains had dwindled away and were replaced by scorching hot weather as detailed in my letters to Sherrie.

3/20/69 (L-60): Temperature = 105 degrees F. "no problem."

3/21/69 (L-61): Temperature = 110 degrees F.

3/27/69 (L-68): Temperature = 115-120 degrees F. "Air conditioner in operating room broke down. Man, we sweated."

3/31/69 (L-70): Even though "it can get to be 100 degrees F in LA, you don't know what hot is until you are in 125 degrees F. And not just for one day, but at night and then the next day and so on."

4/2/69 (L-72): "It is scorching hot." "No place to go for relief."

4/15/69 (L-85): "120 degrees F today." "No water." "No shower."

4/20/69 (L-89): "120 degrees F today."

4/21/69 (L-90): "Tough getting through the day now. It is so unremittingly hot, no respite anywhere. Just ooze sweat, get dirty, work, ooze sweat, breathe dirt, work until the water bucket gets filled and then you just sweat some more, etc. I'm getting depressed more easily and more frequently now."

4/24/69 (L-93): "105 degrees F in the operating room today." "no air conditioning". "Hard grinding day." "All day."

5/4/69 (L-103): "120 degrees today." "Really torrid." "no wind."

5/13/69 (L-111): "120 degrees in the OR." "air conditioning never works."

5/14/69 (L-112): "It is 110-120 degrees F almost every day now, but I am getting used to it."

5/20/69 (L-117): "Today was very hot (120 degrees or more)."

5/21/69 (L-118): "Today was really hot, 122 degrees F, in the shade." "Difficult to do anything."

5/23/69 (L-119): "is at least 120 degrees F." "The heat is torrid." "Every day it is over 120 degrees."

After May of 1969, my letters did not say anything about the temperature until September 1969. I suspect the temperatures began to decrease as Vietnam's winter (and more rain) approached.

9/26/69 (L-200): 115 degrees F.

10/23/69 (L-223): "I can't believe it, but I have a granddaddy of a cold. Can you imagine getting a cold when it is 110 degrees F outside? That's what it has been since the rain stopped 5 days ago. I probably got the cold from my fan blowing directly on me all night."

E. Physical Discomfort Jon Was in Due to a Variety of Other Conditions/Diseases

As revealed in my letters to Sherrie:

1/22/69 (L-8): Insects. "I got so bitten up."

1/22/69 (L-8): "In a malaria infested area." "Rule" is we have to take C-P pills and daily malaria prevention medication.

3/5/69 (L-46): "Everything gets infected around here, even the smallest cuts."

4/3/69 (L-73): "Today we had no water for drinking or showering. The Viet Cong blew up the road so that the trucks that deliver the water could not get through to us."

5/23/69, #1 (L-119): "Went on a nerve gas alert. At all times you must carry your gas mask with you. Plus, you must have some injectable medicine with you as well."

5/23/69, #2 (L-120): "For a month I have had a skin infection called Tinea on my feet ("Athletes Foot"), in my groin ("Jock Itch") and on my body ("Ringworm") (back, arms, chest). It is impossible to get clear of it here. Everything is covered with dirt and dust and you never stop sweating. It is easy to get these infections."

5/23/69, #2 (L-120): Weight Loss. Came in-country at 155 pounds, now 135 pounds.

10/16/69 (L-217): "Weighed 134 pounds. Been eating. Seem to keep losing weight. My skin is infected again with Tinea. Generally speaking though, I feel pretty good."

COMMENT SECTION 4
Intermittently Occurring Long Hours of Non-Stop Work of Saving Lives

As with Comment Section 3, "The Dangers and Physical Discomforts Jon Experienced," Comment Section 4 needs some words of explanation of some general work issues before we get to the specific instances of long non-stop work.

First, I usually knew, from a few seconds to many minutes before, when I had to go to either the med-evac helicopter landing circle, the ER, or Operating Room (see L-94). I always assumed that the soldiers would be badly injured, losing blood, hemodynamically unstable, having trouble breathing, perhaps near death. Some, as they were off-loaded from the helicopter, would already be dead (see L-83). When I had the time (even a few seconds) I would be apprehensive (see L-94), and to some extent, dreaded what I would find. L-94: "I always hated waiting for them (the injured) to come and when they came, it was hard and heavy." If I had a lot of time, I would try to rest (e.g. L-94: "I should close my eyes until the casualties come.").

Second, increased fighting, or increased in-coming rockets, or hearing machine guns, AK-47s, M-16s or Cobra helicopter gunships in the air ALWAYS meant I would soon be going to work in the operating rooms.

Third, sometimes a lot of saving lives work had to be done on the helicopter landing pad and in the emergency room before the patients went into the operating rooms. See L-38: "When the choppers came in" I had to do "IVs, cutdowns, chest tubes, awake intubations." As I sorted through the patients being off-loaded from the helicopters, I had to figure out who was already dead (some were, see L-83 for example), who was barely alive (but had a chance to be really alive if taken to the OR immediately) and who was really alive and could wait a little while

Jon (right) standing inside the very large room (combined ER, PACU, ICU and Ward beds of the MASH Unit) discussing a patient with Dr. John Flora. In many letters, Jon described the long hours that he spent saving lives within this medical area.

1969–Photo of medical evacuation (med-evac) Huey Helicopter used to transport patients. Jon provided intensive medical care many times to many patients, when their care required that they needed to be transported in these helicopters.

(with treatment ongoing), before going to the OR. It was in this setting, receiving patients on the helicopter landing pad and in the ER, where I saw the most gore, carnage and death. Those we took to the OR, even if barely alive, had a good chance of being really alive.

Fourth, saving lives was not just confined to soldiers (USA, South and North Vietnamese Regulars and Viet Cong). Several mass casualty situations were due to orphanages being hit by rockets and the patients were babies, children and mothers (see L-69 and L-80 for just two examples).

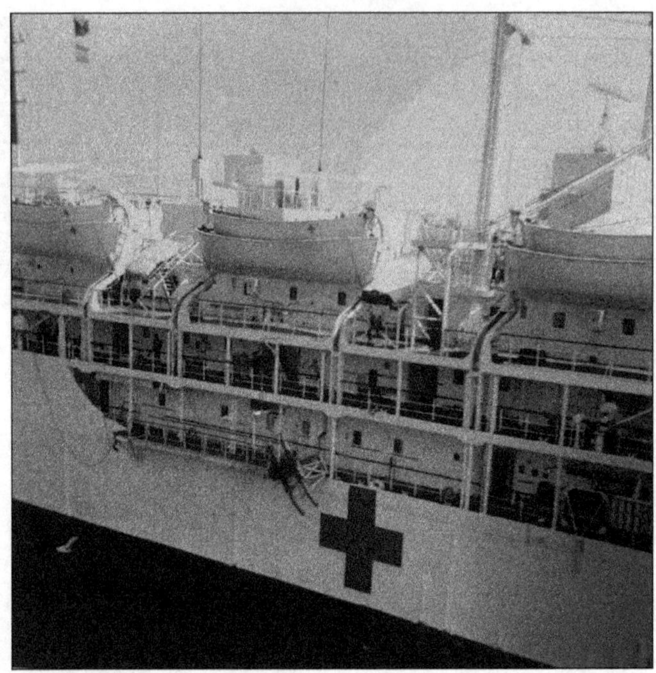

A Navy hospital ship (the Sanctuary or the Repose) that was positioned a few miles off the very Northern coast of South Vietnam. Jon had to bring many patients to these ships. Due to illness, a Navy Anesthesiologist had to return to the U.S. so Jon was asked to work on one of the ships for a few days.

Fifth, my saving lives work extended into the postoperative period where I had to stay and/or repeatedly see all the critically injured patients mentioned in "Fourth" above in the ICU. Additionally, I had to multiple times transport critically ill patients by helicopter to the Navy hospital ships (the Sanctuary and the Repose) lying offshore (see for example L-171 and L-172). On 4/22/69 (L-91), I describe pulling a pilot out of a burning helicopter as the pilot crash landed, barely making it back "home" to Camp Evans.

Sixth, all this work was a strain on me, it took a toll on me (see L-104). Why was I able to work so hard at times? I held the soldiers in high regard. On 2/25/69 (in L-38), I said "They (the soldiers) are so brave, these young men, I will work to exhaustion for them." Also, as said in L-93, "I am a Doctor." I HAD to work on badly injured patients no matter how hot, tired or exhausted I was. As I said in L-93 and L-96, "You cannot turn your back on somebody, while he has his guts hanging out, who might be somebody's husband or brother you know and got hurt just possibly protecting you or me." "It makes it easy to work hard for these courageous young men and boys, when you think of what they are doing, and very possibly for no reason at all." Finally, as I also said in L-93, "I guess I was a soldier, of sorts, and I was in a war."

Seventh, and finally, the reader should remember I had very little training to do what I was doing in Vietnam. In several letters, I commented on the fact I was doing the job with a medical book in one hand and a needle and syringe in the other hand (see L-48 for example).

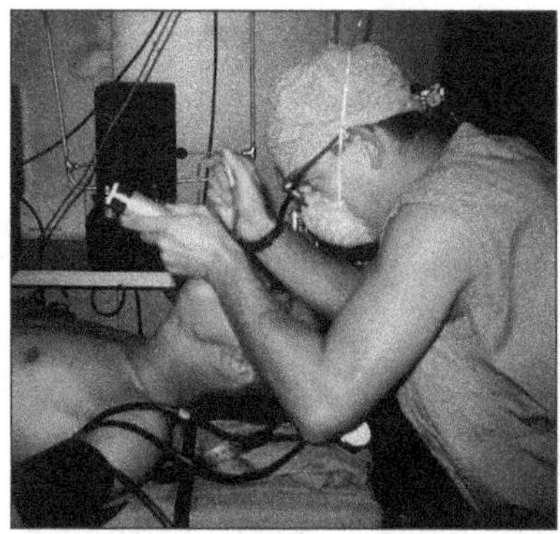

1969–Jon is performing laryngoscopy and tracheal intubation to get a patient ready for surgery. The patient is under general anesthesia and paralyzed.

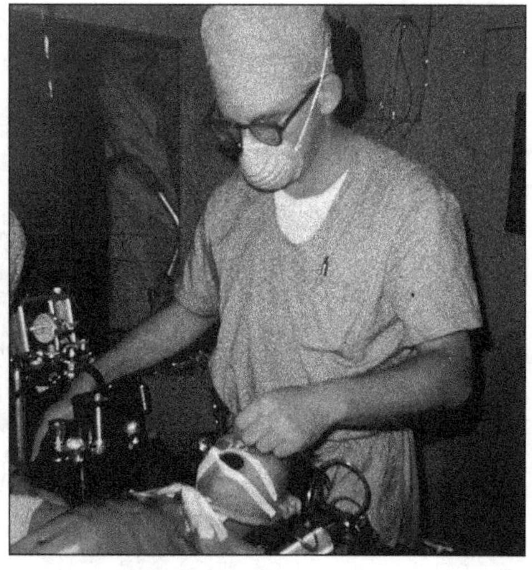

1969–Jon is preparing a Vietnamese boy for surgery. The boy is under general anesthesia, paralyzed, and intubated.

Here are some of the specifics of long hours of non-stop work by actual date of occurrence, the associated number of the Letter, and the actual quote from the Letter.

1/26/69 (L-11): "Worked through the night."

1/27/69 (L-12): "Up most of last 2 nights."

2/6/69 (L-20): "I worked about 36 straight hours in the past 2 days."

2/10/69 (L-23): "Worked through the night last night."

2/25/69 (L-37): "I worked all day yesterday and through the night."

3/8/69 (L-49): "Very drained of emotion and energy right now" after we "lost a patient after 3 hours of resuscitation."

3/21/69 (L-61): "I worked through the night."

3/27/69 (L-68): "When I arrived at the ER there was a "tremendous number of casualties." "I myself ran 3 operating rooms for the next 18 hours."

3/30/69 (L-69): "In OR for 24 hours. Did 31 cases in 1.5 days. Viet Cong hit orphanage with rockets. We got babies less than 1 year old to pregnant mothers."

4/1/69 (L-71): "In the last 5 days I have been in the OR more than 18 hours a day."

4/10/69 (L-80): "We had another all night, and all day, affair in the OR on Vietnamese children and their mothers. The kids are darling."

4/13/69 (L-83): "Would you believe 48 hours of straight cases without a break." Because "Twenty-five, I say again 25, were brought in. A whole platoon was wiped out (6 were dead-on-arrival). They were hit by our own gunfire by mistake."

4/25/69 (L-94): "I'm afraid we'll have to work through the night tonight."

5/11/69 (L-109): "In OR early morning to past midnight."

5/12/69 (L-110): "Spent the whole night and most of today in the OR.

In the last 3 days I have done 32 cases personally and I have helped the nurses with an additional 10."

5/13/69 (L-111): "We had over 20 cases today." "80 cases in the last 3 days."

5/15/69 (L-113): "We've been so busy. I think in the last week we did some 50 cases. The cases are going nearly around the clock and I'm sleeping pretty odd hours."

5/16/69 (L-114): "I've been busy with 20-hour days in the OR all week." "We're slaving away in the OR with the guns going and coming." "I'm just about done." "I hope the fighting breaks for a while."

5/19/69 (L-115): "Cases coming so fast." "Took us to the wee hours of the morning to get them done."

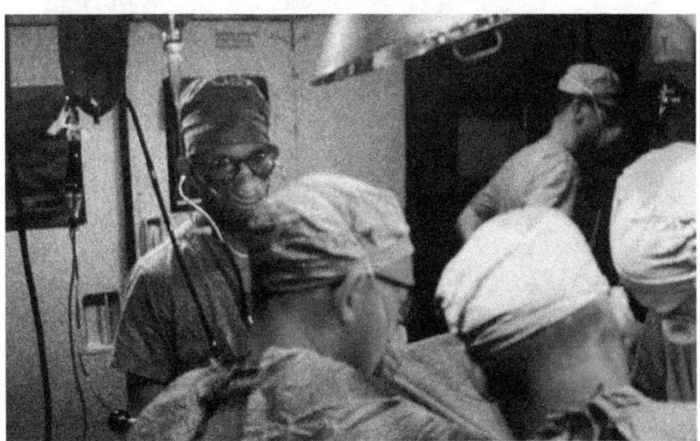

1969–Jon administers general anesthesia to patient. Stethescope allows monitoring of breath and heart sounds. Blood and intravenous fluids administered from a pressurized bag and glass bottle (upper left).

5/19/69 (L-116): "It is unbelievable the steady stream of casualties for 6 days and 7 nights now. The biggest rest I've gotten was 4 hours at one time 2 nights ago. Otherwise I've slept 1 hour here and there."

5/29/69 (L-126): "Busy until 4 AM last night."

I was required/ordered to go to the Navy Hospital Ship ("the Sanctuary") for a week because "the Anesthesiologist on the ship had to be sent home due to a back problem" (from 7/7/69- 7/14/69). I continued to work on "The Sanctuary" and unfortunately continued to have some soldiers die (see L-136 and L-139).

8/6/69 (L-157): "A patrol stepped into a booby trap", "We ran 3 ORs most of the night."

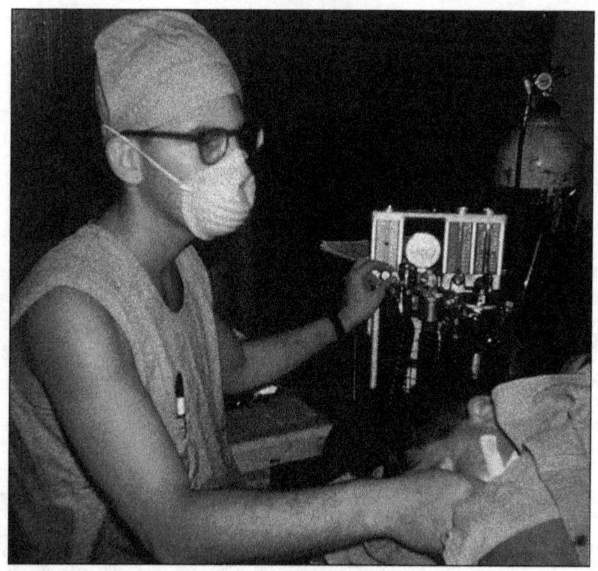

1969–Jon is administering general anesthesia to a prone patient, from a very simple 3 tank field hospital (MASH Unit) anesthesia machine.

8/12/69 (L-160): "Our hospital hit with rockets. Worked all night, half of next day on cases coming in from all areas of our own hospital." "Many from my own unit." "I knew most of the people hurt."

September 1969 was a relatively quiet month regarding work on injured patients.

10/9/69 (L-210): "Today I was 'Physician-on-Duty' (means I was the primary Emergency Room Doctor as well as being the Anesthesiology Chief and always on call for the OR)." "I had a dramatic case come in a little while ago. The patient was a Viet Cong soldier with a sucking chest wound. I rushed him straight into the OR after taking one quick look, put him to sleep, tubed him, and inflated his lung. He had a hole the size of a softball in his chest. Surgeon came, closed his chest."

10/14/69 (L-215): **"I found out today", "I have been nominated "for a Bronze Star", "Very hard to get", "There has been only one Bronze Star given to somebody from the 18th Surgical Hospital." "I feel proud." [author note: It was for a lot of hard work, good work, under difficult conditions, listed above in Comment Sections 3 and 4, and not for any specific individual or heroic event or anything else].**

10/17/69 (L-218): "I worked again through the night last night." "Being Physician-on-Duty (in the ER) and taking anesthesia call, I have been up every night for the last 5 nights."

A major part of November 1969 through December 1969 was involved in moving our MASH (Mobile Army Surgical Hospital) Unit north to Quang Tri which was basically the southern border of the DMZ (demilitarized zone, but really was just a conduit for North Vietnamese forces to flow into South Vietnam). During this period, of moving the MASH Unit, very little surgery was done.

11/25/69 (L-244): Performance of surgery by our MASH Unit in Quang Tri had begun. From 11/29/69 through 12/6/69, I had to take "second surgery call" "in addition to my anesthesia call" because "2 out of 3 of our Surgeons were taking their Board Exams in Saigon" which left us with only one surgeon and me (now the second surgeon). I anticipated needing to do "simple operations", but it is possible I may need "to do major belly cases." "So, I'm second surgeon."

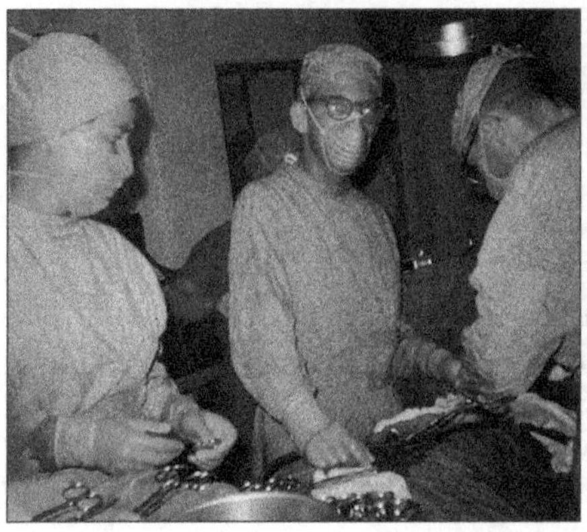
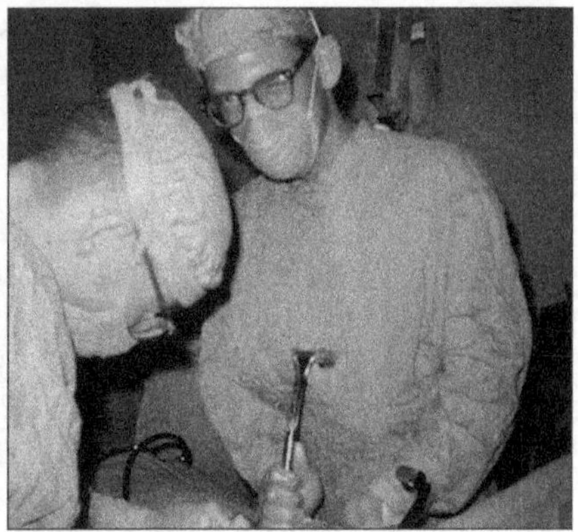

1969–Jon performing surgery.

11/27/69 (L-246): Indeed, I did do surgery. "I worked like a dog for about 15 straight hours today. I did 3 operations and did my own anesthesia for these cases." "And, I resuscitated a cardiac arrest and administered 5 anesthetics that Steve (First Surgeon) did."

11/30/69 (L-249): "I did one case today, a spinal. And I, also, did the surgery for that case. But I'm beginning to dislike doing both on the same case. It's too much of a strain. I worry about the anesthesia, which I can't do anything about since I'm scrubbed up for the surgery. And, I worry about the surgery since everything is so new. Another surgeon is coming tomorrow." "I think I will be relieved of my surgical duties."

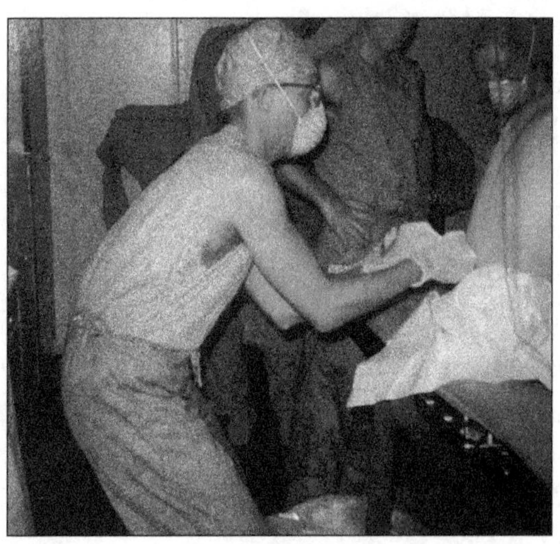

Jon is performing a spinal anesthetic for a patient.

12/1/69 (L-250): "I worked all day from 5:00 AM until 10:00 PM tonight." "My day started with an amputation of the leg. I had to do it myself, including the anesthesia." First Surgeon "was tied up on a big case." My patient did well fortunately. Then "all day as Physician-on-Duty, I had to be on the run." "Today, we got a temporary surgeon, so maybe the load will be eased for me."

12/2/69 (L-251): "If I wrote you that things were bad up until 10:00 PM last night, they got a lot worse after that. Around midnight, I got a comatose Vietnamese 52-year old lady, who I had to stay up with all night. I think she blew an aneurysm in her head, secondary to a hypertensive crisis. I got everything under control now. To boot, a guy came in who shot himself in the belly. And, there were 2 guys who needed to be treated for combat fatigue. Now I have combat fatigue."

12/6/69 (L-254): "Up all night. I then did 8-hour case, 40 units of blood." "Surgeon had a heart attack during the case" (talk about stress).

12/20/69 (L-266): "Last night we had our first mass casualty situation since Hamburger Hill." "There were 25 patients all at once. They were ambushed. I was running around putting in chest tubes, endotracheal tubes and cut downs. Sherrie, some of the wounds were horrible." "We worked through the night and a good part of the (next) day." "I did 3 operations (by myself) and my own anesthesia for them."

12/23/69 (L-268): "Worked all night." "On Vietnamese casualties."

1/2/70 (L-277): In response to a letter Sherrie had written me telling me she felt badly about a renal dialysis patient of hers who had died in the ICU, I wrote her "It's too bad that he died. Know how you feel. I had approximately 20 patients die, on me, for whom I spent more than 6 hours of time or work on (knowing from the beginning they would not make it). They each received over 50 units of blood. For some, I worked 24-48 hours trying to save them. Still, no luck. But, then again, I had 3 make it who received over 50 units of blood. So, you keep trying. The same goes for you."

1/5/70 (L-279): "working straight through for the last 20 hours."

1/6/70 (L-280): "I am just going to say hello. I've just gone another 24 hours in the OR and I can't see straight. The war isn't over. I'm as busy as I was during Hamburger Hill. I pronounced 6 dead today. I counted that I gave 141 units of blood to 6 patients today. That's an average of 23 units per patient. They had such bad wounds. And the injuries were to their arteries, nerves, bones, chests, hearts, livers, kidneys, bowels, just everything. I'm so sick of it."

COMMENT SECTION 5
My Growing Despair and Negative Feeling About the Loss of Life of Boys and Young People in the Prime of Their Lives

As expressed in my letters to Sherrie, there were a lot of strong emotions tied up in me as I did my job to save lives in a war. Sometimes emotions in a positive direction would prevail, sometimes emotions in a negative direction would prevail, and sometimes both positive and negative emotions were in me at the same time. Let me try to unravel and explain, using what I said to Sherrie in my letters to her, how I felt about boys and young men living and dying in my care for a cause that seemingly became more and more questionable as the 12 months went by.

In the beginning of my year in Vietnam (mid-January 1969), as I described in Comment Section 1 (traveling to and getting to the 18th Surgical Hospital), I was flat out scared I could not do the job (see L-5 in particular). Remember, I had very little (10%) of the training to do the job that I was going to do compared to a fully trained Anesthesiologist and I was worried I would hurt the soldiers and make mistakes.

When I began to actually do the work of saving soldiers' lives, I found success right from the beginning and I did not express any negative thoughts.

1/23/69 (L-9): "Cases in the OR went well." 1/23/69 (L-11): "I think I am doing a good job."

2/6/69 (L-20): "Soldiers have terrible wounds, terrible. I did some very difficult cases and I don't mind saying it......I did well." I think I was thinking "I can do this job."

2/11/69 (L-25): After doing open heart chest cardiac massage, with my bare hands, I wrote Sherrie "I really do have inestimable pride in some of the cases I have done."

2/18/69 (L-32): Of course, I "felt very let down when we lost" a patient. I had a great regard for ALL the patients. "These guys are so brave. All of them - Americans, South Vietnamese, Viet Cong. They are all very scared, afraid they are going to die or lose a limb. Yet they control themselves and are cooperative."

To my mind, my first expression of a glimmer of a negative thought began after doing heavy duty saving lives work for 6-8 weeks.

2/25/69 (L-38): I wrote Sherrie "Whenever I saw the soldiers leave Camp Evans to go to fight somewhere, I became emotional and always said to myself God be sparring of them for we will be operating on a few of them tonight." But, more positively, I wrote in the same letter "They are so brave, these young men. I will work to exhaustion for them."

My confidence in my medical competence continued to build.

3/8/69 (L-49): "I know what I am doing."

3/31/69 (L-70): "I know now I can do the job and do it well."

Questions about the war and what the USA was doing there became more frequent in my mind.

3/9/69 (L-50): I told Sherrie I talked with the Chaplain attached to the 18th Surgical Hospital MASH Unit. Because of all the killing I was witnessing, "I was in despair over man's nature." The Chaplain seemed "as lost and searching as myself."

3/30/69 (L-69): "We did 31 cases in 1.5 days", "Viet Cong hit an orphanage and we got babies and mothers." "What a mess." "War is hell."

4/10/69 (L-80): "Worked all day and night on children." It was heartbreaking to see these "darling children" mutilated.

Nevertheless, the good positive feelings that come from success as a doctor saving lives always was the strongest feeling I had. See 4/13/69 (L-83): On this day a platoon of 25 soldiers was wiped out by mistake by our own gunfire. Six of the 25 were Dead-on-Arrival. "We got each of the 19 who were alive off the operating room table alive." "I felt very proud of this positive result." So, in a growing sea of negative thoughts, positive feelings of what I was doing as a Doctor predominated, at least on that day in my letter to Sherrie.

I usually knew what was going on with regard to how the Camp Evans soldiers were doing and sometimes the news was not good. The not good news always led to negative thoughts about the war, anxiety while waiting for the injured soldiers to be brought to the hospital and dread regarding how medically bad the mass casualty situation would be. See for example 4/25/69 (L-94:) "I am very anxious right now." "Big fight going on now." "Four helicopters shot down, can't seem to get the area secured, can't lift out the downed pilots by helicopter." "I hate waiting for them" and "when they come, it's hard and heavy." And 2 days later, much more of the same very bad news. On 4/27/69 (L-96): "Out of 20 gunships parked outside of my hooch (see Figure 1), 8 ships (helicopters) have failed to return. I know most of the pilots, and so far, 3 have been hoisted out of the Viet Cong infested area where they were shot down." "4 miles from us." "I pray so hard that they will all come back." "I don't think they will." "They didn't." Then, on the one positive thought side, I said (in L-96) "It makes it so easy to work hard for these courageous young men and boys, when you think of what they are doing." BUT, on the negative thought side I said (in L-96) that "what they were doing was very possibly for no reason at all." "All so sad" and "after working so hard."

A few days later, on 5/1/69 (in L-100) to Sherrie, my negative thoughts about the war led me to say I wanted "freedom from dirt, dust, guns, wounds and cases and on and on." Nine days later (on 5/10/69 in L-108) I told Sherrie, after losing a Vietnamese soldier on the operating room table after giving him 47 units of blood (giving that much blood to one patient was at least a weekly occurrence) and getting him through 3 cardiac arrests, "I came back to my hooch too tired and too depressed to write." My spirit was being beaten by the war. On 5/16/69 (in L-114), I said "I'm just about done in" by so many injuries, from so much fighting and so much saving of lives to be done. Three days later (on 5/19/69 #1, L-115), cases were "coming so fast", I worked so hard, I felt "so harassed and so tired of cases" (injured young man after injured young man), the thought of yet another case "is infinitely repulsive to me." On the same day (5/19/69 #2, in L-116) my resentment of the war, frustration of seeing no end to the people killing people over our "trying to take one stinking hill (Hamburger Hill) and getting killed for doing it" was very evident. A few days later (5/24/69, in L-121), my frustration and exasperation and despair with the whole war process, namely killing, losing young lives, to gain a hill (Hamburger Hill), only for the 101st Air-borne to give it up again and "then fight for it all over again" was clearly expressed. On 7/15/69 (L-139), I said all of this is "getting to me", I wished "we could pull more of these kids through." "We are doing all that we can, and it just isn't enough." I despaired over this. I said (on 8/6/69 in L-157), "I hated" seeing our "guys all busted up."

On 11/13/69 (L-232): "Massacre took place at Quang Tri last night. Took 30 dead and 70 injured." "I felt really very bad about that ambush." "Just think, those guys were just like you or me. It was so useless, so tragic and so wasteful to lose lives like that." "Should I be risking my life over this war?" "Oh Sherrie, I want to get out of Vietnam so badly."

When my MASH Unit had to move to Quang Tri, in November 1969, some surgeons were permitted to go to Saigon to take their Board exams. When that occurred, we were left with one surgeon and I had to become the second surgeon in addition to being First anesthesia. (See Comment Section 4 for the 11/69-12/69 period). In a letter to Sherrie (on 11/30/69 in L-249), I told her about a particularly heart wrenching experience I had in the operating room as being both the Surgeon and the Anesthesiologist. "The guy I did the surgery on, today, cried his heart out throughout the whole case. (I must have been using regional anesthesia, so he was awake). We failed to resuscitate his best friend and he saw the whole thing. It was so very, very sad. I could find no words to console him.

What could I say? I felt the same way." "I don't think I'll ever forget the loneliness, desolation and despair of being in Vietnam."

On 12/20/69 (L-266): We had a "mass casualty situation" ("25 ambushed soldiers" with "horrible wounds"). Worked all night and the next day. I had to do 3 of the operations, all by myself, while I did the anesthesia for these operations at the same time. I wrote Sherrie "It all made me sick." I was in despair and angry over the situation. I wrote Sherrie "I would like to grab the 'silent majority' (code for those in the USA who thought this war was a good idea) and stick them close to the wounded. Then let's hear them continue to support the war."

The next day (12/21/69 in L-267): my despair and heartbreak over people killing people continued and increased. "Today a helicopter crashed." "They were bringing in 11 wounded soldiers. With the crash, 9 of the soldiers were dead. I felt so bad. I had to go outside and just cry. It is so tragic. Lately, I'm getting very emotional when patients come in and are badly injured or dead. Their bodies are so mutilated. I put endotracheal tubes in people that have no jaws, watch an eye fall into the palm of my hand and put IVs into the stumps of amputated legs. I'm sick of it all. I can't stand much more of this." "I think I will get drunk tonight."

Two weeks later (on 1/6/70 in L-280), I said "busy as Hamburger Hill. Pronounced 6 dead today. Gave 141 units of blood to 6 patients/ average 23 units per patient. They had such bad wounds. I'm so sick of it."

COMMENT SECTION 6
What Did I Do Between Periods of Taking Care of Injured Patients?

Between periods of taking care of injured patients, recreational activities greatly helped me get through the days. Very shortly after I got to my MASH Unit (2/1/69 in L-16), I found that "time goes by very slowly when there are no cases." At times the workload seemed almost too much to bear and at times, when there were no cases to be done, boredom almost seemed too much to bear. This thought/feeling was expressed in 10s and 10s of my letters to Sherrie following this initial L-16 letter. In particular, see the last paragraph in this Section, namely Comment Section 6 (reference to 8/5/69, L-156).

A. Running

I ran a lot. I began running, when I could between cases in the OR, soon after I arrived at my MASH Unit. As early as 2/27/69 (L-40): I wrote "It's getting so I don't feel right if I don't run every day" (when I could between cases). On 3/13/69 (in L-54): I wrote "I don't feel right, anymore, unless I've run once a day." Thereafter as many letters document, I did run whenever I could, come rain (pouring with the monsoon season; see Comment Section 3) or come sunshine (120 degrees F many days; see Comment Section 3). I ran on roads and paths well within the Fire Base, in and around the gunship and Med-Evacs helicopters parked near my hooch (see Figure 1). But, I NEVER ran near the perimeter fence (see Figure 1) because Viet Cong could be lurking and hiding in the jungle just outside of the perimeter fence. I ran every day I could, in my combat boots, for the whole year. When I came home, I was so used to running in my combat boots, and they were so well broken in by running in them, that I ran in combat boots in the United States for several months after I got home. As a humorous aside (to wanting to run in combat boots), I had also learned to love eating reconstituted powdered eggs and I insisted that Sherrie buy some to cook for me. Just shows you how odd situations can make for odd behavior.

1969–Jon working to build a better basketball court.

B. Played Basketball and Helped Build a Small Half Court Concrete Basketball Court

One day soon after I arrived at my MASH Unit (1/22/69 in L-8), I discovered there was "a hoop over a dirt court." I was elated with this finding: "I went wild." "Played for an hour." Within a week plans were made, and then carried out, to mix and lay cement for a better basketball court. By 1/26/69 (L-11) playing basketball "was my salvation." By 2/11/69 (L-25), the enlisted men/boys I was playing with called me "Doc, the white soul brother." Thereafter I ran more and played basketball less because, when the TET offensive began with the late February and March/April monsoon rains, it became harder and harder to get the enlisted men and 1or 2 Doctors to play.

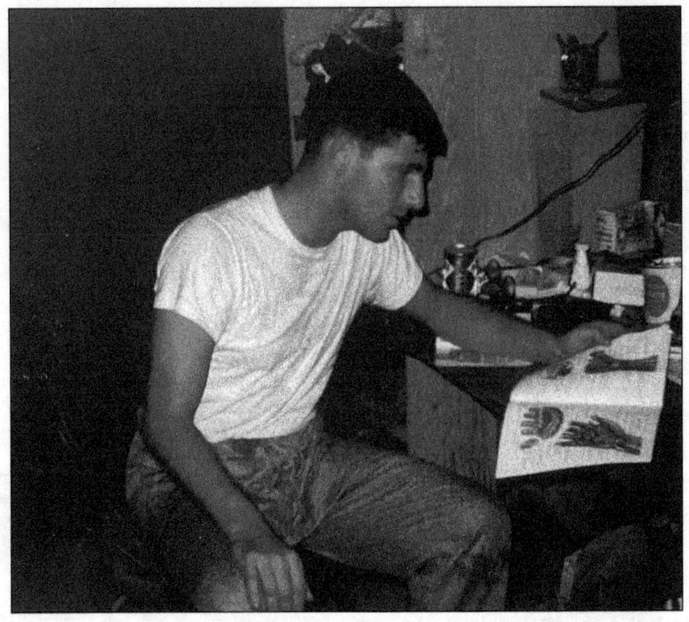

1969–Jon studying from a medical book at his desk.

C. Studied Anesthesia, Intensive Care and Medicine, Here and There, All the Time

My studying activity is mentioned in countless letters. My studying activity was initially fueled by fear of being inadequate, and unable to take good care of the soldiers properly, because of the little training in anesthesia that I received prior to going to Vietnam. As I gained confidence that I could do the job, and do it well (see L-70), the studying was fueled by a desire to improve the care of the injured patients above and beyond what was presently being done.

D. I Read Many Novels

This activity and the many novels are mentioned in many letters. Most of these novels turned out to be bestselling classics by authors who became world famous. These novels were read most of the time by the light of a single light bulb in the hooch, or sometime by flashlight when hunkered down in a bunker, and very occasionally by sunlight on our 'sun deck' on top of our bunker at the back of the hooch (see Figure 2).

1969–Jon reading a medical journal at his desk.

These novels, as I recall, helped to remind me that the non-war world was a real world that was rich in many ways given the fact that my immediate war world was basically kill or be killed, harm the human beings on the other side of the war (whatever you perceived the other side to be) as much as you can. As revealed by my letters to Sherrie, I read, sequentially: "The Prize" by Irving Wallace, "Airport" by Arthur Hailey, "The Fixer" by Bernard Malamud, "Tropic of Cancer" by Henry Miller, "Scarne on Cards" by John Scarne, "Dear and Glorious Physician" by Taylor Caldwell, "The Plot" by Irving Wallace, "The Magus" by John Fowles, "The Man" by Irving Wallace, "Topaz" by Leon Uris, "Georgia Boy" by Erskine Caldwell, "To Brooklyn With Love" by Gerald Green, "The Battle of the Bulge" by John Toland and "The Godfather" by Mario Puzo.

E. I Played Chess and Poker from Time to Time

These activities are mentioned in many letters.

F. For a While I Tried to Learn How to Play the Harmonica

Ultimately (it really happened pretty quickly), I failed to learn how to play the harmonica. The attempts to play the harmonica are mentioned in numerous letters.

Even though recreational activities helped get me through the days, sometimes the combination of "everything" got to me and at times

1969–Jon is trying to learn to play the harmonica.

I probably had clinically significant anxiety and depression. "Everything" meant dealing with watching young men getting mutilated and dying, rockets coming in, extreme heat and periods of rain, dirt/mud everywhere, and, yes, boredom when I had no cases and did not want to do any type of recreation. After 4 months in-country (and with regard to boredom), I wrote Sherrie on 8/5/69 (L-156), at a time we were NOT busy with injured patients and there were NO attacks on us: "I'm keeping a stiff upper lip but sometimes I get scared that I'm not going to make it. Sometimes I can't see any way to the end" (going home). "I can't see my way through the gap" (my remaining 8 months) "to my future."

COMMENT SECTION 7
Drinking Alcohol and Alcoholism

The following chronology details the evolution of my drinking alcohol in Vietnam to alcoholism in the USA after the war. The chronology also contains my present thoughts about what I think my drinking in Vietnam meant in terms of alcoholism.

1/22/69 (L-8): On the day I arrived, at the 18th Surgical Hospital, I wrote "I think I should develop some good habits here. I've drunk very little here." It appears I started my year in Vietnam as a normal drinker of alcohol.

2/2/69 (L-17): "Drinking much less than before." "Most I have is 2 beers in one day." The "Drinking much less than before" implies that I was drinking more alcohol before I left for Vietnam. My memory is not clear on this issue.

3/2/69 (L-43): I wrote that at a sing-in (sing along) with the enlisted men "I got really plastered (drunk) for the first time since being here." "I was so sick today." It should be noted that getting drunk, as a one-time event for a 26-year old, is not an unusual event but getting "plastered" is an abnormal endpoint of drinking alcohol.

3/9/69 (L-50): I wrote a lot about drinking to Sherrie on this day. "Last night the Officers' Club opened." The Officers' Club was located inside Camp Evan's main underground bunker (see Figure 1). The door leading to the underground bunker was a red door which had a sign on it that said "Rathskeller" (beer parlor). Not surprisingly, the Officers' Club promoted the drinking of alcohol. BUT, I wrote Sherrie "I have become one of the few non-drinkers here." "I have about two beers per day." Most of the men (Doctors included) drink quite a bit each day." They "get very mean" "when they get drunk." Their "whole nature changes." I "knocked out" "with a few punches" a drunk Doctor who entered my hooch and woke everyone up.

5/23/69 (L-119): "Last night everybody just sat around and got drunk" (me included). Once again, it should be noted that getting drunk as a one-time event for a 26-year old is not an unusual event. BUT, "getting drunk" is an abnormal endpoint of drinking alcohol.

7/28/69 (L-149): "Really got plastered (drunk) last night." Not an unusual event. BUT, getting "plastered" is not normal drinking of alcohol.

8/1/69 (L-153): Two days later at a 'toast' to an OR technician, who was leaving to go home, "I got smashed." Getting drunk, 2 days apart, was unusual and not normal drinking. In retrospect, the drinking behavior is worrisome and consistent with the beginning of alcoholism.

8/11/69 (L-159): I told Sherrie if l did not have to work in the OR that night (I did end up working in the OR that night), I would have gotten drunk (the reason being that I hated and was fearful of boredom). That is a disturbing, bad attitude and abnormal cause and effect thinking. It is alcoholic thinking; i.e., alcohol will diminish negative feelings in my heart and replace them with 'feeling better/good'. Looking back, 50 years later, the frequent extremely high intense periods of work and danger may have contributed to the relative inability to deal with the low intense periods of having no work to do on patients, no danger and the fear of having nothing to do.

8/19/69 (L-165): "Got smashed last night." Third time in 3 weeks.

Troublesome. Alcoholic behavior.

9/6/69 (L-181): In terms of understanding the development or onset of my alcoholism, this is an important letter. I wrote "USUALLY... (then list of activities I did until 10 PM)" and "IF not in the operating room" "THEN (I would) have a couple of drinks in the Officers' Club." I now think the two drinks were a minimization of the reality and the beginning of regular drinking of alcohol if it did not conflict with taking care of patients in any way.

9/29/69 (L-203); I got "slightly sloshed" playing (and losing in) chess.

10/8/69 (L-209): "Last night I got sort of smashed".

10/19/69 (L-219): "I was drunk" on this day. This was the third time in the past 3 weeks. Again, this is behavior consistent with the beginning of alcoholism.

12/7/69 (L-255): "Tonight I am off" (duty). "I will have time to drown my loneliness and misery in booze." (How shocking it is to go back and see that my drinking of alcohol was deliberate and misguided).

12/21/69 (L-267): After an incredibly tragic mass casualty situation on this day, dealing with/receiving many dead soldiers and badly mutilated soldiers, the horrific situation briefly forced me to step outside and cry (See Comment Section 5 on this letter: 12/21/69, L-267). After all the soldiers were cared for, I wrote Sherrie "I think I will get drunk tonight." Clearly this cause (hard to imagine the magnitude of this tragedy) and effect (getting drunk) is understandable (perhaps poignant), but still undesirable. Treating/medicating negative feelings with alcohol (and having some success in that regard) is paving the road to alcoholism.

1/5/70 (L-279): After working for 20 straight hours, and not expecting to work any time soon, I told Sherrie "So, maybe I'll do some serious drinking." In retrospect, it seems to me that alcoholic drinking behavior is setting in.

COMMENT SECTION 8
Coming Home to No "Welcome Home" or "Thank You for Your Service"

The letters to Sherrie do not say anything about the fact that Veterans (including me), returning from the Vietnam War, did not receive a "Welcome Home" or "Thank you for your service" upon arrival in the USA by the public. The obvious reason that the failure of the public to recognize military service is not noted, in my letters to Sherrie, is because it is something that occurred to me after I returned home (from Vietnam). The failure to recognize the contribution of all these servicemen, to their country in the Vietnam War, is now widely recognized as having been very hurtful to these individuals. I am including this Section 8, in the commentary on all the letters, because WHAT WAS IN ALL THOSE LETTERS constitutes the reasons I should have received a "Welcome Home" and "Thank you for your service."

First, I think it is important for me to reiterate I was apolitical when I went to Vietnam. I was neither for or against the war. Due to the special circumstances of where I was in my medical training, and the intensity of the war, I basically had to go into the military. If I had not, I would have received some sort of significant punishment. Nevertheless, I can say that if I had to go to the Vietnam War, I was certainly for the prospect of saving lives if I could. The vast majority of fighting young men/boys went to war because they were drafted and were simply doing their duty to serve their country. To me, it is understandable to be against those who created the war (being against those who created the war was a viewpoint I was sympathetic to when I came home) and against the reasons being proffered by those who created the war as justification for the war (being against the reasons being proffered to support the war was a viewpoint I was sympathetic to when I came home). But, it is not understandable to me to be against those who were simply doing their duty to serve their country. In summary, I was simply trying to save the lives of those doing their duty to their country. As a general proposition, we should have received a "Welcome Home" and a "Thank you for your service" from everyone. We did not.

Second, there were many specific reasons, as told in my letters to Sherrie, I should have received a "Welcome Home" and a "Thank you for your service." In general, I had worked as hard as I could, for as long as was ever necessary and I cared about the patients as much as one can care. All the while I was in considerable danger and discomfort.

More specifically:

for all the carnage, mutilation of humans, and death I had to deal with;

for all the open and closed chest cardiac massages I had to do;

for all the clamps I had to put on openly bleeding vessels;

for all the intravenous lines, breathing tubes, and chest tubes I had to put in;

for all the extreme heat, and the relentless rain, I had to endure;

for all the hours of taking care of patients on ventilators and the many times I transported critically ill patients by helicopter (multiple risks).

For all my intense involvement in, and doing the activities listed above, I should have received a "Welcome Home" and a "Thank you for your service". I did not get any of that, from the public, for many years. In my heart, I always silently cherished my Bronze Star and Purple Heart "thank you" that was given to me by my immediate Commanding Officer and by the men and women with whom I served.

Fifty years have passed since I returned home from Vietnam. I did not live these 50 years being bitter about not getting a "Welcome Home" and a "Thank you for your service" from the public. In fact, I hardly ever actively thought about it. In recent years, if by chance the topic of my being in the Vietnam War comes up, occasionally someone will recognize my service. The only time in my life that I knowingly felt really bad, and openly cried, about no "Welcome Home" and no "Thank you for your service" was when I visited the Vietnam War Memorial in Washington DC. At least the 58,000 dead soldiers got this post-mortem "Welcome Home" and "Thank you for your service." I know an ache in my heart exists about the failure of the public to appreciate the service of those who went to Vietnam. Nowadays, when someone says to me (at 78 years of age) "Welcome Home" and "Thank you for your service", only then do I realize how much those kind words are now appreciated and how much they would have been appreciated in January of 1970.

SHERRIE'S LIFE WHILE JON WAS IN VIETNAM January 1969 – January 1970

We had only been married for 6 months when Jon had to leave for Vietnam, for a full year, as directed by his orders from the Army. This, of course, was very emotional for both of us. But, we aimed to be strong supports for one another so that each of us could get through the 12 months of separation.

We committed to writing to one another daily and we did that faithfully with very few exceptions. Some of our letters, to one another, did get lost in the mail system. But, even so, I ended up receiving 282 precious letters from Jon. These letters were an intimate and loving connection to Jon and his life in Vietnam. And, they sustained my life without him in Los Angeles. The letters, from Jon, kept me in touch with what was happening in his daily life and his feelings about his life in Vietnam and the War. In addition to the extremely long hours of work that he described (the tragic loss of life and the stories of success in saving lives), he tried to keep his life in balance with other activities.

It was comforting to me that he was successful in establishing good working relationships with all the Operating Room (OR) staff and the other Doctors. It was great to hear that he garnered the respect and admiration of them and the Army's top Officers. It was wonderful to know that he was doing a lot of reading of medical books, journals and novels, playing basketball, playing cards and chess, listening to his favorite music recording artists, running almost daily, building some of the furniture that he needed in his hooch, cooking and sharing meals together with his friends, trying to learn to play the harmonica and constructing a cement basketball court with fellow soldiers. Jon's letters were very descriptive of his life, his longing to be home with me, wanting his year in Vietnam to be completed, his thoughts and feelings that this War had no winners, no purpose and had impacted so many lives with such extreme devastation and loss.

In his letters, he never failed to tell me how much he loved me and that my letters were his lifeline to being able to survive emotionally in Vietnam. Because of this, I wanted to live the best life I could in his absence. I always told him, in my letters, how much I loved him and that we would get through this year together. To make his life a little more comfortable, almost weekly, I mailed him care packages filled with all kinds of food items that he requested. Included in those packages were what was to become his very favorite cookies for the last 51 years (Banana Oatmeal Chocolate Chip Cookies—see recipe next page).

I, also, made many tapes for Jon, singing the songs that he enjoyed hearing (he always loved to listen to me sing).

To be strong for Jon (and for myself), I kept as busy as possible. I was able to be rehired to work full-time as a Registered Nurse (RN) at Los Angeles County General Hospital (LACGH) in the Renal Dialysis/ Kidney Transplant Specialty Unit. This was the same RN position that I had before we got married. This was extremely important to me as I already knew many of the staff there. I have remained friends with four of them (all RNs) since 1967, when I first worked with them. They are Maureen, Maribeth, Judy and Sheila. I could not have endured the year that Jon was in Vietnam if they weren't in my life at that time. They knew Jon and they reached out to include me in activities outside of work. In turn, I decided to work double shifts when needed and weekends and holidays so that they could spend extra time with their significant others. I figured the extra work would keep me busy and I could make more money for us to save. I, also, worked extra private duty RN shifts at Cedars-Sinai Hospital and Children's Hospital in Los Angeles to keep me busy and to make extra money.

My future education goal was important (a Bachelor of Science Degree in Nursing), so I took some classes at California State University Long Beach. Also, I took guitar lessons, swimming lessons, did some sewing of dresses for me, refinished some furniture for my apartment and started frequently jogging a mile or two. I wanted Jon to be proud of me and I wanted to improve myself and my abilities. I, also, maintained contact with Jon's medical school classmates (Greg, Stu, Rich) and encouraged them to write to Jon in Vietnam (which they did). As busy as I kept myself, the longing for Jon to be home never subsided and his letters were so very important to me. Our faithful writing to one another sustained us both in what was a most difficult time.

Banana Oatmeal Chocolate Chip Cookies

Sherrie baked these cookies and sent them often to Jon while he was in Vietnam. He speaks of them frequently in his 282 letters.

INGREDIENTS

1 1/2 cup flour
1 cup granulated sugar
1/2 teaspoon baking soda
1 teaspoon salt
1/2 teaspoon cinnamon
1/4 teaspoon nutmeg
3/4 cup cooking oil
1 egg (well-beaten)
3-4 large ripened bananas (mashed)
2 cups Quick Quaker Oats
2 (12 ounce) packages of semi-sweet chocolate chips

These cookies are also the favorite of our adult kids, their spouses, and our grandchildren. They all bake the cookies and now they share them with us.

DIRECTIONS Oven Temp = 350 F

Mix all ingredients (in the order listed). Stir carefully after each ingredient is added. Drop teaspoonfuls of mixed batter onto an ungreased cookie sheet. Bake for about 12 minutes or until golden brown. Makes 4 dozen cookies.

(1st Letter

PART 2:

282 LETTERS FROM JON'S HEART

Dearest Sherrie,

I've been on the plane for nine hours ... just about going out of my gourd. I've never been so lonely in all my life. I feel so alone, but holding together. I've read, went to the bathroom and dozed a bit. I guess a movie is coming up soon (Doris Day). As soon as I left you, they put us on the plane. We stopped in Honolulu for 30 minutes.

All my love and thoughts,

Jonny

Dearest Sherrie,

Ending the plane trip soon (about 1 hour). Total time is 22 hours. I've never been so lonely. I hope you got to L.A. without incident. Tell me about your stay at Nat's. Remember, if you need money, my folks are anxious to help with anything.

Thinking of you constantly,

Jonny

5:30 PM (2:30 AM your time)
Dearest Sherrie,

Well, I'm here ... it's so hot and humid. The Vietnamese are indescribably impoverished. The Army stinks. All I can tell you now is that I'm going to Da Nang tomorrow night by plane at about 2:00 AM my time. There are six hospitals up there (it's very near the DMZ) and I'll find out which one I'm at when I get there.

I love you very, very much.

P.S. On the way in I saw bombs go off all over the country. If you write anybody, just tell them what I tell you.

Dearest Sherrie,

Miss you a great deal, think about you all of the time. Today, I'm in jungle fatigues passing time waiting for my flight tonight to Da Nang. I obtained a PX catalogue today and it contains so many things we need: stereo, cameras, recorders, projector, ad infinitum. I saw a fur I'm going to get you and a watch. I changed my thinking a bit. I may spend $2000- $3000 here. The buys are great. I may need you to send me a big check in a few months *(like $1000) and I'll buy a lot and send it home all at once.*

I love you very deeply,

Jonny

Dearest Sherrie,

I've been thrown to the wolves. I have a terrible assignment. It is at the 18th Surgical Hospital at Camp Evans. We service the 101st Airborne Special Forces and dig this, I'm on my own in 15 days- me Chief. I have so many deep emotions right now. It's such a challenge, but I'm so scared. My APO is 96383. See return address.

Sherrie dearest, I love you so much. Please think of me.

Dearest Sherrie,

I don't really understand this card (birthday), but at least you know I remembered. As you know, I've been assigned to the 18th Surgical Hospital at Camp Evans-60 miles North of Da Nang and about 20-40 miles South of the DMZ. This is where the 101st Airborne are. In the words of the Colonel who assigned me ... "I've been thrown to the wolves" because the Board Eligible Anesthesiologist who is there is leaving in 15 days. Everyone seems to be bracing for an expected TET offensive which will begin in about a week. All I know is that the guns, from off shore, are constantly shooting and the planes and helicopters fill the sky. I'm in Da Nang now waiting for a helicopter to take me to Camp Evans this P.M. or tomorrow A.M. I feel thrilled by the challenge of being Chief of Anesthesia during TET offense, but I'm very shaken and scared inside. They tell me I'll be frightfully busy during TET. Maybe it's what I need. I need to get to work rather than thinking about it. I need you very much. Absence has made my heart fonder, but so much sadder.

Dave Thompson is here at Da Nang. He had a Port-of-Call January 12. I had supper with Roberta Johnson January 17 in Bien Hoa- enjoyed seeing her immensely. Spending time with Dave while I wait. Please write my Mom and Dad, Nat, Des and tell Greg and Stu the details for me now. I'm too up in the air to write to them now.

The food has been good, but I've completely lost my appetite. In just a few days, I think I lost 5 pounds. So far, I've slept on cots in barracks. At the Surgical Hospital they have started barracks, so I won't be in a tent long and that's good since the monsoons will be coming in 3 months. Getting used to the heat now. Everybody wears fatigues and boots all of the time, even in the O.R. The PX's have had nice things to buy, but I'm going to wait till I get to Camp Evans. Most things will be sent directly to you. The hospitals are all pretty safe, but most places expect to get some shelling during TET. Well this is Jonny the Soldier signing off.

Love You–can't wait for R&R, back rub???

Dearest Sherrie,

I still have not made it to the 18th Surgical Hospital. I'm in Phu Bai, 20 miles away, waiting for my last helicopter. I just sent you $400 from where I checked in at finance. You should get it in 7 days or so. It's per diem.

Four hours later ... Just got to Camp Evans–in the boonies. Oh yes, $650 per month will be coming in now. How I miss you so very much,

Jonny

Dearest Sherrie,

Well today was finally a happy day for me, at least in contrast to the others, which involved lugging my foot locker and two full duffle bags on and off jeeps, on and off planes and helicopters and living in poor quarters. I arrived here (18th Surgical Hospital) last evening. As you know, I sent you $400 out of $550 which I got for things like travel pay, per diem, wages for December, part of January, etc. Please write me of your receipt and, also, please send me my extra pair of eyeglasses. Tonight, the ones I was wearing cracked. Why, I don't know. One night, enroute to here, I got so bitten up.

I'm now in an infested malaria area and so it is a rule that in addition to the C-P pills, we have to take every week, we have to take a daily malaria prevention medication.

Let me tell you about the place and my day. Today, I woke up at 9:30 AM. The hospital has been very quiet, very few cases. We are quietly waiting for the TET offensive. So as you can see, there is little to do. I spent the morning building myself a combination cabinet-closet and shelves. I think it's great, for me, and I'm building a desk next. I'm really doing it on my own ... no help. It's very simple. It's surprising what you can do when you want to. It's so humid here. Everything (like my closet and shelves) will need light bulbs, so what I'd like you to send me is an extension cord with socket receptor at the end of it. If you can, also, a light bulb with 100 watts and prongs on the end to fit into the extension cord socket. Just go to a hardware store.

At 1:00 PM, I did a gunshot wound of the abdomen. No problems, case went smoothly. I then went back to work on my cabinet. After supper, I found a real good basketball player and guess what? The guys have a hoop over a dirt court. I went wild and played for an hour. I guess you can imagine how the basketball, the smooth gunshot wound case and building my cabinet-closet lifted my spirits.

We live in barracks for 4 people (MDs). Pretty nice guys, but the only one I like is the basketball player. The others are either too much like MDs or uninteresting to me. But, I think I'll get along with them. We use an outhouse toilet (ugh) and have sort of a shower. The hospital is surrounded by bunkers and machine guns which are about a 1/4 mile to a 1/2 mile away. Last night, the artillery was busy and there were flares in the sky all night. Most of us have guns. I get one tomorrow.

I've been pretty well received here. I guess most are really waiting to see how I do when we get busy. There is one board eligible Anesthesiologist here and 3 Nurse Anesthetists. All will be gone, in 1 month, with one very inexperienced Nurse Anesthetist coming. So, everyone is acting towards me as a "soon-to-be-Chief". The board eligible Anesthesiologist is going in 8 days and he is not very well thought of. In return, I'm approaching everything very energetically, with great interest and instituting new ideas that I got from Des. So far, I have attentive ears. I think I can do a good job.

I've lost 5 pounds. Get with it, I don't want my wife to be jealous of me when we are in Hawaii. I'm so anxious to be with you. I think of you very frequently. We're going to have such a good time in Hawaii. I think I should develop some good habits here. I've drunk very little. I'm much more energetic and doing things like building furniture that I've never done before. Next week, I plan to mix and lay cement for the new basketball court.

In a few weeks, I'm going to be buying things (radio, recorder, etc, etc) and you will start receiving them since I am having them sent directly to you. I am getting you a little fur wrap for your birthday. It won't arrive for months, but at least you know you'll be getting it.

I love you very much. I hope this letter shows it. I feel close to you. I don't feel like writing to anyone else now so, in your letters and conversations with people (Mom, Dad, Nat, Des, Greg, Stu, etc), tell them what I write you. I want so much to hear from you. I'm told it takes 2 weeks to get the first letter. Payday is at the end of the month.

All my thoughts and desires are for you,

Jonny

(I'm called "Ben" here)

1/23/69
Letter 9

Dearest Sherrie,

I miss you very much, but I was quite busy which helps a great deal. Today, about 10:00 AM, a whole bunch of cases came in. I did 3 of them (out of 7). One was a general on a 6 year old Vietnamese boy shot in the shoulder (big case), general of his Mother (7 months pregnant) who was shot in the leg with a fractured femur and his Father with gunshot wound of the abdomen- for which general was done. Oh yes, a fourth was a spinal on an American boy (19 years old) for a gunshot wound of his buttock and leg. All went well. Tomorrow, I'm taking first call. Up until now, I've just been doing the cases to familiarize myself with things and establish myself. The cases took a good part of the day. After that, I worked on my closet-shelf cabinet, then ate, played basketball for an hour, then showered and now I'm writing you. I always seem to miss you the most after I've played basketball and the whole evening and night faces me. All the guys just sit and talk small talk which I hate, but I participate some since I don't want to be antisocial. But, that's when I pine away for you. Tonight, I'm going to play chess with one of the guys.

Tomorrow, I have to buy an electric shaver. My old one is no good. I don't know what it is (maybe the cord is shot). I'm going to send it home along with other things that I don't need.

I guess tomorrow I'll get a camera, also, and start shooting photos. Naturally I'm eagerly awaiting your first letter, but I know it takes time for the channels to open up and the Army to locate me. Then the letters will come much quicker.

Think I'm going to play chess now and then read. You're such a lovely far distant vision to me. Won't it be fun to have children, a home (I can build now and all). Perhaps today's pick up in casualties signals TET?? I don't hear the guns right now. Tomorrow, I'm helping build bunkers.

Goodnight Sweetheart,

I am your Jonny

Dearest Sherrie,

Today was such a slow day. Not one case. Worked a little on my cabinet, went to the PX by jeep (carried a gun!!!) where I just bought some food and bathroom articles, read, ate supper, played some real good basketball, showered and now writing you. Listening to the guys talk, I apparently misunderstood something. The TET offensive is on, but the shooting isn't supposed to begin until February 15–at which time, I'll be alone in the Anesthesia Department. What the Viet Cong are supposed to be doing is tunneling in now. In return, we are putting up bunkers around our hooches (barracks). Today, I was second call. Tomorrow, first call. Should get a case, I guess.

One of the surgeons bought a pair of tape recorders, for $50, which he doesn't think he'll be able to use. If not, I told him I'd buy them. They should come in about 2 weeks. I'll let you know.

Please send me that light bulb and cord as soon as

possible. February 15 is supposed to start the monsoon (the Viet Cong are using the good weather to tunnel and then when it rains- boom) so the light bulb will keep my clothes dry. I made up a package today of my boots, broken shaver and field jacket to send to you. I don't need that stuff.

Last night, I won in chess. We're playing again tonight. I didn't get anything at the PX today. I'm going to wait just a bit. After writing you, I'm going to go through some catalogues.

Boy, I'll be happy when I get a letter. Dammit, 354 days to go. I wonder what you are doing?

Love you very much, Dumpling

Jonny

These letters make sort of a diary, don't they?

Dearest Sherrie,

I didn't write yesterday because I was very busy. Had a lot of cases ... kids, South Vietnamese, Viet Cong and GI's. Worked through the night. I'm kind of tired right now. It seems as though the South Vietnamese are the ones who are getting injured the most. In the past two days, we've done about 15 of them compared to 2 Viet Cong and about 5 Americans. Think I'm doing a good job. They have a medical meeting every week and I was asked to speak at a meeting, in about a month, on respiratory care. Thank goodness I brought that book on respiratory care. I'll just more or less vocally paraphrase the book.

I'm still going through periods of severe depression and loneliness. I haven't made any real good friends yet and I'm beginning to think I'm not going to. I get along alright, but most of them are older and have been together for a long time. We'll see. I do enjoy doing cases and basketball every evening has been my salvation. After playing ball tonight, I felt quite sick and I took 2 salt pills. I feel a lot better now. Must have been salt depleted or Sherrie depleted. Naturally, I miss you a great deal. Most of my free time, which can be considerable when nothing is happening, is spent reading and do little jobs here and there. Wish so much they would send your letters through to me. I had one of the fellows take a picture of me, today, so I could send it to you. It'll take about a month before you get it. My hair is even shorter than before I left.

Love you very much,

Jonny

Hi Sweetheart.

I'm so tired. I've really been bombed these last 3 days ... up most of the last 2 nights doing generals, spinals, difficult intubations, etc. Did a Viet Cong big shot or so intelligence (Army, not mine) tells me. Supposed to be the biggest catch in a long time. Two guys were brought in dead last night. I was so sorry and sad for them. Nice looking young guys. Such a shame.

I was thinking, today, of how wonderful and giving you

have been in our marriage and I'm so thankful for having you. I think you have tried hard and for the most part were successful. That is in lieu of my faults, which at times can be considerable. You've done a great job. I think that I shall be able to be a better husband now that I've had a chance to collect myself. I've been so busy these past days that I have not sent that box yet nor purchased anything yet. The way things are going, I don't know if I will be able to until after TET. It definitely seems like the Viet Cong activity is increasing and more are being seen every day. I wrote Des a letter and Gary Fletcher a postcard yesterday.

Gee, I hate to think how long I have to go. Where would you like to go (my next assignment) after Vietnam? I think Fort Ord in California would be best and second choice would be New York. What do you think?

Today, one of the corpsmen took 2 pictures of me working in the O.R. I'll send them to you when I get them, but I don't think that will be for a month yet.

I'm going to read a little and then go to bed. I'll talk to you tomorrow night. I hope nothing comes in tonight. Wish so much they would put your letters through.

Love you,

Jonny

Hi Sweetie,

Today was such a boring day. I had no cases since I was first call yesterday. I read, wrote my Mom and Dad, filled sandbags and did nothing. Tomorrow, I stand a good chance of going to the PX and think I'm going to get a camera for $108 that sells for $300 in the U.S. It takes very good slides and I'll buy a $40 projector and have it sent, to you, so you can project the slides. I'll take lots of shots.

I still haven't got a letter. That's so disappointing to me. Last night, dust-off (the fly boys) had a party, but I didn't stay long because all male parties were never very appealing to me. Most of the humor involves insulting somebody and that somebody always looks to me like he isn't enjoying himself because of the insults. Even though I was never the butt of the jokes, I didn't care for it, so I went home. I made a list of all the things I expect to buy and it comes to about $1200. Not bad. Here is a quick list: watches– one for you and one for me= $26, radio= $44, stereo= $300, color TV= $419, electric knife= $10.65, mixer= $6.50, shaver= $18, camera= $108, projector= $40, movie camera= $70, movie projector= $62, screen= $10, binoculars= $10, two recorders= $50, fur= $70. Can you think of anything else?

I daydream of you all the time. This is getting me down being here.

Love you very much,

Jonny

P.S. Sherrie, please send me a cheap air mattress. I need one.

Today, I got 5 letters ... 3 from you, 1 from your folks and 1 from Nat. That was great, made me feel good- especially after last night which I'll briefly tell you about. We took some rockets (we were fired on) last night and there was a great deal of return fire all night from tanks, planes and machine guns. We spent about 4 hours in bunkers with guns. With all the noise, it seemed unusual to me. I had difficulty, at first, telling what were incoming and what were outgoing rockets. The only thing that scares me really is a direct hit. Otherwise, I feel confident. The closest shell hit at the beginning of an airstrip, across the way from us (about 1/3 mile), where the 101st Airborne group is. It's amazing how loud and close it can sound. A half mile away, the percussion is terrific. Anyway with the coming of TET this is supposed to be, I'm told, a nightly occurrence and that I will become an old pro at shitting in my pants. Little do they know how good I am at farting. Eh, girl?

I think my Board scores are somewhere in the metal file. If not, try opening my diplomas. Maybe I stuck them in there. If not, I guess you'll just have to go through everything till you find it. Remember, there is a part one and part two. Let me know if you found them.

I do not need a hot plate or refrigerator. The Docs here use one collectively. Everybody loved your cookies. Send more. I don't need anything else right now. I would enjoy very much seeing some pictures of you. Don't be self-conscious. Just take a few of yourself regularly and send them. I enjoy them and liked the one you did send. You looked so pretty.

Today, I had 2 cases which went fine. I'm on tonight and I suspect it's going to be busy. I think the Viet Cong are dug in now in some hills to the West of us.

Can't see them because there is jungle vegetation covering. Adding together the number we are catching, and the rockets, our own casualties are increasing. It comes to pre-TET activity. That's what the amateur Generals around here think, so I think it. I'll write your Mom and Dad soon- in a few days.

Your Dad's letter was enjoyable. Tell him I said so. Your Mom's was nice, too, but too much on the prayerful side. Know what I mean? Nat wrote a nice letter. Thanks for talking to Greg, Stu and Bill. It sure would be nice to hear from them.

The wind has shifted here and I'm told that it means the monsoon rains are coming. I see that you have had one of your own. The monsoon is important because it coincides with TET and offers coverage for the Viet Cong. I don't mean to dwell excessively on these things, or try to scare you, it's just what everybody talks about and consequently thinks about. I'm really pretty content doing my job and I'm fairly busy doing cases. When I'm not, I play basketball, eat, and write letters to you. And, like today, worked about 2 hours building (or rather cementing) our basketball court. We talk about the war and I try to get another Doc to play chess. Yesterday, I filled sandbags for awhile to bunker our hooch.

Remember, we are 25 miles South of the DMZ and the closest town is Da Nang (40 miles South of us). Don't worry, Honey. I couldn't get into trouble even if I wanted to, which I don't. I love you very much, miss you a great deal and think of you all the time.

I really miss you,

Jonny

Dearest Sherrie,

I got your carnation milk today, but part of the package was torn so it had fallen out. No loss though, we have regular milk here. Don't send anything unless I ask for it, otherwise it's just wasted and you know how I am about that. Two things I would like you to send, in addition to the other things that I specifically asked for, are: about 6 pairs of medium thickness socks and a book called "Scarne on Cards" (or "Games"). It's something I want to read so I can play blackjack when we go to Las Vegas (it seems so far away).

I'm sort of getting a sneaking suspicion, which has me greatly upset, that you are not getting my letters. In the note, in the powered milk package, you asked me to tell you what I've been doing and what you can send me. Damn it, aren't you getting my letters?? I write every day. Please let me know exactly how many letters you have received. I'm not angry with you, just distressed that I might be out of communication with you.

I'm very glad you're singing. You know I'm your favorite fan.

Today, the monsoon rains have started. Everything is wet including me. Today, we had long meetings on how to best deal with the TET offensive and how to make the hospital more efficient. When the attacks start, I'm going to be very busy I think. I was the only MD not put on duty in the admitting ward. They think I'll be lucky to get out of the O.R. Maybe time will go by faster. Please answer my questions and requests specifically.

I love you very much as always. I think I'll be very happy when we are together again.

Jonny

P.S. Please send me a cheap electric blanket as soon as possible. I forgot to tell you in the letter about that.

Love You

2/01/69
Letter 16

Dearest Sherrie,

Well, today began with a real bang. Just before dawn, we got hit with 4 rockets again and this time closer than I like to think. I woke up and was crawling, in the mud, into the bunker although half asleep. The worst of it is that it's impossible to get dry. Absolutely everything is wet, including me. It hasn't stopped raining for 3 days and it will go on for weeks.

Time goes by very slowly when there are no cases to do. We have here 7 board eligible Surgeons, 1 On-the-Job Trainee (OJT) Anesthesiologist (me), 1 Internist, 1 GMO (General Medical Officer), 3 Nurse Anesthetists and the rest are Nurses and Corpsmen. We are surrounded by 101st Airborne, but it seems like the Viet Cong can hit us with rockets when they want to. They are very difficult to find. I can see the jungle from my hooch.

We just had mail call and I enjoyed hearing from you. That was a nice letter. I am so anxious to be with you again, also. I want to answer your questions before I forget. Did you see that on the back of my letter, yesterday, I requested an *electric blanket? I did, so please send it. Please send another flashlight. I lost the first. Did you find the Part I and II National Board scores? Did you get the money I sent ($300-$400, I forget exactly)? I play chess with one surgeon fairly regularly (about every other day). No cards. When we're busy, we're very busy.*

I got another letter from Nat today. She's sweet. About cameras, I'll tell you what I'll do. I'm going to get a cheap camera very shortly, take a couple of quick rolls, send the camera to you and then buy at a more convenient time a good expensive one. Even the cheap flash camera, I can get for one-half or three times less than what you can. I've had about 5 pictures taken of me to send to you, but they won't get to you for about a month. That's all for now. The only thing I really look forward to is hearing from you and writing to you.

All my love and thoughts,

Jonny

Dearest Sherrie,

Today, went pretty fast. I had 2 cases which took most of the day. One of which was interesting, for me, because the patient did not breathe for over 1/2 hour after the operation and presented a very interesting differential diagnosis.

I got a very nice letter from you today. That's what I need most, to hear from you. I feel very strong with you behind me. Your letters have been interesting, funny, mature and have done wonders for me.

I was a little distressed to find, from the nature of what you said about getting my letters, that there is apparently quite a lag in your getting them. I write you every day. Again, tell me how many letters you've gotten as of receipt of this letter so I can get an idea of what the lag is. The letter I received, from you today, was dated January 28, 1969 (Tuesday night). Of course, I'm a day ahead of you (I think).

It's still raining and getting chilly. What can I say??

It just goes along with the rest of the bull-shit here. Guess what?? Last night, after I wrote you, we got shelled again with rockets and we all hit the bunkers. Well, a poker game started up and I watched for about an hour. Then they needed another player, so I figured I'd try. They were all pretty experienced. Well, I won $20. Now they want me to play again, but I told them they would have to wait at least a month before I'd play again. I really had a lot of luck, but I also obviously didn't know what I was doing. Don't worry Sweetie, I won't play again for a long time. John Stevens is slightly South of Saigon, so he is quite a distance from me. I wrote him a card the other day.

My closet and shelves have been done for a week, except for the bulbs you are sending. Since the rain, we have not been able to mix and pour cement for the basketball court. I miss playing.

Too bad about the rent, but you still got a good deal.

Listen Honey, I'm quoting you "I do so badly want to make sure that our savings will grow this year". Sherrie dear, I don't want to be hard on you- but, not only are our savings going to grow, they should and will grow to between $8000-$10,000. I won't accept less. There is no reason why it should be less.

Glad to hear about your weight. I think that's terrific. You certainly have will power. I have lost about 7-8 pounds and the reason is because I'm not eating bread, potatoes and cake. When we are together, I don't want to ever see that on our table. Remember me asking for steak and peas? I'll have to admit that probably my drinking so much less than before is important, also. The most I've had since coming here is 2 beers in one day.

I am most anxious to play with you, too. For the business part of our being together, it would be very nice if you could learn to play chess. Since I met you, I have really only had eyes for you and it's silly of you to think I would really look at someone else on R&R or elsewhere. You know there are so many girly magazines around here, but I am singularly unimpressed with the girls in them compared to you. I'm sure love has something to do with it, but I think you are very beautiful too, inside and outside.

Your Jonny

(1st Letter)
Dearest Sherrie,

I got two letters from you, today, which made me very happy. One enclosed the letter from Uncle Ruby. It means a lot to me to get something every day. I still can't tell, from your letters, if you are getting my letters. Are you?? Please let me know. I enjoyed getting the Lil Abner cartoons and stuff on the Lakers. Keep sending them. It's very difficult to remain interested in the world. I don't even know if I want to. I mean it. I don't care anymore. All the Docs are this way and I can understand it. We are so isolated and concerned about getting through each day that the world is meaningless to me. I appreciate your efforts, but don't send any news to me except Lil Abner cartoons because it makes me smile and maybe the Lakers. Newsweek is ok and Sports Illustrated is ok, but it hurts to see the day to day stuff.

The board eligible Anesthesiologist is gone and I'm on my own. But, it should really be no different than when he was here. I was acting Chief anyway. Cases still come in bunches (ambushed patrol, booby-trapped squad, etc) except for an occasional appendectomy. Glad to hear Lonnie is back. Give him my best. Oh yes, got a very funny letter from my Uncle Abe. Thanks so much for doing a terrific job in keeping me in touch with everybody. I love you so very much, you are so good to me. Glad you got the money. Dammit Sherrie, are you getting my letters??

I haven't played any basketball because it's still raining. And, it's become very cold (about 50 degrees) and so damp. The bad thing about this 50 degrees is that there is no place to get warm. I was so cold today. I wore a scrub suit and two pairs of fatigues all day and a field jacket. I've lost 10 pounds ... look pretty slim. I hope you send an electric blanket soon. Also, a sweatshirt. Please hurry. It's not expected to stop raining for a month. Eagerly awaiting the bulbs and extension cord. I can use them.

I was overjoyed to learn that you sold the three pillows. Good girl. Maybe I'll make a business woman of you yet. I was especially pleased to hear of your school plans and the fact that you are only a year away from your B.S. (full-time, that is). Whatever you take is fine, just study hard. I'd be delighted to have you try for your Masters. I agree that you could do it even when we have a child. You certainly won't have to work.

Sorry I'll miss Glen Campbell's show. Sounds great. Please DO NOT send a portable record player. Most of the Docs have tapes so there is enough music around.

Today, I bought an instamatic camera for $15. I'll shoot about 3 rolls of film and then send it to you. Then, I'll get a camera for $100 which sells in the U.S. for $300. The film I'm shooting comes out as slides and I'll be sending you a projector as soon as I can get one. I'm going to shoot everything as slides so I can build up a collection and show them on a projector.

Since I plan to write my Uncles, your folks and Nat tonight, I'm going to close now. Thanks for being such a wonderful wife and friend. I love you very much. I realize, now that you're gone, what a close companion you were to me. Goodnight, Honey. See you in my fondest thoughts.

With much love,

Jonny,

(2nd Letter)
Dearest Sherrie,

I'm going to rush this letter. There are about 4 cases to be done in a 1/2 hour. We were lining up for supper when rockets hit about 10 miles North of us. Last night, they hit South of us. Tonight, most think it's going to be us, but we are well prepared. Six other Docs, and I, spent the whole day building up our bunker. The way it is now, it can definitely take a direct hit by mortar. And, when we finish, it will take a rocket. I'm so sore. We have the best damn bunker for miles around.

I was so disappointed, today, in not getting a letter. I'm enclosing a type of cocoa I'd like you to try and get for me.

Don't send any other kind.

Every day here is like a year. No matter what you do, the time goes by slowly. Within a month (this one), two of the Docs I'm living with are going home. How I envy them.

Sherrie, are you getting my letters? I wish it would stop raining.

I hope to be able to send some pictures in a couple of weeks. Send me some Sherrie. I'll be furious if you don't because you are self-conscious. How are you doing? Job, friends, home, bank ... what's going on in the real world? Got to do cases.

All my love and thoughts,

Jonny

2/06/69
Letter 20

Dearest Sherrie,

Sorry if you missed getting a letter from me, yesterday, but I have been extremely busy. I worked almost 36 straight hours in the past 2 days. Must have done upwards of 15 cases. Terrible wounds, terrible. I did some very difficult cases and I don't mind saying it ... I did well. A couple of the cases were at least as bad, if not worse, than the guy who got caught between a tank and pick-up at Ft. Knox. I'm turning out to be a pretty good Chief of Anesthesiology.

Aside from work, life is miserable. It hasn't stopped raining for one minute. It's driving me crazy. It's become cold too and every day I wear a tee shirt, scrub suit, two pairs of fatigues and a poncho on top of that just to keep warm when I'm not in the O.R. I don't know how the troops survive out in the field without any protection.

Things to send: (1) Your phone number- One of the surgeons is getting out in about 20 days and he will call you from northern California, where he lives, to say hello for me. He has lived in the same hooch with me. (2) An electric blanket- Please hurry, I'm freezing. (3) More of the soups you sent and some more juices-V8 juice, tomato juice, orange juice ... and, the kind of cocoa I sent in one of my previous letters. (4) Your love.

I got the eyeglasses and extension cords and bulbs you sent. Everything came in fine shape. Thanks a lot.

You know, I realized today how frequently I think of you. You are really quite beautiful. I look at your pictures often. Please send me some more soon.

One of the surgeons had to fly out, today, to the U.S. because of an emergency at home. It seems that he has a boy who is brain damaged, from birth, and his wife was unable to cope with the situation by herself and had a breakdown. I think he will be able to get a compassionate reassignment. He was very kind to me. I was sorry to see him go, but I hope he doesn't have to come back to this hell hole.

I'm going to get supper now and then wait for the mail to see if there is anything you want me to reply to. Natalie has been sweet ... she's written 3 times.

Guess what? I didn't get a damn thing at mail call. I've got to get a letter tomorrow. I'm gonna write your folks a note (I didn't the last time that I said I was).

I miss you so much it hurts,

Jonny

Dearest Sherrie,

Today, I got a fair amount of mail. Two packages and a letter from you and a letter from my folks. One of the packages (with raisins, soup and silverware) was dated January 19. The letter contained a picture of you taken at Stu's and Erica's. I was delighted to receive it and happy you went over to Stu's place. I've been staring at your picture for an hour. Your figure is just great! I prefer your hair longer and swept more forward on your face and closer to your head. I guess you cut it?

Tell me about your weekend nursing job for Desi Arnez. I bet it was interesting. We haven't had any rockets for the last 2 nights, but it's still raining steadily and it's cold. Now that we haven't had any rockets for 2 days, I can see and recall the tension their presence made in me and everybody else. Man, I hope they give up on us.

Lonnie sounds older. I'm sure he is. Maybe he knows about the 2 hospital ships (The Repose and The Sanctuary) just off shore from us. Give him my best.

So far today, I have had no cases. I'm on third call. But, really on first call for spinals, axillary blocks, IV regionals and the big horror shows. Days like this drive me crazy. I tried to study some, read, etc. The time crawls so slowly. Every day seems like a week and I have so long to go yet. Did you get my electric blanket off yet? More pictures? I wrote Des a rather technical letter, yesterday, telling him of the equipment we have, procedures I used (which has been just about every little thing he taught me), etc. I don't think I'll write until I hear from him. I wrote my Uncle Ruby thanking him for his letter to you and, also, to my Uncle Abe and my Mom and Dad tonight. Everybody here says you can tell your real friends by those who write you. I was frankly surprised to see how bitter they all were towards those "friends" of theirs that never wrote them. Letters become so important here. I'm curious to see which ones of my "friends" will write. I think Stu will because he is generally considerate. I wonder if Greg will. I doubt Bill will.

Oh yes, I got the brownies and they tasted fine and fresh. In case you were wondering, I would always prefer to receive a letter from you instead of a package, except for the things I specifically urgently asked for. And, very important- send me a plastic covering or album to keep all the pictures you are going to send me.

I've shot half a roll of pictures and as soon as we get some sun (see I still have some optimism left), I'll shoot the rest and send it on to you to be developed.

Remember, you will need a little viewer to see them (until I can get to a PX that has a projector) because they will come out as slides. You can, also, get prints made from the slides because slides are really negatives.

I love you very much and miss you constantly with all my being,

Jonny

P.S. Are you getting my letters? Please try to give me some idea. Did you get the package? Send me your phone number, Baby (every girl needs to give their number to one guy). Seriously, one of the surgeons will call and say hello for me when he leaves the country in 20 days.

Dearest Sherrie,

Happy Valentine's Day, Honey. Every beat of my heart is for you.

Nothing much happened, today, except the rain let up for the first time. I was so glad. Hope it holds up for a while. And, also, no rockets again last night…… 3 days in a row. No cases today. Tomorrow, I'm first call. Probably will be busy since we haven't had anything for 2 days. Hope the Viet Cong are not getting ready for a ground attack.

No letter, today, from you (pout, pout, sigh, sulk). Got one from your folks (your Mom). She said she sent some coffee. Tell her I don't drink coffee.

VERY IMPORTANT! (1) If you should ever have an emergency, or need me to know something quickly, contact the Red Cross. They can get me the quickest. The guy who went home on emergency leave, I told you about yesterday, was contacted through the Red Cross. (2) Call Greg and Madeleine and get Rich Anderson's address. I want to write him.

The guys have been asking me to play poker every day since I won that night. Maybe I'll play next week.

Tonight, I played basketball and had a good time. Got real muddy and took a freezing shower. We have no hot water. I've pretty well decided to request a transfer, to another hospital, after six months. The living conditions are supposed to be much better at most other hospitals. It's a pretty big base, where I'm at, but the Viet Cong have us isolated. The only contact we have, with the rest of the country, is by helicopter. We know the Viet Cong are North, South, East and West of us because that is where the rockets come from ... all over the perimeter.

Sherrie, I miss you so much. My only companion is gone. I'm really slim now ... lost about 12 pounds.

I love you. I've burned a hole through your picture, I've looked at it so much. Please send me Anderson's address. I still am not sure you are getting my letters.

Send me pictures. I've got to have something to look forward to.

Again, I love you my Valentine,

Jonny

2/10/69
Letter 23

(1st Letter)
Dear Sherrie,

I worked through the night this past night. Had some very interesting difficult cases. Saved one, but lost one. He had so many holes in him it was impossible to bring him back.

I have to write this quickly because the mail goes out in a few minutes, and I want to try to get this off, so you can get something from me every day.

Got the air mattress. Thanks. What did you spend for it? Got the card with it. I can't wait. Got a note from Des. He said you had called them. Did you? If you did, I hope you had fun talking to them. His note was funny.

Goodbye, Honey. Happy Valentine's Day.

(2nd Letter)
Dearest Sherrie,

Hi Kiddo, how are you? Received 2 letters from you today which made me happy, a Valentine's Day card from Nellie Griffy and some chocolate chip cookies from your Mother. Would you please concentrate and try to give me some idea of what time lag there is between my writing to you and your receipt of the letter? I've asked you so many times. What gives? I want to answer your questions. One possible explanation of your dream is that the violence projected toward us, as bystanders, symbolically was the Vietnam War. Can't think of anything else right now. Don't dream, poor baby, you must have been all trembling and big-eyed. Sounds like you're making the rounds with our wedding pictures. I do not think the Army will give us W-2 forms at all. No one in Vietnam gets one. They give us 18 months after you get here before you get one. Incidentally, the first $500 per month of my salary is not taxed. There are 2 possibilities for obtaining my Part II Board scores. Best avenue, or approach, is write the National Board and tell them of my situation and request the scores. Second, ask Dean Nehrlich's secretary to see if the medical school has them on record.

As I wrote you hurriedly, this morning, I had a busy night last night. Got some sleep this morning, but this afternoon we had four more cases, all Vietnamese soldiers. Yesterday, during the day, I played ball for about 4 hours- football (scored 2 touchdowns for the officers versus the enlisted and we won) and basketball. I am so sore. During the cases today at 3:00 PM, while I was in the process of intubating one of the Vietnamese soldiers (which means he was paralyzed and could not breathe), would you believe we got rocketed - 2 big rockets came in. Well, I tell you everybody hit the floor. But, I couldn't because I had to get the tube in. I was so scared. I almost needed to tube myself. Nothing like starting a case with a bang. They landed on an airstrip on the other side of the hospital. You'll see when I explain my slides, to you, when I come home.

That reminds me, I want to criticize you lightly for something. In your letters, you hardly give me any feedback or comment on my letters. Are you getting them? Am I talking to a wall? Every day I wait for you to say something, but you never have a response. Will you send me some pictures? If I sound exasperated, I am a little. But, that gives you an idea of my need to know.

We've had 2 or 3 days of beautiful weather- about 90 degrees and sunny. After TET and the monsoons (about the end of February), the other Docs tell me that the weather will climb to 120-130 degrees. I wonder how hot that will feel? Suffocating, I bet.

Sherrie, I am quite tired and over-worked a bit, I think. So, I'm going to close now with love for you. It comes out of every pore and lifts me up to look forward to a future.

How I wish this year were over and I could be back with you.

Jonny

Dearest Sherrie,

I got 5 pieces of mail, today, from you! Three were newspaper articles, your nice Valentine's card with the picture and most importantly 2 letters (both long). What was of great relief and joy, to me, is that I got my first real indication that you are getting my letters. Although, you're getting my letters quite late (over a week) and in a ragged and unpredictable fashion. I write one a day and I guess you are not getting one a day.

Since you asked so many questions and spoke of so many things, I will take each point by point. I feel the same way as you do when I write to you. I feel as if I'm alone with you. I was very pleased to learn, in detail, of your phone call to Des and Madeline. I just always perceived them as good friends, and as a couple, just as they perceived us I'm sure. I expect my friends to like you, as well as me- aside from those that I just play basketball with or tennis. Dig?

Otherwise, they really couldn't be my friends. Right?

Dammit, Sherrie ... guess where I am now? Flat on my stomach in the bunker. Our area was just hit with 8 incoming rockets. What a noise they made. Anyway, you should see me with gun, helmet and flak jacket. Boy, I look tough. Anyway, back in the hooch.

You bet I'll be a good Daddy. Just wait and see. I'm having one of the guys shoot some pictures of me as I was tonight when the rockets came in.

About buying things.... I think I'll get a week's leave, in August, to go to Japan where I'll meet you and we will buy *everything together. Yes, things are about 1/2 price. I will send you an instamatic, next week, on which I have taken 3 rolls of slides. You will get these in 2 months (takes time to get them back). And, today, I bought us a $40 slide projector. You should get that in 2 months, also- along with a $16 watch I bought myself. I thought I'd let you pick out your own, in Japan, along with a fur. Do not send any golfing stuff. I don't need it. I play basketball and run and between cases that is enough, not including the rockets. I've read all of the books that we bought, before I left, and enjoyed them- especially "The Prize" and "The Games". Most everybody has novels, so there are plenty around. You can send "Airport".*

I have a small refrigerator. It belongs to my hooch. I did try to call you, once, but could not get through. It's by radio to the U.S. and I'm afraid that even if I did, it would be very unsatisfactory because of static and you can only talk one way at a time. The Docs say you are better off not trying.

We lost another young boy, on the table, last night. Too bad. Eight hours on the table and I finally could not bring him back from his third arrest. He was bleeding from every imaginable artery. With my bare hands, I was squeezing his heart. His buddy made it. But, I really do have inestimable pride in some of the cases I have done. Some were very difficult, but we brought them through. I have established a great deal of camaraderie between myself and the surgeons. I think they like me.

Your thoughts were good ones on where to ask to be located when I get back. I'll probably do what you suggested.

I'm very happy you are in touch with my folks and Nat. I've written them both and my Grandma. All I can do is state the facts. I have not lost interest in you or forgotten you. I have more interest in you and I promise no second bests. I'm the only one who won't hang any pin-ups on the wall because I have pictures of Sherrie which are much better. I, too, hope *you see my Uncle Abe. He's a great and knowing man. You told me we have $650 in the savings account. What about the checking account? You are already a super duper wife. I really think you are terrific. The grocery store man is nice. Thank him, for me, for his prayers. I'm sure he is sincere. Nights like tonight, I think I need them.*

Today, I was paid a nice compliment. You know I play basketball every day. Well, the guys I play with are 6-7 black Enlisted Men. I'm about the best basketball player and they call me "Doc, the white Soul Brother". What do you think?

Love with all my heart and will and desire to survive to be with you again,

Jonny

Dear Sherrie,

I had a real good day today. Ran 3 miles, played basketball and studied about 4 hours. And, then was topped by 2 letters from you, 1 from Ben Ezra's wife and 1 from my Dad. Thanks so much for informing everybody of my address. I'm going to make this letter a little short because I want to write John Stevens, my folks and Ben. I think it's great you are running with Dottie. I'm running, also. I plan to eventually do 5 miles every day. Remember, Honey, you have to run till it hurts to do any good. That means more each day.

Sherrie, a bunker is an underground cave so the fragments from mortars and rockets go over your head. It is surrounded (as everything here is) by sandbags which are big bags filled with sand. Sandbags are used because they absorb the shock and fragments of near hits.

I am enclosing my W-2 form which I got today. Remember, you can sign my name since you are my Power-of-Attorney. Please go to a guy like we did last year. Also, very important- if you are not sure of my deductions (like I spent over $100 on books), send me the list of possibilities and I will fill it out.

No rockets since yesterday. Weather has been nice (about 90 degrees). Hard to believe it was so cold just a few days ago.

Glad you are enjoying your work. It gives me comfort. Please be very careful about hepatitis. It can be dangerous. Take your globulin shot, you chicken. Remember, if you ever get seriously ill, tell me. And, tell the Red Cross to notify me. If you can get a Doctor to write the Red Cross that you are seriously ill (if you really are), and that my presence is necessary, it could get me home right away for a while. I want you, in your very next letter, to acknowledge whether you understand what I just told you (or not). I don't want to keep wondering and asking you. Dig?

I've tacked up your 2 pictures on my cabinet door. Look at you all the time.

Every beat of my heart is for you,

Jonny

Dearest Sherrie,

Received your letter of February 8th, today, informing me that you are getting my letters. Great! I received the air mattress. I don't think I really need it, but what the hell. Same thing with the flashlight. There is so much shooting going on at night. Our forces put up flares all night and they really light everything up. Also, I probably won't need the socks. I took a few from supply, but they certainly won't hurt. I, also, got the glasses.

Marcia and Ben Ezra are very nice. I hope we do see a great deal of them. You might return her short note. When I get back, I automatically get 30 days leave. Isn't that great? But, it seems like it will never come. I will probably get a week's leave in July or August and I will meet you in Japan. This will be at the 5th or 6th month point of my tour of duty. Then, at 8 or 9 months, I will get a week in Hawaii. How's that?

Also, I found out today that under the GI bill I get $150 per month during my residency. That comes to $3600 for 2 years. Nice surprise, huh?

Here's someone for Judy to write to, one of my Nurse Anesthetists. He rides in rodeos, in civilian life, and plans to go to medical school when he gets out. Very nice guy, he's 26, very natural and will probably be one of my better friends here. He said he would like to hear from Judy. He is not writing anyone now (he is single) and he is very good looking. Here is his address (same as mine): Lt. Dan Doren, 18th Surgical Hospital, APO SF 96383.

Would enjoy hearing about "Hair," especially your thoughts and interpretations.

Worked very hard (8 cases), today, but found time to run and play basketball. The temperature is really beginning to get up there.

Love you very much, think of you all the time.

Jonny

2/14/69
Letter 28

Dearest Sherrie,

Enclosed is a picture of none other than yours truly. Found somebody 2 weeks ago, with a camera, and he just got back his photos. The things on top of the truck are machine guns. Most of the jeeps and vehicles are equipped with guns here.

No letter today from nobody. I'm wiped out. At times like this, it seems like I will never get back to the world.

There is something that I want you to pay very close attention to and give me some comment on, in return, so I know you understand. Remember I told you about one of the surgeons being contacted, by the Red Cross, because his wife was unable to cope with the fact that one of their children had problems? Because her physician contacted the Red Cross himself, and wrote them a letter (something in writing), he had enough evidence to get out of the country for a month and probably will get a compassionate reassignment. Now if you should get ill, or anything happens to you of serious nature, contact the Red Cross. But have Dr. Berne, Dr.

Barbour or any others you can get to contact the Red Cross in writing that my presence is needed at home and that you are critically ill. It could get me home. Now don't go get sick, but if you should become ill, use your brains. Now, please write me back that you understand or don't understand this point. It will be especially hard for me to get home being Chief of an Anesthesiology Department. They are so short of Anesthesia personnel, but you can never tell. They might let me go.

Tonight, the hooch next to mine is having a party. But, I'm not going to go because I don't particularly care for them and I don't feel any genuine warmth on their part. They invited the female nurses (there are about 5 or so of them) who are career Army nurses.

They are very difficult people to work with. The other Docs verbally say this, but they still socialize with them. In spite of my feeling particularly lousy and lonely, tonight, I can't go over because if I do then I'm not relating to people on my own terms- but, on their terms and then I'd be robbed of my identity which personally I have pride in. The people who have been here for quite some time together are pretty clicky, but the hell with them. I've got myself and you and that is enough.

Somewhat forlorn tonight, but always full of love for you,

Jonny

Dearest Sherrie,

Boy, was I busy today and the night still lies ahead. Had many cases today- 2 generals, 2 spinals, 2 axillary blocks. One of them was a North Vietnamese Army regular who intelligence found out from (after the operation) that his battalion was on the way and is still on the way to attacking Camp Evans (that is where my hospital is) by ground. Oh, brother! We are hoping the 101st Airborne will intercept them (ambush) and turn them back. I don't know what the hell I would do if they broke through the perimeter. I wouldn't know where to go or who to shoot at. I'm definitely a liability in this situation.

Here is a heartbreaking tale. A Board Eligible Internist, who was here only a week, was assigned here and then had his assignment changed to go out to the field (a General Medical Officer's job). Meanwhile, his Father had a stroke a week ago and he can't get emergency leave (30 days) because he does not have substantiation (evidence) of this through the Red Cross- nor any Doctor's opinion stating his presence is necessary in writing. Sherrie, I'll have a stroke if I don't get some indication that you understand this matter of what is needed if I'm needed at home.

Here is another heartbreaking tale. For the second day in a row, I didn't get any mail. I'm dying, Sherrie. My life depends solely on your letters. Is everything ok? Are you running? Oh, if I could only get back to the world. I miss you so much.

Goodnight my love,

Jon

Dearest Sherrie,

There must be something wrong with the mail service. No mail now for 7 days. How depressing. I hate this place ... no mail, shitty food, hot and it's getting hotter (this is the cool season), hitting the dirt all the time because of rockets, cases when they come in fantastic numbers- otherwise boredom and on and on and on. I find myself constantly trying to get a grip on myself. I get by, by withdrawing into myself. It's the only place I can find any strength to continue. I am studying the books I brought, read novels, run track (should be able to do under a 5 minute mile pretty soon) and play basketball. I don't want you to feel badly. It's just something that I have to cope with, for my entire existence here, every minute. I have to accept it (and I do accept it)- but damn it, I don't like it.

Incidentally, I found out a little more about the Red Cross. Usually, all you have to do is tell the Red Cross who your Doctor or Doctors are and they will call them and verify your illness and that my presence is needed. The reason I keep mentioning this is because I was not aware of this before I left and it is so important in case an emergency does arise. So much time could be lost in writing direct letters (at least a month). Please tell my parents about what to do in case of an emergency and do it soon. How I hope that I hear from you tomorrow night.

Goodnight my love,

Jon

Dearest Sherrie,

Hi Honey, what's new? What have you been doing? Do you go out at all? See movies? See anybody? What do you do after work?

I finally got a letter, today, from you ... first one in 5 days. What's wrong? Anything? I'm glad you are receiving my letters regularly. But, as I've said before (and I'll say it again now), your responses never reflect anything I say to you. I don't want you to feel hurt, but I am so frustrated in writing you. I hardly ever get a letter back that would show that you took note of anything that I said. I feel like I'm talking to a wall at times. That is why I mention the Red Cross everyday just to get one answer from you. Please don't be hurt, Honey, just try to make your letters a little more conversational with me, a little more responsive to mine. Like in your letter, today, you asked about when you might receive more money and where. I told you some time ago (twice), in 2 different letters, that the money (the allotment) would probably come during the first 2 weeks of March and every month thereafter. The $400 is pay for part of December and January, travel, etc. Please don't be upset by this letter, but please acknowledge at least that you are aware that I feel that we are not communicating as well as we might.

My simple questions are not casual or polite ones. Please answer them. Will you send some pictures? I should be able to send some more of myself pretty soon. I don't care about some snow storm in New York. I want to know how the call made you feel (happy, sad, better, worse, easy, tense, etc, etc)? How are my folks? Any thoughts you might have exchanged, etc? Sherrie, Darling, I cherish you. I cherish every memory and every vision I have of you and every letter you write. I'm talking to you like I have many times in the past when you or I were upset. So please, don't feel unwanted or rejected or hurt. Just think a little about what I expressed here.

Very busy here with cases. Fun being Chief. Did an IV regional block this morning with success. Everybody gathered around to gape at the new anesthesia. Right now, the cases are coming in at a rather steady rate instead of bunches. But, we're keeping up. Do you love me? Really? Really, really? I'm so lonesome here.

I love you very much, Jonny

Dearest Sherrie,

I'm going to make this very short because it's late and I had an unbelievable day again in the O.R. (and a very depressing one). Six South Vietnamese soldiers came in. I took the worst one and he was on the O.R. table 6 hours and then expired. We sweated over him. It was so hot in the O.R. Then, he died. I had given him about 35 units of blood. I felt very let down when we lost him. These guys are so brave. All of them: American, South Vietnamese, Viet Cong. They are all very scared, afraid they are going to die or lose a limb. Yet they control themselves and are cooperative.

Heard from my Mom and Dad today, Uncle Ruby and Aunt Norma. They all had said many, many nice things about you. I know better than anybody else how terrific you are. My mind is such a blank right now. I think I'll just say goodnight for now and write you a better letter tomorrow.

Love you with all of my heart, desire, soul. You make everything mean something to me. Without you, I think I'd be lost.

Jonny

Dearest Sherrie,

Hi Sweetie! How is my favorite wife? I am going to start reading through the letters of yours that I got, today, and answer them as I go along. Would you believe Toby and Tania sent me cookies? They did. Happy Valentine's Day to you, too, Dearest.

About Hawaii ... anything you want is fine with me, but remember I'll see you in Japan before Hawaii in July or August. You will have to make reservations for Tokyo. I will suggest areas or hotels that other guys have been to and send you your tickets for Tokyo.

About the projector, the one you showed me is good, but I already bought one for $40. You should get it, in a month or so, along with a watch. It shows 40 slides, at a time, which I thought was adequate. I should be getting my first 20 slides back soon and I'll send them to you as soon as I do. I'm sending another 20 to be developed, tomorrow, and you should get them in a month to 6 weeks. You should get our first allotment ($650) the first week of March. I was given a tape recorder by another Doc, for free, which works but *does not have a microphone and one other part. Take it to an electronics shop, get it cleaned (it's dirty) and fixed up, etc. Let me know when it's ready, and we can start exchanging tapes, since there is another Doc here who will let me use his recorder. It's the exact same one I am sending you. Please give me answers to all of these things that I have mentioned. I will send the tape recorder with the first group of slides as soon as I get them.*

Today, so far, no cases. I need the rest, but it was over 110 degrees and that is hot. Ran a mile anyway (nearly passed out), played basketball (nearly passed out) and worked on cementing the basketball court (nearly passed out). We have a long way to go yet on the basketball court. Should finish it in a month. I have not been sick at all since coming here. Feel fine. Have lost 15 pounds (weigh 145 pounds). I am eating now, but I continue to keep on losing. When I get below 140 pounds, I'll start worrying.

I am happy you remember me warmly. You know the times that I was grouchy or withdrawn could have made you think less warmly of me. Thanks for having so much faith in me. It makes me want to be all the things you think of me ... for you.

The things you have sent are more than enough. I can't even read all that you send because between studying, reading novels and cases- there is no time.

I built myself a desk today with shelves. And, someone gave me a desk fan so I'm really sitting pretty. I will have so much fun explaining the slides to you.

I enjoyed Rod McKuen's poems. I had read "Channing Way" several times before. Hey Girl, glad to see the ole bean is working. Great. Keep it up. I'm sure you will be teaching me soon.

I exist for you in thought, action, feeling, hope,

Jon

Sherrie, sweet Darling,

Honey you are an angel, not for any specific reason, but just because you are you. Here are 3 pictures of me in the O.R. with the negatives. Please get the negatives developed so my sister and parents can each get a set. Explanation: Picture #1- I just intubated patient. Picture #2- During case, surgeon is irrigating, I move machine and myself down to the right of patient. Picture #3- End of case, before dressings are put on, I am observing his breathing and eventually decided on a tracheostomy. You can include these explanations to my sis, and folks, so they can understand it better.

I got a very funny letter from Greg today.

Sorry you had such a screwy schedule. Did you get by ok?

Your letters have been wonderful. Enjoy reading them immensely. Can't wait to see the pictures of you. Keep them coming. Hope your cold is better.

I'm making this short for several reasons. One, I have to write to John Stevens, my folks, Nat, Aunt Norma, Uncle Ruby, Greg. And two, believe it or not, I got a great idea for a research project. I'm reading and outlining how I'm going to approach the problem. It's a special kind of respiratory death in non-thoracic trauma that some of the patients are dying of. I've done a good bit of reading on it and the surgeons are integrated enough to give me their cooperation. I'll tell you more about it in the future. I'm in the swing of things with running, reading, writing letters, basketball, etc.

Hope you like the pictures. The patient, I think if I

remember correctly, was a Viet Cong. I'm much thinner now than in the pictures. Oh, I love you!

Please send my Goodman and Gilman "The Therapeutic Basis of Pharmacology". It's a big blue text book. It's for my friend Dan Doren. Did Judy write him? Send instant ice tea, brownies, chocolate chip cookies, tuna fish and salmon (canned), peanut butter and crackers. Thanks!

It's raining again now. But I have my electric blanket, from my Sweetheart, to keep me warm.

All my love and devotion,

Jon

Dearest Adorable Sherrie,

Our generator was hit last night (I'm getting so used to rockets, I slept through the noise, it's about 1/2 mile away), so we have no lights. So, this will be short. I got another wonderful letter from you, today, with Rich Anderson's address. And, I also got my first set of slides back today. I'll send them off to you, tomorrow, along with the tape recorder I got for free. It needs a little work on it- like cleaning, buy a microphone for it, etc. But, it works. The slides came out great with the instamatic. I'm going to keep this camera and you should continue to use Lonnie's. You really only need to take some pictures of yourself periodically, for me, so you don't need a camera all to yourself right now. When we are in Japan, we can decide about what to buy then. Don't throw any of the slides out. They all mean something and I'll have lots of fun explaining them. It's raining, again, like before. Ugh! No cases will be done until the generator is fixed.

Don't worry about your figure and tan so much. I love you the way you are. I don't know how tan I will be when I see you. I don't get outside so often. I'm fairly tan, now, but it doesn't show up so well in the slides. Incidentally, you have to look at these through a projector or viewer. Your projector should come in 2-3 weeks, so hang in there.

You are the most wonderful person in the whole world!

I love you so much,

Jon

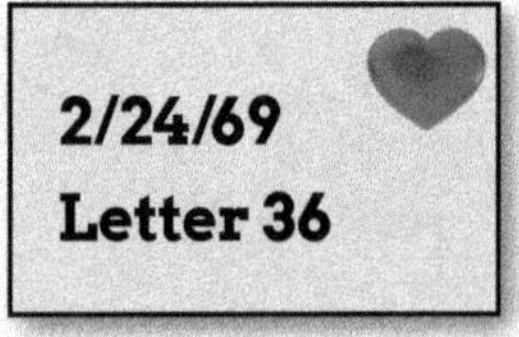

My Dear Precious Sherrie,

Hi Baby, I'm very involved with my research. Mostly reading journals, at this point, but soon I expect to translate it into patient care. We are still pretty busy. And you may have read, in the papers, there were widespread attacks by the Viet Cong last night. Still found time to run (1/4 mile around the airfield) and made up a package for you. It contains 2 pairs of shoes (one of them my sandals which broke, you might get them fixed), the tape recorder and the first set of slides. Look for the box of slides in and among the paper cushioning in the box. If you can't find the proper microphone, for the tape recorder, let me know. I can get you one. I'll get the package off as soon as I can get to the post office.

I got your package of juice and sweatshirts. Thanks. I'm wearing the blue sweatshirt in your honor.

I heard from my Mom and Dad, Uncle Abe, Greg, Grandma and Mike. Maybe I shouldn't write so much. If it keeps up, I won't be able to keep up. Did my friend call you? What did you have to say? Did you like the idea?

Glad to hear the applications are complete. You are the prettiest, most efficient and talented secretary I have.

Please don't get any ideas about getting hepatitis. It's never a happy parting when somebody has to go home on emergency leave. I would much rather go home the regular way.

Make some more chocolate chip cookies with lots of chocolate chips in them. They were delicious. I weighed 148 pounds tonight. I weighed 164 pounds when I came here. Ooh la la.

Bye for now, Sweetheart.

Love You, Jon

2/25/69

Letter 37

(1st Letter)

Dearest Sherrie,

I'm sorry I missed writing you yesterday, but we have been extremely busy. I worked all day yesterday and through the night. We still have a 6-8 hour back log of cases, but most of them are simple and the nurses can handle them. I was really going yesterday. For most of the time, I was running 3 rooms at one time by myself: (1) A spinal in one room in which a surgeon monitored the patient after I put the spinal in. (2) A second room in which a surgeon, also, monitored after I put it in. (3) A third room in which I was doing general anesthesia. The Marines and Calvary Divisions have been in vicious fights for 2 days now and a big push is scheduled for tonight. The fighting is going on in Ashau Valley, in case you read about it, and up on the DMZ- both of which are very near us. The Valley is only 5 miles from us. Well, such is life. I've got to go to bed to get ready for the work tonight.

Incidentally, we will almost definitely be together in July or August in Japan. That is leave, not R&R. R&R will be in October or November in Hawaii. The package with the tape recorder and slides should get to you in 2 weeks. Let me know about that, also, when you get the slide projector and watch. I already shot 80 slides.

I'm keeping the instamatic. It takes great slides. So, why spend $100 for a better camera in which the slides are only slightly better? How's bridge, chess, running and school?

You will have to make reservations for Tokyo, Japan. You might like to know I, too, am very anxious to be with you. There was never any question, in my mind, about spending the $700 for you to come.

I think I'm getting all your letters. There is a 6 day lag. I've got to go. I may not be able to write every day for a few days.

All my love,

Jonny

(2nd Letter)

It's 10:00 PM and we are still waiting for the casualties to come. I thought the most pleasant way to pass these anxious moments (all hell breaking loose when the choppers come, IV's, cutdowns, chest tubes, awake intubations and then off to the O.R. in 10 minutes from arrival) was to reply to 2 letters I received from you today. My greatest pleasure is reading your letters and you looked infinitely lovely in the pictures. I hang up all your pictures on my closet.

I'm glad you like my family, since they are so much a part of me. I'm glad you are down to 110 pounds. I know you put a lot of willpower into your dieting. I weighed 146 pounds today. I've lost 18 pounds since coming here, but I suspect I will level off around this point. Could you, also, send some more juices (but, only orange juice, V8 juice and tomato juice)?

It was interesting to learn Harbor General did a heart transplant. I'm sure the Chief Resident did the case under staff supervision.

Good for you going to the Police auction and getting the nursing journal.

I know you write every day. I'm sorry to hear you were so distressed and anguished when you heard I wasn't getting any mail. I hope tomorrow's letter doesn't find you more upset. You are very good to me and don't think I forget that for one minute.

About what friends I have here ... I am liked by all, I think. But, I am only really close with one of my Nurse

Anesthetists- Dan Doren. He is a great guy, warm, sincere, unassuming, pleasant and nice to work with. I'm sure we will remain friends for a long time. He is in a position much as I was with Des. There is no question about who is boss anesthesia-wise, but I try to cut it out once out of the O.R. We live in the same hooch and spend most of our time together (which is mainly concerned with anesthesia). But, we eat together, talk, etc. I've gotten into such a solid routine of studying, reading and running that my time is spent so much more constructively out of the O.R. In the beginning, I was somewhat bewildered and lost by the lulls between cases.

I just witnessed a very inspiring sight. A company of tanks and infantry, stationed near us, just left for the Ashau Valley (5 miles away) where the fighting is going on. On top of each tank was a Company and American flag waving and the boys cheering. I'm probably basically very emotional so all I can say is "God, be sparing of them" for we will be operating on a few of them tonight. They are so brave, these young men. I will work to exhaustion for them.

Oh yes, remember I can get a microphone for the recorder if you can't get one. But, it would be 2 months before you got it. As soon as you get the recorder in working shape, tape a reel and send it to me and I will do the same. There are recorders here I can borrow of the same type.

All my love,

Jonny

Dear Sherrie, Sweet Precious Friend,

Last night's surgery wasn't too bad. Got to sleep at 3:00 AM and had nothing to do today, but study, run, basketball and read. Got a letter full of questions from you, today, so let me answer them. Ran 2 rooms by myself last night.

About the taxes- did you deduct things like books, the first $500 of my income, journals, magazines, etc? What did you deduct? Glad you got my narcotics stamp renewed. Don't forget in June.

I will keep the instamatic. It shoots good slides and there are only minor differences between it and a $100 camera. Like with a $100 camera, things in the pictures appear nearer to you. But, that is not worth $100 to me. Use Lonnie's camera. If you could send me pictures of you once a month, it would make me very happy! Even sooner, if possible.

As you can see there is a slide of me, enclosed in the letter, building our bunker. Those are 2 other Docs in the background. If I were you, I would go ahead and buy a good but cheap screen so you can start projecting the slides I am sending you. I have shot over 80 already. Twenty are on their way to you. The projector should be on it's way. I'm looking forward to getting your pictures eagerly. It will be so good to look at you. "How sweet she is." The screen type should be like a roll down for $10.

Don't send any more books. I'm 3 behind already. I'm reading the "Dear and Glorious Physician" by Taylor Caldwell. I have yet to read "The Fixer", "The Tropic of Cancer", a science fiction book and the book "Scarne on

Cards." My textbooks have kept fine, but the 120 degree–130 degree heat has yet to come. We'll see.

If you have the time, some pastrami would be nice to have. But, you will have to wrap it real good. Try sending 2 pounds. Need more V8 juice, chocolate chip cookies and raisins. Potato chips would be nice.

I'm so glad you are writing to people. I've not heard from Ronny Broudy (he is the only one), so I'd go easy on letters to him.

I am a bit concerned about the Bilchick's, too. If I were you, I would call her at the address you have and try to find out what is going on. Friends should certainly be worth a couple of bucks if they have had any trouble.

My sister is wild over you. See if you can get her to come down to visit, with Rachel, for a couple of days. She has a whole week off in 5 weeks from today. You can introduce the idea by saying I wrote the suggestion. All my family, each one, has had nice things to say about you. You are a terrific wife! I love you very much, think of you constantly, hunger for you.

Oh well, someday, someday. Jonny

Got the picture of you tonight. You looked so beautiful and lovely and pretty. Boy, what I am missing. You looked especially good in the pictures where you were 110 pounds. Your hair is not bad, but I prefer it longer. Such a pretty face. Dan (my friend) thinks I'm lucky. Please keep them coming. Send some pictures on a regular basis. I would rather get pictures than any package or food or whatever.

We will have a real spending holiday in Japan: TV, stereo, radio, fur, movie camera, projector and many other things. Around June, we will see what we have in the bank and decide how much money you should bring. It will be very hard for me to go back, to this hellhole, after living with you for a week and being human again.

Got a card from Des and letters from Nat, John Stevens and your Mom.

It has been pouring again, for 3 days, but at least now I have the electric blanket and sweatshirts. They really help. Ran a very stiff, fast 1.5 miles today in the rain. It's getting so that I don't feel right if I don't run every day. Studied a lot today and read from "Dear and Glorious Physician". It is about St. Luke.

Hope this rain doesn't screw up the mail delivery like it did last time (when I got nothing for 5 days).

Have you seen any movies? Nat wrote she might be coming down to L.A. on June 14th or so. That would be nice, but remember she is pretty slow in translating her desires into action. So, if you feel up to it, encourage her all you can. Hate to think of her becoming so isolated, all alone by herself because of something that she had nothing to do with. Perhaps, she would now be young and happy in her heart if Doug had not died.

I counted that I have 322 days left today. Seems like forever.

Everyday my understanding and awareness, of my love for you, grows larger. You radiate warmth, giving, love, life and friendship. And, your being is becoming always more fully and completely integrated with mine as one. I think I mainly see myself in terms of you and living for you.

Jonny

P.S. Do you think you could send me a large portrait photo of yourself? Please?

Dearest Honeydew,

Business before pleasure ... Today, we were paid and this is what you need to know. A $650 allotment went out to you. In addition, I was given $369 in cash of which I am including in this letter $175 in money orders. Therefore, I kept for myself $200 or so. Now what you should do, upon receipt of this letter, is check carefully with the bank everyday that the $650 is deposited properly in our savings account. Do what you please with the $175 enclosed in this letter (preferably to be put in savings also). Part of the money given me was back pay. And, I think they also took out $150 that I owe them (partial payment for the $900 I got at Ft. Sam Houston). Next month, when I get paid, I probably will send home most of what I get because of the large amount I kept out this time (which I don't expect to spend). Have you paid off those pots and pans yet? Please do. I don't like the idea of our belongings being strewn between your apartment and your Mom's house. I'm not criticizing you nor am I angry at anything or you. These are just things I would like to see done.

No letter from you, today, but I am sure the rain is interfering with delivery. The whole base got only 14 letters, today, and there are 3000 men here. I did get a package or box of food from the Reillys. Don't send me anything that has to be heated. It's too difficult to prepare. I wish I had some of those chock-full of chocolate chip cookies of yours. They were so good (brownies, too).

Had 2 cases today. Then after that, the Colonel (the

Commander of the whole place) personally lent me his jeep to go to the PX. He is very nice to me and I think he is satisfied with my work (an On-the-Job-Trainee as Chief of Anesthesia could wreck a whole hospital if he was shitty). I got more film and flash cubes, for the instamatic, as well as a soap dish and envelopes. It was fun driving the jeep. I took Dan and another surgeon. We all took guns and the whole bit.

Well, that ends today. Just think I have 321 more wonderful days ahead of me. Just think, I go wild over getting to a stinking little PX (it is smaller than my hooch). You know the old saying "you can't polish shit".

All my love, thoughts and just everything for you,

Jonny

Dearest Sherrie,

So Sweetie, how are you? Today, we had a break in the rain for a short while which was nice. This morning, we were hit with rockets again. But, I think the reason was because a General (two star) was near where the rockets landed. Nobody got hurt, but it sure made a big boom.

We have been working sporadically ... a spinal here, a general there, etc. I'm reading and studying a lot, but I may be heading for a depression. When I get bored, with the things I like to do, I'm in trouble.

Today, also, I rated (evaluated) my staff (4 Nurse Anesthetists and 10 Operating Room Techs). I gave everybody outstanding and recommended that my Chief Nurse Anesthetist (a male Major who is leaving in 2 months) be given a Bronze Star for meritorious service. He is regular Army.

I hear from Natalie very frequently. She writes concerned letters. Maybe she is getting outside of herself more. What do you think? Heard from the McMilin's today and, also, Nellie Griffy.

I can't take my eyes off your pictures. You look so pretty! I'm waiting for my second batch of slides to come back so I can send them on to you. I am very anxious to see how you like the projector, when it comes.

Glad to hear that you got out to see "Funny Girl". Wish they would show a movie or something around here. We don't have anything and many other places do. Miss you a great deal, think of you constantly. You know when I run track and the pain in my legs and lungs is great, I think of you to ease the pain. And, then I run farther and farther.

Cheer up, Honey. When it's all over, it will be finished and done. We will just look back with less pain than we have now for this period of our lives. I am beginning to think I shall never forget this year or war.

All my love, Jonny

Dearest Sherrie,

Received your letter explaining your difficulties at work that day (February 25- Tuesday) and enjoyed it. What do you mean "patient had a possible embolus somewhere"? Why do you think so and where was it?

That was an excellent idea of yours to send my harmonica. Very good Sweetie, you're on the ball.

No, I'm not puzzled by Vietnam. I believe I understand my feelings for the situation pretty well, as well as the South Vietnamese, Viet Cong, North Vietnamese, Chinese and the U.S. It is difficult to discuss all of this in a letter, so I won't. But, I would just say that I believe that war and conflict and suffering are inevitable events in human life. They are a constantly recurring characteristic of history whether it be history for a day, week, year, decade, century. This is just a thorn in the cactus of man's struggles.

Last night, I had a very good time. We had a sing-in with the enlisted men until the wee hours of the morning. Several of them played guitar and one of the Docs is an excellent drummer. We all sang and sang. I got really plastered (drunk) for the first time since being here. I was so sick today ... nauseous, queasy, etc, etc. I can't look at another can of beer for a week. Oh, how I enjoyed singing. Many were my favorites, except nobody knew Tim Hardin's songs. But, we sang Beatles, Dylan, Rock n' Roll, etc. It was sort of a spontaneous party and it started after I had written you last night. I always write to you about 7:00 PM, because we get our mail at 6:30 PM.

Enclosed is another slide one of the other Docs took of me when it was raining. We had gotten rocketed, so we are wearing guns. I had just come out of the bunker behind me which is on the side of my hooch. We have a trap door cut out of the side of the hooch. It leads directly into the bunker through a passageway of sandbags that are directly behind me. Helicopter just landed at the hospital, so I think we got some business. Bye for now.

Love you very much,

Jon

I received your package of goodies today. Thanks. I hope I can learn to play the harmonica without driving anybody crazy. I'll be able to get to "Airport" in about a month. I've got so much to read.

Today was nice. It stopped raining. I ran my fastest 1.5 miles (9 minutes), played basketball, had no cases, read, studied, slept and dreamed of you.

Last night, though, I had my most exciting cases of all. You'll see what I mean when I tell you about it. The guy had a gun shot wound in his abdomen and fractures of both legs and one arm which, in itself, is not a big deal around here. But, after 8 hours, we finished at 3:00 AM and I extubated him and sent him to the ward. A half-hour later, I went to see how he was doing. The two surgeons had just left thinking he was ok. I thought he looked bad and got a chest x-ray which showed complete collapse of the right lung. I put in a chest tube and did a tracheostomy myself and put him on a ventilator with oxygen. Well, they were dumbfounded when I showed them, this morning, what they had missed. They said that I made a very astute and good clinical diagnosis (suspecting the lung was out), etc, etc. Always enjoy one-upmanship when it's in my favor. Carried to an excess, though, this kind of thing can be demoralizing.

Today, I finished another roll of snapshots and am getting them off tomorrow. I'm waiting for 2 batches to come back tomorrow.

Could you give me a better idea of how you spend your time around the house or what you do to pass time?

Your Mom sent some cookies, but they weren't chocolate chip cookies. So, could you tactfully remind her to only send chocolate chip ones? I appreciate her sending the cookies, but they are the wrong kind.

Miss you a great deal. Think I will try to learn to play some songs on the harmonica. I love you my precious darling. You are the only one for me.

All my devotion and love,

Jonny

Dearest Sherrie,

Today, I got 3 wonderful letters from you and in most you seemed happy, quite happy. One included the letter from Ruby and one told of a nice meeting with Stu. Since you told me you had a nice conversation with Stu, I'll return his letter. Ruby certainly writes nice letters. Got a nice one from my friend Ben. I've worked a very long day and I'm tired, so I'm going to be brief in answering your letters. So, please understand.

Glad to know you understand about the Red Cross. As far as residency goes, I'm leaning slightly towards Harbor General. But, Columbia is very close behind. I'll just have to let it sit in me a few more months. I don't need a fan.

The area I live in is a little wooden sort of bungalow (but really, less than a bungalow). The hospital is at one end made up of inflatable giant balloons. There is one public shower and toilet. No cement except by the hospital. We will be cementing the basketball court in 2 days! We got the cement from the engineers who mix it for us in a truck. It was a lot of work trying to get the ground level and ready for the cement by hand.

About your apartment ... without going into detail, my advice is if you are really that disturbed about paying $165 per month then I would move to your old apartment on Cornwall. It is fine. I want you to know that I do not object to paying $165 per month for your rent. I do not think it is excessive. If you think you would be as comfortable on Cornwall Street, as where you are, then I can see moving. I definitely think that safety, and closeness, to the hospital are most important. You probably would enjoy having a pool in the summer. Remember, it can get very hot and a pool would be nice. That's what I think. It's really your decision. I never mind saving money, but I am not foolish in my quest to do so (save money).

Bill Rader has not written. Glad you got the globulin shot. I'll let you know all about Japan in due time (what you have to do, etc). Don't worry. I'm very glad you feel proud of being Jewish. Let's create this feeling in our children. I'll let you know more about my research in the future.

All my love, Jonny

Dearest Sherrie,

I have worked very hard, today, from early in the morning to 2 AM tonight. I am very tired, but I don't want you to miss your daily message from me. Namely, I love you, think of you all the time and miss you a great deal. Missed hearing from you, today, but I am sure I'll hear tomorrow. Hang on Sloopy.

Dan has been sick and one of the nurses is on leave, so I'm being called on for everything. This is the reason why I have been so busy these past 3 days. Dan has an infection. Everything gets infected around here, even the smallest cuts. I've been lucky, not even a sniffle. The rain never stops. I think this is where Noah built his ark. Out of the last 30 days, 25 have rained.

All my love and devotion,

Jon

Dear Precious Sherrie,

Well here I am, alone with my Baby again. How are you Honey? What's with the apartment? Did you get the slides, recorder? The allotment? Have you heard from my family recently? Tell me all about yourself.

I didn't get any mail, today, again. I'm sure it's the weather. It has to stop soon. It seems like it's been raining forever. Aside from a few sunny days, I haven't seen the sun.

Today has been quiet, no cases so far. I slept till 1:00 PM today. I was so tired from the past few days. I'm happy if each day I can run, study and get some mail. I'm playing the harmonica a little each day. But, I'm really bad. After 3 days, I can't play do-re-mi-fa (etc) yet. My tongue is always in the wrong place. Maybe, in 6 months, I'll really be swinging along with Yankee Doodle. I weighed 146 pounds today.

I hope you took some more pictures. Please send some

chocolate chip cookies. I was crushed to find that even you sent the wrong cookies to me. How could you? Also, you could send some small cans of tuna with lemons or lemon juice. Otherwise, I don't need anything. I finished "Dear and Glorious Physician", pretty good book. I have "Tropic of Cancer", "The Fixer", "Airport" and a science fiction book waiting in line.

There is some talk that I will be getting On-the Job-Trainees to train in anesthesia (General Medical Officers from the field or other hospitals). That will be fun, I guess, but means more work too.

Well, that's about it. Can't think of anything else to tell you except to say over and over that I love you.

Jonny

Dearest Darling,

Received two nice bubbling letters from you, today, filled with love and many "Ha's". Today was quiet again and I saw many, many troops come back from the Ashau Valley ... got some shots of them. Today, I got forty slides back from the developer. What I am going to do is include 4 slides, every day, in my daily letter so you can have an extra surprise each day. They have a little caption on top, but each has a little story to it. I'll make them come to life when I show them, especially just the scenic ones which will not mean much to you.

I was delighted to hear you are doing skin tests and drawing blood. That is wonderful. Makes life more interesting the more things you learn and are capable of doing. I've done some nerve blocks here with the book in one hand and the needle in the other. See if you can get the interns and residents to let you start some IV's.

Sounds like the coming package is a good one. Look forward to it.

I think buying the bike was a very good idea, but only if you work at it. Physiologically, it does you no good to run or bicycle if you don't do it to the point where it hurts you ... that is to exhaustion. That is the only way to build up your stamina and muscles. Next package I send you will include a book on this subject (the relative values of different exercise and how you should do it). Since you decided to do what I suggested, a couple of days ago (concerning the apartment), I won't say any more about it.

I'm very happy Ed Carlson called you. I begged him to call collect, but I doubt he did. He is very nice, yes?

Oh yes, take good care of the slides Honey.

I was looking over the prices, today, of stereos. The one I liked cost only $230. Can you imagine that? It is without a cabinet (which I'm not sure I want anyway), but includes two speakers, 3-speed player, tuner-amplifier and AM-FM radio. I am almost debating whether to buy it through the mail or have it sent to you now. Or, wait until we are together in Japan and buy it then. What do you think?

Still stuck on just the scale with the harmonica. My Yankee Doodle sounds like a funeral march. That is a literal interpretation. How about some pictures, Sweetie? Come on, produce.

All my love and thoughts Darling,

Jonny

Dearest Sherrie,

I'm very drained of emotion and energy right now, so this will be short. We resuscitated a GI for 3 hours, tonight, and finally lost him. We came close at times, but obviously not good enough. He had both legs and one arm blown off, but I was hopeful for him because 3 weeks ago I resuscitated an identical injury (got him alive out of the O.R.). Well, I guess you win a few, lose a few. I am pretty certain that God giveth, but who taketh? We or God?

In retrospect, I was somewhat flattered tonight because there is a trend here at the hospital (I think) where in situations like this the other physicians have delegated the leadership to direct the resuscitation to me. I don't mind. I know what I'm doing and I believe my new ideas (my quasi research) are good ones. And, nobody has offered any substantial arguments against them. Well that's it for tonight. Enclosed are more slides.

Love you a great deal, Jonny

(1st Letter)

Dearest Darling,

Today was a very gloomy day. It just seems to rain

harder and harsher. It hasn't stopped now for 2 weeks and everything is getting wet. The one bright spot in the day was 2 letters from you.

I'm getting the hang of the harmonica. I can now play the scale and "My Country Tis of Thee". In fact, a guy here tuned his guitar to my harmonica. I played every note perfectly. The guys in my hooch have been making fun of me, but I showed them tonight.

Dan said the letter, that he got from Judy, was one of the nicest letters he ever received. She is a nice person. Got a nice letter from your Dad and my Mom.

Last night, the Officers' Club here opened. It's in the main underground bunker with the red door leading into it. It says "Rothskeller" on it (beer parlor). I am always most lonely at these times and surprisingly have become one of the few non-drinkers here. I have about 2 beers per day, but most of the men (Docs included) drink quite a bit each day. A lot of the men get very mean when they get drunk. Their whole nature changes and I can't believe it's the same person. After me and Dan were asleep (in our hooch), Doug and Chuck, another Doctor, and a board eligible Internist all came in and started to make a lot of noise in our hooch, waking us all up. The Internist threatened to send Chuck (who is a General Medical Officer) to the field and he is Chuck's boss. I told him to get out and he challenged me, so I knocked him out with a few punches. It was easy to do. I was cold sober and angry. And, he was drunk and mean which always is accompanied by bluff and is nothing to fear. He recovered quickly and wasn't badly hurt. We haven't spoken to one another yet, but I have said publicly that I felt no personal ill will. I would have stood up to anyone who disrespected our privacy. I'm sure the incident will soon be forgotten. And, I'm sure the Internist Doc will think twice before he acts again with me, which I take as progress.

I am much relieved you received my package. In order that I can purchase a recorder that is compatible, with the one I sent you, I need to know the number of the Sony recorder I sent you. All Sony recorders have a number. It is probably on the machine, although I forgot to look. If it isn't, find out from the repairman or some electronics store what Sony number it is. The table in the slides is one I made. It is covered with a blanket that is tacked down with nails. Looks good, eh? It's my desk. Don't send a fan, we have plenty.

Since you are making pictures of the slides, I think it would be nice if you would send some on to my family. Enclosed in the letter is one of me as I sort of look now. It's labeled "skinny" in my Bermuda shorts. I think my Mom would especially enjoy having a picture of me like that since I looked so skinny as a child. Make a picture, of that one, for her.

I understand about Bill. I'm sure he was uneasy. Just say hello to him for me. Ben Rosen is an extremely nice, considerate person. Please tell him hello for me. And, tell him I'm playing flanker on the football team here thanks to his astute lessons in football. I have not met or heard of his friend.

I'm very proud of your blood drawing dexterity. Very good, keep it up.

Please convey my best to Lucille Smith and Jim Smith. They are, I agree, very nice people.

Look forward to getting the package. We are out of snacks, at the moment. Don't send any more frosting for the brownies, it's too rich for me. I'll try to send the plastic containers home in my next package. I got the album.

I strongly suggest you read "Dear and Glorious Physician". Not so much because it is a story about a physician, but because it tells a beautiful story of St. Luke's search for Jesus Christ. Don't let your glory hallelujah Baptist upbringing get the better of you. I'm reading "The

Fixer". The Jew is so courageous and real.

I think you ought to call Gloria Bilchick's parents and find out where she is. If you can't, I will try to find his whereabouts. In fact, I'm going to do it anyway.

I had a very interesting long talk with the Chaplain attached to the hospital. He agrees that God certainly defies any definition in any traditional sense. I respected him because he was honest. It is hard not to despair over man's nature, especially in a war as we are. He seemed as lost and searching as myself.

Well, that is it for now. Think of you all the time. I sympathize with "The Fixer." I'm in a prison, too. Many of the same elements are present in kind, but of course not in degree.

Could you please write to: Williams and Wilkins, 428-E. Preston Street, Baltimore, Maryland 21202 for the: Journal of Trauma, Volume 8, Number 5, September 1968. I would love to have it. I just want that one journal, not a subscription.

All my love and devotion,

Jonny

(2nd Letter)
Sherrie,

I think the statement is correct. What I would do, since I'm not sure either what all the terms on the form mean, is call Ron Mogen. You have his card, remember? Ask him to come to your apartment. Tell him it is next to the one where Harold used to live.

When he comes in to L.A. to play basketball, he can help you out with the form. I'm sure he would be more than willing to do so. Besides, it's no trouble for him since he is in L.A. and near the hospital so frequently. Ok? Do it please.

Love you so much,

Jon

Dearest Beloved Sherrie,

Hi Sweetheart, how is the apple of my pudding dumpling eye? Quite an opener, eh?

Today was uneventful, except for a peripheral nerve block I did today that I never did before. Book in one hand, needle in the other. It worked well. I, also, played a great deal of ball and ran today. I am back on speaking terms with the Doc I punched around the other night, apparently no hard feelings. I, also, got a haircut today. The Colonel lent me his jeep.

I am going to send you a package, in the next few days, whenever I can get to the Post Office. It is 3 miles round-trip, but I dare not walk. The path leads close to the perimeter. And, there is some dense jungle foliage there which could conceal Viet Cong. I'll wait for the Colonel's jeep again. It is protected. And, I go with Dan who sits behind with a machine gun. The package will consist of the transistor radio, my O.R. shoes, a few books, some slides, my galoshes and a few odds and ends. I don't need these things. I was given a nice pair of jungle boots for the rain. The radio is too weak as we are too far North.

I got your package of food. Thank you. Dan especially likes your cookies. He thinks you are a great cook, which I readily agree with. Don't send any more pudding. It really doesn't taste very good.

The reason I'm sending home, the above mentioned stuff, is because I don't want to be burdened with unnecessary things in case the hospital has to move. As things are right now, I couldn't take everything with me.

Got to go and practice my harmonica, so I can play songs for you when you sing. Are you singing?

I'm sending off another 20 slides, I just finished taking, to be developed.

All my love Sweetheart,

Jonny

Dearest, Dearest Sherrie,

I cannot tell you how excited and happy I was to receive the acceptance to Columbia. I am filled with a tremendous sense of accomplishment. I cannot say whether I will accept, but I am very tempted to. One reason that I might is that, after finishing at Columbia, I could probably walk into any job or situation in Anesthesia anywhere in the country (including the crowded competitive West coast). Private groups, which are difficult to get into (if they are at all established), would accept me much more readily if I came from Columbia. Pub-

lic jobs (like being Chief at say Santa Barbara or Harbor) or at least an esteemed staff position would be much easier to get. I'll probably let it ride, for another month or two, but I must admit I'm very proud of being accepted. I think more so than any other place.

I'm following Smitty's course (post-op) with interest. Glad she is well.

I'm hoping to hear soon that the allotment was received and put away correctly. You wrote we have $826 in the savings account. What about the checking account? In the future, whenever you tell me what is in the bank, tell me both accounts.

That book "Doctors' Wives" sounds like trash. Why don't you throw it away? I don't think there is very much in this world that one can hold onto that means anything outside of your family and your mind, so you better hold onto your wife or husband.

I got a very nice letter from an old friend that I used to know when I played basketball with Ben Ezra (from whom he got my address). They both are on Long Island, New York.

Eating your cookies. They are delicious. Still raining like crazy. Got my package off to you. It, also, has a pair of eyeglasses that I don't need. Please put it away carefully. Miss you very much, Darling.

I love you,

Jonny

Dearest Darling,

I just got back from a case and found my package, with the books, waiting for me. Just think, some of my brains just came.

When you make up your next package include some orange juice, V8 juice and oranges.

No letters, today, so not much to respond to. Still raining steadily, but I ran today anyway. I don't feel right, anymore, unless I've run once a day.

This letter contains the last of the slides that I have. The rest are in the package I sent two days ago. I have 40 slides being developed right now. I hope that as you receive the slides you will put them in boxes, that have the month of the year on them, so they will be roughly in chronological order.

I weighed 148 pounds today. I will probably level off near this weight. I've been within 1 or 2 pounds of 148 for a couple of weeks.

Did I tell you I heard from Lonnie? Nice letter, will naturally answer it.

We got mortared yesterday and one of the gunners, on the South perimeter, got killed. At the time I heard all the noise, I thought it was all outgoing stuff. First time I've been wrong. But it's, also, one of the few times we have taken mortars. I'm sure with just a little more unwanted practice, I will be able to recognize mortars as well as rockets (which I don't have any trouble recognizing). We got hit with them so much.

What's new on the home front? Do you watch TV? What do you do on the weekends? Are you sending pictures?

Nothing new on the rumored move. Rumors are all over the place and none, I'm sure, are well founded. I heard some guys talk about going to Korea. I'm sure we will stay right where we are. The bad thing about a move is that we would have to sleep, on the ground, in tents for several months wherever we went. Things like tape decks, stereos, recorders (etc) would have to be left behind. That is why I am reluctant to collect anything of value around me.

I bought some clothes for $130. It was a package deal and included 1 suit, 1 sweater, 2 pairs of pants, 2 shirts- all made of real good stuff. I should be getting them, in a couple of weeks, and will send them on home.

Miss you a great deal, as always, and always look forward to that very far off distant leave in Japan with you. Take care of yourself.

All my love, Jon

Dearest, Dearest Sherrie,

Poor little Sherrie. I was called to the O.R. very early this morning (6:00 AM) and was there all day. I did not get one chance to mail the letter I had written, last night to you, so it will go out with this letter. It means you will probably be disappointed one day next week.

Today was a pretty good day. I worked hard in the O.R. most of the day, but I got out in time to run. Then, I had a refreshing shower and then got your 2 letters. Here I am now writing to you and I may write to somebody else. But, then I'll practice the harmonica for a little while, read, study and then go to bed.

I enjoyed hearing about your days off last Saturday and Sunday. I was so pleased to learn that you enjoyed talking to my parents. A close family is very important, to me, and I couldn't be more pleased if you and my parents genuinely like one another. I think it's fine if you are taking just one course. But, study it hard and do well (all anyone can ask is that one try to do their best). I'm sure you'll be able to go back to school full time during my residency.

Again I want to repeat, if you don't mind at all moving back to your old apartment, I certainly don't mind saving money. With that said, it is your decision.

I hope you have been able to land a private case occasionally. The money sounds good.

About Japan, I too would only take my cousin Jerry's friend's apartment if we were alone. This is the first time I've heard of this, so let me see what the deal actually is.

I'm looking forward to getting those brownies and cookies very much. You're such a good little cook. And the pictures, I hope they come soon. I think if you would like to buy the knee-high boots, you may. Try and decide for yourself, when you buy them, if you think they make you more attractive or not. Think carefully, but be brave. Have you bought a pair of decent bell bottoms yet?

It is me who puts the tape, on some of the letters, to hold them together. It is so wet here that some of the old envelopes get completely stuck together.

I would love to hear you sing "Yesterday" (on the tape) and "Going Out of My Head". And, most of all "Gentle on My Mind" and "Reason to Believe".

Don't let the VW people cheat you. Demand your rights on the guarantee. Get your Dad to help if there is any question

All my love and thoughts and hopes are of you and for you.

Jonny

Dearest Darling Pumpkin Head,

Hi Honey. How is the sweetest flower of them all? Blossoming, I hope. Shed a little petal my way, will you?

Had one case today. It was a little 2 year old Vietnamese baby, burned from a mortar blast. Ran as usual and studied. And, believe it or not, I'm getting a little better on my harmonica. I think I may be getting the hang of it. "Yankee Doodle" though still gives me fits. I can play "My Country Tis of Thee" pretty well. Dan has been shooting pictures of me. I'm trying to include myself in more shots. I have 7 shots of myself in the roll of film that is presently in the camera. Dropped down to 145 pounds today. Today was the first day it didn't rain for several weeks and everybody is hopeful the sun will come out tomorrow.

I got a funny letter from my Dad and a nice one from Bob and Leslie Kopel. They tell me they wrote you, also. They are warm, aren't they? I, also, got 2 letters from my Sis. Sigh, nothing from you, but I got 2 yesterday and probably will get 2-3 tomorrow.

I, also, got a card from PACEX (Pacific Mail Order Exchange) today. These are the people I ordered, and bought, the slide projector and watch from. They told me they got my money. The order will be filled in 20 days, so you have an idea how much longer you will have to wait for the projector (say a month or so). Should you have any questions concerning the projector or watch (their condition when they arrive, etc, etc), when you write them you should give them the order number (#046078). The money I sent them (which *included packaging, mailing, etc) was $69. I don't think you will have to pay duty on the package, but you may. It will only be about $5, if anything. Their address is: Japan Regional Exchange-PACEX, PACEX Mail Order, APO, 96323. Hang onto this information since I will probably purchase other stuff through them and may need it in Tokyo. We will do some shopping here (PACEX) when we are in Tokyo.*

Much love Sweetheart, Jon

Dearest Sherrie,

What a disappointment. After our one day without rain yesterday, first time in several weeks, it rained again all day today (seemingly harder than ever). In addition, I couldn't run, had no cases and was cold and miserable. These are the hardest times to take, nothing to do. I studied a fair amount and read "Airport" some. "Airport" is the ninth novel I'm on. I've read one textbook, a whole journal and parts of 3 other textbooks. Man, when I come home, am I ever going to be primed and sharp with medical knowledge. Looking to the future residency. It seems like it will be very easy mentally. I'm packing away so much knowledge now.

To top everything off, today, I didn't get any mail either. Just what I needed.

There are two things that I want to discuss with you. (1) I will attempt to call you after I get a reply, from you, concerning the following information. The call is by radar, from here, even though you can get it on your phone. It is not private. There can be 20 people listening at one time. When you speak, it is one way (meaning that when one person speaks the other can only listen). When you have finished speaking, you must say "over". Then the operator or radio transmitter will switch over, to me, so I can speak. Then, you will have to listen until I say "over". One can't speak and listen at the same time. We will only have a maximum of 3 minutes to speak. So, you should say all you can quickly and then say "over" and listen. Make up a list, beforehand, of the things you want to say. Finally, send me your phone number again. I lost the other copy or gave it to Ed. (2) The other thing I wanted to ask you to do, or find out, is how much it would cost you to fly from L.A. to Hong Kong. And, also, what it is from L.A. to Tokyo. Please call the airlines and write me back soon. I want the round-trip price. We may take my leave in Hong Kong, so take care of this, ok?

They started showing bi-weekly movies here. I haven't seen one yet, but I guess I'll go one of these days.

Remember, answer me in regard to phoning you and Hong Kong. Would you like to go there? If it doesn't cost too much more to go to Hong Kong, for you, we might go there. The prices there are the cheapest in the world. And, it's much like Tokyo otherwise. We'll be buying so much.

I really think of you all the time.

All my love,

Jonny

Dearest Darling Sherrie,

Today, I received a package of brownies and cookies from you. Also got a letter from you, Nat and my Mom and Dad (including 3 snapshots of themselves). They looked terrific, but I still can't get over how darling and pretty you looked. Tonight, I skipped supper and made a big fat sandwich of pastrami, had a brownie and 2 chocolate chip cookies for dessert and then an apple to clean my teeth. I pretended that it was just as if you had made it for me and enjoyed it very much as I sat down to read my 3 letters. It was the nicest meal I can remember having for a long time. Hell of a lot better than waiting on a long line for a greasy, grubby, tasteless, lukewarm meal in a dark dingy mess hall (with plastic eating ware which breaks and no salt or sugar because it is too wet).

Yesterday, I got awakened from a deep sleep to go to the O.R. Today, I was told by the tech (who woke me up) that at the time (just prior to waking me up) I was hugging and kissing the pillow. I remembered, very distinctly, I was dreaming of kissing you at the time. I remember, now, what a funny look he gave me.

Today, finally was a nice day. I ran like the wind (2 times) and played some on my harmonica, outdoors, where everybody heard. Naturally, there was some good-natured kidding, but I really didn't do too badly. I played a little basketball and now will read and study tonight. I got sunburned today. I hope so much we have seen the last of the monsoon rains. You've got to see it, or be in one, to believe it could rain so much.

Dan says "Hi" and says thanks for the goodies. He is a big fan of yours. Naturally, he has good taste. He thinks I'm lucky to have you, so do I. Boy, sounds like a big fight just broke out just outside the perimeter. Man, you should hear the noise. When they shoot 1/2 mile away, our whole hooch shakes. Oh well, another idyllic night coming up.

Sherrie, make sure you put the slides away carefully. Yes, Baby?

Only yours forever,

Jonny

Dearest Precious Sherrie,

Today was beautiful. Looks like maybe we have the monsoon season behind us for good. I got very sunburned today. I suppose, if this weather continues, I will be very tanned shortly. The only catch is that very quickly it is supposed to be sunny, only it gets up to 120-130 degrees. Well, I guess I'll get used to it just like everything else.

I have something very important I want to tell you about. As you know, I bought some clothes for $130 (six weeks ago) from a Hong Kong dealer. Today, they arrived. I showed them to the Docs and they unanimously thought they were worth $250-$300. I myself thought it was a real good deal. I bought them so soon, after arriving, because I was carrying too much cash and this seemed an excellent buy to lessen my cash load. Now, for the important part. I am sending them, to you, within the next few days. They consist of a sharkskin *gaberdine perma-press suit, 2 pairs of perma-press worsted flannel and worsted silk slacks, 2 shirts and a beautiful mohair sweater-jacket (that is worth $60 itself). I am going to insure the package for a lot, but I want you to keep an eye out for its arrival. Now, when I was originally measured (for the pants and suit), my waist was 32 inches. I figured I would lose an inch and ordered them to be made to 31 inches. Well, today, my waist measured 29.5 inches. The pants were too large in the waist and the hips by 1.5 inches. Today, I weighed 144 pounds. Now, I think if you allow for my gaining back an inch (which would make my waist 30.5 inches), they would still be a 1/2 inch too large. I don't know whether to ask you to have a 1/2 inch taken out of the central back seam (from waist to crotch) or not. Most of the seams, incidentally, are hand stitched. What do you think we ought to do? Do you think we should wait until I come home for good? I don't see what good that would do since, if anything, I would be as thin or thinner. What do you think? The clothes are beautiful. The suit looks like an $80 or $90 suit itself. We'll get you a good $100 or more worth of clothes in Japan. Don't worry, I didn't forget about you. I am quite pleased though with what I got.*

About your logic course, I don't think you can or should try to review the course by yourself at home. I think it would be a very frustrating and uninspired undertaking. I don't think you or I or anyone, for that matter, could learn the material that way. Remember, you work and have other classes. I emphatically think that you should sit in on the classes at the college, do the homework along with the class and attend as faithfully as possible. This approach is much more economical time-wise since you would not spend many hours trying to figure out the problems (you have trouble with) when the instructor can clear things up in minutes. I do believe you should attempt to erase that incomplete.

I have stopped smoking cigarettes, for the most part, so

I'm in need of another pipe. Please send me a pipe, of your liking, that costs around $2.50 soon. I'm trying to eat the pastrami as fast as I can since it is beginning to spoil rapidly. I'll have it for supper now, but I don't know if it will be any good tomorrow. I've eaten about a pound of it.

Well, I can't think of anything else to rant about except that I love you very much and think about you all the time. And, I hope that through my letters you can see that you are an integral and inseparable part of my life, being, feelings and thoughts. Glad to know you are hanging on Sloopy. No letters today (sob, sob).

All my love, Jonny

My Dear Sherrie,

Today, the thermometer crept up a little bit more and was 105 degrees in the sun. No problem. Ran 3 miles, laid in the sun for an hour, read, studied, etc. Have had very few cases lately. But, I think the 101st Airborne guys are going back into Ashau Valley to clean the Viet Cong out and we'll get busy again. Before I forget, please send me another can of cherry blend pipe tobacco and a pipe. There are more rumors that the hospital is going to be moved to the Ho Chi Minh Trail in Laos. Nothing substantiated, to the rumor, that I know of.

I got 2 nice very chatty letters from you today, a card from Des and a letter from Nat. She said something about seeing you in 2 weeks. True?

About novels, I finished "The Fixer" a week ago. I

thought it was pretty good and, to some extent, I sympathize with his situation. I'm in the middle of "Airport" right now and enjoying it. I plan to read "The Plot", next, by Irving Wallace. It's a long book though, 900 pages. To date, I have read 9 novels. "Topaz" sounds good. Send it.

I made the package up containing my clothes and I, also, put the air mattress in it. I really don't need it. It was such a good one, I would hate to ruin it here. Probably would be nice to have in Japan and Hawaii. I would love to continue my training regime, while on leave and R&R, by swimming and then resting on the mattress in the middle of the pool. It is so hot here that the thought seems like a mirage to a guy stuck in the middle of a desert. I'll get the package off as soon as I can find somebody who is going to the PX (the Post Office is near it).

Sorry you couldn't enjoy the party. I sympathize with you.

Dan is delighted that Judy is baking something for him. Between you and me, he is very anxiously awaiting a reply from her.

About the tape recorder, I will probably borrow one until I get to Japan. Then, we can buy one that is compatible with the one you have. It will only be $24, in Japan, for a similar one. Incidentally, it is important for you to ask the repairman "How many channels does this recorder have"? I need to know this. For instance, a 2 channel recorder plays 30 minutes on each side. And, a 4 channel recorder can play up to 120 minutes. If you play a 4 channel tape (from a 4 channel recorder) on a 2 channel recorder, you get a double voice since both tracks on one side are playing at the same time. You should buy about 4 or 6 appropriate tapes and then we can send them back and forth. They are $3 a piece here, I think.

I think you should only make chocolate chip cookies and only every other week. The brownies spoil too quickly.

I smiled at your surprise that I enjoyed Luke's search for Christ. I have nothing against a man's sincere and honest search for God no matter what religion it is. In fact, I admire religious honesty and integrity. I despise, however, self-deception, hypocrisy and insincerity. Often the difference is very subtle, and seemingly slight, but the significance and meaning between the two is really infinite. The word infinity as used has a double meaning in case you didn't notice.

I am very glad to know that you have trimmed down to 105 pounds. I'm sure you look terrific. What did you weigh in the pictures you sent? I was very surprised, today, when I got on the scale and found that I weighed only 142 pounds. I'm getting to the point where I had better watch it.

You wrote that you were going to do private duty the next day. I think that is very good and we could use the money. How many times have you done private duty? You know that you have travel fare to Japan and Hawaii alone that will cost over $1000. Not complaining, but I'm not complaining about you doing private duty either. But, don't knock yourself out.

These are the last of my current bunch of slides. The one where I am standing up projects beautifully. You might send out a copy (a photo) of that one to the family.

Take care. I love you with all my heart and soul.

Jonny

3/21/69
Letter 61

Dearest Sherrie,

Well tonight, I have to console myself with your pictures. No letters, today, from anybody. I'm very glad I have them to look at.

I spoke too soon, last night, when I wrote you that it was quiet. Just after finishing the letter, we got in 10 cases. I worked through the night until about 10 AM. Had some interesting cases.

I still haven't been able to mail the clothing packages yet. I'm considering going to the Post Office myself, tomorrow, but I hate to put on the uniform in this heat. It was 110 degrees today. I wear my surgical greens all the time. Last time I put on my uniform (a couple of weeks ago), to go somewhere, it caused quite a stir when everybody saw me in uniform.

Last night, I finished another roll of slides and I'm sending them off to be developed. Takes me about 3 weeks to get them back. I believe I have two rolls being developed right now. The roll I am sending in, tonight, has about 15 shots of me or so. So, you'll have plenty to look at in a month.

Send pipe and pipe tobacco (cherry blend).

I am very tired right now. I can't think of anything especially to say, except you know the universal constants of my life are the same. I love you, miss you, think of you all the time and wish I was out of here.

Jonny

Dearest Sherrie,

Right now, I feel like I'm not living life, just hanging in there or just hanging on. About the only thing I sense or perceive is the passage of time. I mean "sense" like you see something or hear a noise or smell something. I am only aware or sense or feel time pass because each day I do something like wash my socks, run, do a case, read, etc. I remember that this is exactly the same thing that I did, at the same time, the past day. Sometimes I feel as if I'm in limbo, living in a one-dimensional world, namely time, length, width, height. And, most important: emotion, love, happiness, etc. are non-existent. I feel dulled, shocked. But like I said above, when I occasionally feel something about my present situation, I feel that I am hanging in there. I reserve thoughts of you, and past life, as belonging to another world. If I brought them emotionally into this world, I don't think I could tolerate it. I would even lose my dimension of time, even though I am floundering in it now.

Today, I went to the Post Office and mailed the clothing package off by air mail. It cost $13, but I was told it would take 60 days to go by boat. This way, you should get them in 10 days.

I could summarize things by a sign like this. "Tomorrow was cancelled due to lack of interest, God".

I know this letter is not very bouncy, but I took the liberty of being depressed and melancholy tonight.

Maybe God will call tomorrow off, after all. I wish he would. My area is a very hot war zone. The fighting is fairly intense. Everybody could do with a break.

I have had some success with my research and I'm writing everything up in a paper. I may submit it, for publication, in a few months.

As you can see, there is not much new to tell you today. So, I'll sign off with fond remembrances of my glowing, sunny, shining, happy, love-filled past life with you. You are the sun on the horizon of my life.

Jonny

Dearest Sherrie,

I am not sufficiently aroused from my depression, to be jovial, but I have brightened up somewhat. Mainly because I've started writing a paper, which if nothing else is keeping me occupied. The paper is entitled "A Review of Pulmonary Insufficiency and Its Relationship to Shock". It is really sort of a synopsis of my "Respiratory Care" and "Care of the Critically Ill" books that I have read. As well as several journals, I have read, and my clinical experience here in Vietnam during the past 2 months that I have been here. The paper will serve as the basis for a talk I am giving in 2 weeks. And, it will be useful for an on the spot talk anytime during my residency as well as putting my notes in a more readable form. I expect it to be fairly long (in the neighborhood of 20 pages) by the time I'm finished.

Otherwise, nothing is changed. In fact, if anything, things are worse. Simply because more of the same thing as before makes the same things worse. Understand?

I received more slides, today, but the bunch doesn't

contain very many of me. Most will need a projector to be visualized. To the naked eye, they are hard to make out.

I am doing pretty well on the harmonica, but I need to play more songs I know the words to and, also, the tunes in order to make the songs comprehensible. Several days ago, I requested you to send the music for several popular songs I like and know the words and tunes. I hope you are doing this. In addition, send me (as soon as possible) one or two other harmonica books with songs in them for a harmonica. The book I have now is very limited in that I know the words and tunes to only a few songs. The book doesn't have any words.

I finished "Airport". It was pretty good. That makes my 10th novel.

Your package of cookies arrived, but it had ripped open and things were sort of a mess. Thanks anyway. I miss you very much.

All my love, Jon

Dearest Sherrie,

Today wasn't so bad. I'm well into my paper. And so far, I have been able to put into words what thoughts I have. I'm reading a good book called "The Magus". It's a movie out now, I believe. Later tonight, there will be a little drinking party on behalf of the Colonel's birthday. The Colonel is Commander of the hospital and a very nice guy. I got a nice letter from you, today, and some magazines.

I wrote Lonnie, today, and tried to write like a brother (which, in truth, I suppose I am).

I'm glad you like the slides. I'm sure you'll enjoy them much more once they are projected. One of the guys here has a little viewer and even looking at them, through the viewer, makes a big difference compared to the naked eye.

I will probably type my paper in duplicate and send a copy home to save. You'll be able to read it that way. I might want you to show it to a few people for me.

Tonight, we had beef stew. Boy, did I ever stuff myself. I loved that meal. But, I love you much, much more Pumpkin. I'm going to work on my paper some more now. Talk to you tomorrow.

All my love and thoughts,

Jonny

Dearest Darling,

I almost didn't write, tonight, because I'm very tired. Last night, I just couldn't fall asleep. I was in agony just lying there all night. I'm sure the heat (which is oppressing) had something to do with it. I resolved during the night to really knock myself out, during the day, so I could fall asleep tonight. I was fortunately called for a spinal at 6 AM. After the case, I ran a couple of miles and then had another case. Then, I ran a couple of more miles this evening, played basketball for hours and now I'm exhausted. I'm so tired I didn't even mind not getting any mail.

In addition, I climbed the airfield observation tower (which is about 6 stories high) by a rickety old ladder on the side of it. Boy, was I ever scared! I took about 10 photos of the Camp, and the countryside, from that height. Did this with Dan. I'm sure I got great shots. Sent them off to be developed with this letter. I guess you will start getting them in 5-6 weeks. You can clearly see the airfield observation tower above the hooches (as seen from the airfield). That's where I climbed up today.

I'm hoping to hear about our bank account (total) soon. Any more pictures of you on the way? What is happening with the tape recorder?

Last night, the Colonel had a birthday party. I had a pretty good time. We have one TV, here at the hospital, but usually it is impossible to see because of the constant shooting by big guns and the passage of airplanes overhead. But last night, for some reason, a Glen Campbell show (with Judy Collins) and a Tijuana Brass special came through really well. I thoroughly enjoyed watching both.

I am about 70% through writing my paper. I hope to start typing in 2-3 days.

The following is something that I think is true of all people and perhaps reflects my religious attitude and why I enjoyed St. Luke's search for Jesus. "We shall not cease from exploration. And, at the end of all our exploring, will be to arrive where we started and know the place for the first time."

All my love, my Precious Girl, Jonny

(1st Letter)

Dearest Darling Sherrie,

I got 2 love-filled letters from you, today, and a large picture of you. I'm very busy right now, so I only have time to respond to your letters. Nothing new, except that I'm slowly losing my marbles. It's very hot right now. I often wonder who is going to get me first? The bugs or the Viet Cong? The answer is, of course, you are.

Thanks for the information on the recorder. Enjoyed hearing about the Unit and Ida Bryant. Yes, I remember her. Very sad. Please give my regards.

I don't remember Dr. Steiger, can't place him. I know Dover. Ben Rosen is very nice.

Terrific of you to send the telegram to my Mom. Just great! I completely forgot. Thanks for writing to everybody. They love you.

Too bad you hurt from your shots. Here is a big kiss to help you forget.

I've got to go. I've got some nerve blocks to do, in the leg, that I have never done before.

I love you very much Darling Sweetheart.

Don't forget that,

Jonny

3/26/69
Letter 67

(2nd letter)

The blocks worked well. No problems, lots of "oohs and aahs" over the finesse and poise of the Anesthesia Chief. I forgot to include the last of my current batch of slides, in my letter, so here they are.

Dan really appreciated getting the cookies from your folks. I share everything I get from you. And, so do my other hoochmates with the stuff they get. It was a very nice thought on the part of your parents. Tell them for me.

I'm really haggard out.

Remember, I love you with all my heart.

Jon

3/27/69
Letter 68

Dearest Sherrie,

Last night was a big horror show. I couldn't fall asleep because it was too hot. The guns were constantly going and the sky was filled with choppers. I tossed and turned until 4 AM and then got called to the emergency room. I knew before I got there what had happened. Our very own Camp Evans was under a ground attack. When dawn came, the dead Viet Cong were being picked off the barbed wire fence right on our perimeter. They had gotten in so close. The fighting during the night had been very intense. What greeted me, when I arrived at the emergency room, was a tremendous number of casualties. I myself ran three O.R.'s (more or less continuously) until we finished the cases at 4 PM or 5 PM today. What made it very hard in the O.R. was that the temperature (outside) was around 115-120 degrees and the air conditioner (in the O.R.) broke down. Man, we sweated.

So, I'm very tired and I have a premonition that more of the same is coming tonight. I'm going to go to sleep. Wish the mail would come more regularly. All I got today was a nice note, from Ann Stevens, with a picture of her baby. This is driving me crazy. Dan was out running, today after the cases (as I did, also), and someone dropped a tear gas grenade. Dan nearly choked to death.

All my love. Wish I was with you.

Jonny

Dearest Darling,

War is hell. I've been in the O.R. for close to 24 hours. Would you believe we did 31 cases in the past day and a half? The Viet Cong hit an orphanage with rockets. We got babies from less than a year old to pregnant Mothers. What a mess. Only one died though. Didn't even see the hooch, so I obviously didn't write. I'm tired, so this will be short. Got 2 nice letters from you, one from my Mom and cookies from your Mom. Dan has eaten half of them already. Your Mom wraps them in tin foil and they keep better than with saran wrap. Also, you've got to make your packages stronger. They are frequently torn open when they arrive.

How's the bank account? I think it is great that you are picking up easy money by working private duty. I am all for it. Of course, when school starts, you'll need all the time you can get to study. So, don't work extra. Always remember, I think your education is more important than making money.

Did the projector come (in addition to the watch)? Yes, I'll wait to have the clothes altered. Did they come?

You should get another allotment around the first week in April. Watch for it. I await the pipe, tobacco and pastrami with eagerness.

I finished my paper and will start typing tomorrow.

I think it's pretty damn good. I, also, think you are pretty wonderful, too. I am tired.

All my love, kisses, caresses,

Jonny

Dearest Wife,

We continue to be extremely busy. And so, again, this is just going to be a reply to a nice letter I got from you today. The fighting is fierce, each case seems to go over 5 hours and new problems arise.

Honey, it can get to be 100 degrees in Los Angeles, but you don't know what hot is until you are in 125 degrees. And not just for one day, but at night and then the next day and so on.

Don't buy me anything for Japan. I'll let you know what to bring when the time comes. You know, it will be sometime in August probably (not July) when I can get to Japan. I will not know when it will be for a long time yet.

Oh yes, today was payday and I may send you $200 in addition to the allotment which is already on the way. I can't even get back to my hooch hardly these days, let alone to have time to get a mail order.

I'm very glad you got the VW fixed for nothing, as it should have been.

I may be sent to be Chief of Anesthesia at a larger hospital. I'll let you know more about it tomorrow. No sweat, I know now I can do the job and do it well. I think I'll be on my own for the rest of the time while I'm here. There is a good chance I'll be Chief of a department back in the U.S.

I've got to go to sleep, Honey. I think I'm days behind on sleep.

I weigh 146 pounds and it contains all my love, devotion and thoughts.

Jonny

Dearest Sherrie,

We continue to be busy. I think, in the last 5 days or so, I have been in the O.R. more than 18 hours a day. Getting a lot of great experience and doing a good job, but I would prefer it in less concentrated doses.

I got some good slides back, today, so I'll start sending them again.

So, you went to the beach. Very good. Weather sounds lovely. Wish I could join you.

I'm looking forward to getting some more pictures of you. I'm sure you look lovely and look like you are loved, because you are you know.

I'm falling way behind in my letters to other people. If you are writing anybody, explain why.

I hope you have sent some music for me to play. I need it badly.

I'm glad you got the clothes. We'll get you some in Japan.

Honey, is everything alright? Your letters seem to have changed their tone a little bit. I have a vague suspicion that perhaps you are not getting enough love from me. Something seems not quite right. Is anything wrong? I very much want an answer, so please do let me know.

I do love you very much. The thought of returning to you keeps me going.

With much devotion and love,

Jonny

Dearest Precious One,

The mail should be here in a few minutes, but I started writing you early tonight. "The Graduate" is being shown. I'll go see it and then, hopefully, an NBA playoff game will come on the one TV we have.

It is scorching hot. No place to go for relief. I think I'll feel funny if I am not sweating.

I almost died, today, when a call came in saying 30 burn patients were on their way to the hospital. We have been working so hard that I think that, if we had gotten the 30 patients, it would have been the straw that broke the camel's back. As it turned out, we didn't get any of them, so I got a chance to rest today.

I was paid an indirect compliment, today, by the Chief of Professional Services (a surgeon). A lot of the Doctors switch, with Doctors on the hospital ship, for 2 weeks at a time (just to get a change of scene). I asked if I could switch, with the Anesthesiologist on the ship, and the Chief eventually said that he didn't feel that the 18th Surgical Hospital would get by nearly as well without me. This is because he felt that my supervision and teaching, of the nurses, would not be followed by the new guy. I am teaching them spinals, axillary blocks, IV regionals and other nerve blocks. Well, that sure is a nice way to say no.

I am two-thirds of the way through reading "The Magus". Terrific book, #1 book. The Vietnamese say #1 if something is good and #10 if something is bad. I didn't get any mail today and that is very #10.

Haven't got very much of my paper typed because we have been so busy. What's with the tape recorder?

As you can see, from one of the slides, I am very forlorn and lonely without you.

I love you very much,

Jonny

Dearest Sherrie,

Today, I got a very love-filled letter from you. I want you to know that the thought of you does sustain me most of the time. But I guess, at times, I'm inherently too much of a realist to get lost in daydreams for any great length of time.

Last night, for instance, they did not show "The Graduate". Everything here is a disappointment. The only redeeming feature, to the place, is that perhaps the next disappointment will be smaller than the next. Another example, today, we had no water for drinking or for showering. The Viet Cong blew up the road. So, the truck that delivers the water simply turned around and went home. I ran anyway and doused myself with what was left in my canteen. I'm dependent on the cokes and beer, that we have left, for survival.

I went to the Post Office, this morning, and got money orders for $200 (enclosed within). As I figure it, I have sent you $2080. I believe we had $600, in the bank, when I left. This means that if you saved nothing up until now (from your own work), we should have $2700 in the bank. Is that correct? What do we have in our saving and checking accounts? I, also, got a haircut and took before and after snapshots for you.

I know that you will be a wonderful wife in the future. You already are. The only way you can go is downhill, Sweetie. It'll be hard to improve on what you are already.

Could you send me some cans of beef stew? I bought a pair of size 30 shorts, today, and they were big on me.

Hey, they are showing the movie in 10 minutes. I look

forward to getting the pictures of you and the music.

Love you very, very much,

Jonny

Dearest Sherrie,

Got a nice letter and package from you, today, in addition to a package and letter from my folks. Thanks for the juice. My parents sent a lot of Passover goodies (chocolate covered matzos, etc). I used to eat them as a kid.

My regards to John House. Extend my sympathy that he is going in the Army. If he goes to Vietnam, it will be an experience unlike anything else (unfortunately) and not a desirable one. I was thinking, yesterday, that I'm doing a lot of things here that I might not have done if I was at home. So, I'm making the most of my time. The other guys are amazed at the amount of time I study and I'm learning a great deal. I'm in excellent physical condition and I lost that extra weight. I'm way ahead in Anesthesia and residency should be no more than a job. For me, this interlude in Vietnam (since it came), came at the right time. But, I would have much preferred I didn't have to come. Maybe, when it's all over, I will be glad for the experience and the things I was able to do for myself here. But, right now, the only positive things I find in life are the physical and mental improvements I am making on myself.

Honey, I hope you realize that you should send me your new address and phone number before you move. And, let me know on what date to start addressing my mail there. I *think you will miss having a pool (etc), but it's up to you. The savings is approximately $90 per month and it's for you to gauge the relative values of each place. I really don't mind if you decide to stay at San Pablo Street.*

Please answer all of my questions, in previous letters. Honey, Sweet Darling, you are beginning to slip a little. Your letters are beginning to be less informative.

I have been so busy that I have not been able to type on my paper at all. I'm going to try now. Goodnight, Sweetheart. See you in my dreams.

All my love,

Jonny

Dearest Darling Wife,

Dig the typewriter. First letter you got from me that you can read, eh? I just finished typing some of my paper. Very smart sounding paper. I hope that I've said something. How are you, Honeybunch?

Last night, I was very scared. I thought the world was coming to an end. It rained so hard, I can't describe it to you. Each drop seemed like the size of a grape. The shutters were banging and the wind was howling. Even if I had been a good Boy Scout, I think I still would have been afraid. At one point, I was going to tear down the hooch and build an Ark. What I did, though, was curl up in my electric blanket and go to sleep. For once, it was cool enough to sleep. And, I slept right through to 1 PM today.

Got a letter from you, Nat, Stu and Uncle Abe today. Abe sends his love to you. Did you know that he was recently sick? He was, but apparently not too badly.

Work in the O.R. (the past few days) has not been too heavy, just steady. Dan is in Phu Bai (20 miles away), tonight, and called me on some business. He is going wild over eating, on a tablecloth, with real knives and forks, etc. Boy, I don't know what I'm missing anymore. I'm so numb, mentally, to the real world. All except you, because you are the one thing that makes it worthwhile for me to even want to go home. Everything else is really unimportant.

Did you send pastrami? Get recorder fixed? Get money from me and the allotment? Answer all my questions other than these? Do I love you? Yes!

Miss you terribly Honey,

Jonny

Sherrie, my Sweet Darling Wife,

Tonight, I'm happy. I received another wonderful letter, from you, and a package today. In addition, I got back another set of slides which came out very well. Five are included. It will be fun to explain the slides to you, someday, and tell whatever stories might be related to some of the slides.

The second reason why I'm happy is a difficult one to believe, but hold on, here it comes. I was asked by the Commander of the hospital to give a talk (my paper that I'm writing) at a meeting that is going to include all the Doctors from the Corp I area of Vietnam. That includes everybody, I think, from South of Da Nang to the DMZ. Which means there will be Doctors from 7 hospitals and the 2 hospital ships, to say nothing of whatever General Medical Officers might come. I wonder if John Stevens could get permission to come? He is in Corp III or IV. I'll write him. I am excited, but I don't feel nervous because the Surgeons here have assured me it is a good paper and I will not look silly. I am about two-thirds through typing the paper. Obviously, that is what I'm doing tonight.

I could kick myself. I forgot to bring your letter, with me, so I don't know if I am forgetting to answer any questions. I was overjoyed to get the harmonica books. It's just what I wanted. I'd love nothing better than to be able to play a few of those songs. In fact, that is what I am going to start practicing as soon as I finish your letter. I think the pipe, you sent me, is not much good. Would you send a new one (about $2.50) to me? The cookies are delicious as usual. I have a question for you. What will be your April 10th paycheck and how much of it is going into the bank? Just checking, Honey. Got to keep you on your toes. What happened to the exercises? How is my beautiful schoolgirl doing? Don't let any of those young bucks, at school, get too frisky with you. Tell them that your old man (me) is doing alright for himself at age 26 (27 pretty soon), eh?

I got a headache tonight. Think I'm wearing my eyeglasses too much. Maybe it's another symptom of me losing my marbles. Sounds like you are getting to be a real renal expert over there.

Well Tiger, so ends another day. I love you with all my heart. I am truly very happy with you and I know I will be in the future. I sincerely think I will end up, for all practical purposes, devoting myself to you much more than I did in the past. I've got faults (not many, of course), but I intend to improve on them. Stick with me.

I love you very much,

Jonny

4/07/69
Letter 77

Dearest Sherrie,

Got your oranges, today, but no letter. Again, I don't have your letter of yesterday, but I think I remember what I forgot to respond to. Your courses in school sound fine, but it will take a good deal of will power on your part to attend classes faithfully and try to get something out of them. Naturally, it is much easier to do problems and work out the syllogisms at home if you are interested and like logic. You should always keep in mind that you are not really just a bystander, in the class, because I'm sure your exams will require you to know something.

Still working on the paper, running, reading, etc. Some days seem to go fast and some slow, but in the main, I've got to admit it looks like I have a long way to go. We heard a lot of machine gun fire on the perimeter today. And, the 852 bombers were hitting the Ashau Valley again today which means another big fight is brewing. We may be pretty busy in a short while.

All my love, thoughts, desires are of you,

Jonny

My Dear Darling Sherrie,

The mail must be screwed up. Second day in a row, I didn't get a letter from you. Nat wrote that she is going to visit you this weekend. I guess she means it. I think she will have a great time at Disneyland. And, when she lets loose, she can be a lot of fun. I know you are the best hostess in the world. I'm very proud of you and feel proud that I am your husband.

Studied a fair bit today, ran a hard 2 miles, did a regional block and now (as you can see) I'm back working on my paper. I have typed up 16 pages complete with graphs (etc) and estimate another 6-8 pages to go. After this, I will read it over and over to myself (sort of memorize it) so I can give a fluid presentation. The big day has not been set because I want to review and go over it with 2 board certified Surgeons here first.

Those were excellent oranges you sent. Only one was smashed. I hope you got all the money that was sent to you. With your pay added to mine, I would think that we would have (in the neighborhood of) $2000 in the bank. I figure that you get roughly $800 per month from me and that you can get $300-$400 of your monthly pay saved. Yes? No? Maybe?

You never did tell me when it would be most convenient, for you, to get off work to meet me. Is there any special time that would be best for you during the summer (July or August)? Remember, you need to consider school, too. Let me know and I will try for the dates you suggest. I'd rather meet as late as possible (August rather than July). Because remember, after a glorious reunion with you, I have to come back and face a war. And, I want that to be as short a time as possible. It will be no fun to come back here.

All my ever loving soul and heart to you,

Jonny

Dearest Sherrie,

I got a letter from you, today, but naturally my appetite for you was not fulfilled by just a letter. We have not been very busy lately, so I am taking it easy, running a lot, reading and working on my paper. The temperature has not been too high, these past few days, so that is something good I guess. Time goes by slowly, nowhere to turn, nowhere to go. I guess I'm a little depressed right now. Think I will play poker, tonight, and live dangerously. Did I tell you I won $6 about 10 days ago?

I am very anxious to know what has become of the projector that is supposed to be delivered to you. There really should not be that much difference in time of arrival of the watch and the projector. I would like you to go to the Post Office and see if there is a package, for you, just in case it came and this escaped your attention one way or another. Also, at the same time, write PACEX (in Japan) and ask them if they sent it. It cost over $40 and I don't want it lost.

Also, I am curious about the car. I didn't realize the mechanic was keeping it for a few days. How are you getting about? How did you pick up Natalie? Don't let them keep the car forever. I think with cars, service is the worst. Takes a lot of time, and in the end, many are unfair and dishonest. You've got to really hound them. Well, that is all for today.

I love you very much. You know that I wish I were with you, don't you?

I do very much,

Jonny

4/10/69
Letter 80

Dearest Sherrie,

Got 2 wonderful letters from you, today, describing Nat and Rachel's stay with you. I was extremely happy that you all had a nice time. I felt like I was there myself. One of the letters included Dr. Papper's second request that I answer him. I am afraid that I will have to soon. This is very important, obviously. In fact, I've decided. We are going to go to Columbia Presbyterian.

I've just come back from trying to call you. I stand a chance of getting through tonight. I hope you remember what to do. I hope to God you are home. I'm so damn excited, I can hardly finish this letter.

I spoke too soon, last night, when I said we weren't too busy. We had another all night, and all day, affair in the O.R. on Vietnamese children and their Mothers. We worked about 16 hours straight. Some of the kids are just darling.

I have only a few pages to go on my paper, but I'm too excited to work on it tonight.

I hope the pictures, you have taken, come soon. I love to see my loved ones (you most of all). For a few moments, they lessen my isolation. Well, I have to take up my vigil by the phone.

All my love Darling,

Jonny

Dearest Sherrie,

I spoke to you about 1.5 hours ago (11:30 PM on April 10th here) which I think was 7:30 AM (April 10th) your time. It was terrific. I didn't understand a word of what you said, but I got the gist of it from the operator. You don't know what it means, to me, to have a girl like you who is so willing to help me and sacrifice for me. I knew it would be alright (before I called), with you, if we went to New York for a couple of years. I mainly called to let you know that I really and sincerely wanted you to know that I don't now, and won't ever, do anything that is not a reflection or expression of our unity. I just wanted you to know that I'm thinking of you. And, although I made the decision alone, it was not without a great deal of thought as to how it would affect you. I realize that you are leaving behind good friends, an environment that you are used to and like and leaving your parents. For me, I am not leaving behind very much. I don't think any of my relationships (Greg, Stu, etc) were meant to be lifelong and the residencies are academically poorer than Columbia. The only thing I'll miss is the weather. But, I promise you that we will have good times and new things to do (shows, movies, eating out, lots of friends over and to visit). We'll buy a boat for water skiing and put it on a lake in New Jersey (or maybe a sailboat). We'll have a baby. That will be really something, won't it? I'll find myself a track and run my body like the wind. I mean it, Sherrie, we'll be ok. With my old friends, and new ones that we make, we'll be fine. We both like people. When we finish, we'll both take a long look at where to go. But, wherever we go, we will know who we are, what we are and what we both want to do.

I imagine you were beside yourself, with excitement, when you got the call on the ward. I suppose it was maybe a good thing that I didn't hear you. I'm not sure if you made sense. Were there many people around? The Doctors' hooch, I made the call from, was empty. All the Doctors were very courteous and left me alone. My Sweet Little Sherrie, so excited and so surprised. I made it person-to-person (charged to our phone 223-7448). I tried, or rather the operator tried, you at home first (there are 3 operators that have to relay the calls). And, when there was no answer, I was about to give up. Then, I remembered you would probably just be going on duty. I pulled the hospital number out of left field at the last moment. That is really thinking under pressure, Baby.

I've got to go to sleep now. I haven't been to bed in 2 days.

I think I'll spend the rest of my life showing you just how much I love you.

Jonny

Dearest Sherrie,

Well, I had an exciting day. Did a case this morning, with Sam Clark (surgeon), and then went out to the ship "The Repose". The helicopter ride was very exciting. I sat right in front of the open sides of the chopper and I was so scared. I hope some of the pictures I took caught that aspect. The whole side of the helicopters are kept open all the time and I was sitting inches away from the side. Unbelievable! Bought a lot of stuff and got some very good anesthesia equipment I needed for the department. I bought 2 pipes, a $22 electric razor, a bunch of small stuff and pearl earrings for you (which I will send pretty soon). They cost me $7, but the guy said (and so did Sam) that they would be $20 back in the world. Spent a total of $40 and am now anxious for payday to come because I have only $20 left. But, it will be enough. I spoke to the 2 Anesthesiologists, on the ship, but they had nothing to offer me intellectually. They weren't even aware of studies that I have read about, in journals, that actually came from "The Repose" in 1966. You would think that they would at least know what had been going on in their own hospital.

Didn't get any mail today, but I'm very tired, so the pain is somewhat diminished. I took 2 rolls of film today (slides) and started a roll of prints that I found by chance tonight. The slides are all about the trip, today, and the prints will be just of me. Twenty shots of me are so you can adorn your wallet with new pictures. You will get them, I suppose, in a month or so. How about some shots of you? Did you get the projector?

I'm tired, Sweetie, so I'm going to say goodnight and I'll talk to you tomorrow. Finished my paper. I heard from the Kapels, and John Stevens, a few days ago.

I love you very much and you are always with me in thoughts and in feelings.

Jonny

(1st Letter)

Dearest Most Wonderful Wife,

Would you believe 48 hours of straight cases without a break? Yes, it's true. I've got so much adrenaline running. I think I'll tell you all about it before I go to sleep and sort of unwind in the process. I cooked the hot dogs (with a few beers, too). It all started with that delivery I mentioned in my last letter. The Mother was in the O.R. at about 11 PM (no saddle block). She then took about 3-4 hours, with a very difficult labor, and delivered a completely BLUE (cyanotic, no respirations, no heart beat) baby. Well, I grabbed the infant and intubated it immediately and breathed for it for an hour. The baby came through like a champ (pink, crying, etc). Well, after the baby was ok (and much mutual back-slapping among the Doctors- none are Obstetricians), I went to bed about 5 AM. That lasted about 50 minutes when I was called to the emergency room. Twenty-five, I say again 25, Americans were brought in. A whole platoon was wiped out (6 were dead-on-arrival). They were hit by our own gunfire by mistake. Well, then the circus began (chest tubes, cutdowns, amputations, 8 hour cases, etc). We got every single one of them off the table alive. I had some good success with my ideas that are in my paper.

I got a terrific letter from you today and the hot dogs (which I just ate), a letter from the Kapels and from my Mom. Incidentally, those Hebrew National hot dogs were just like the ones in New York. Send more!

I've got to go to sleep. I don't think that there will be any gap in the delivery of this letter. You won't miss getting something, every day, if I can get one of the guys to run this over to the Post Office before the mail goes out today. It already left Camp Evans. We don't have our own Post Office.

I think it's terrific that you are good at drawing blood. And, even more wonderful that you are taking such good care of the car. You are really great, Sherrie. My "bag" is you and if ever I'm "doing my thing", it's being your husband.

Love you with everything I have, which is plenty. Just ask me, I'll tell you.

Jonny

(2nd Letter)

Dearest Adorable Sherrie,

Hi Pudding Dumpling. Poor Baby, I received a letter from you, today, when you were so depressed and didn't get a letter from me and you cried. Since the call was subsequent, to that letter, I can only hope that you have cheered up somewhat. I got some freeze-dried food from your Mom, today, and a letter from her. I haven't tried reconstituting the food yet, but it seems like a good idea.

Things are ok with me. We are moderately busy and I'm very involved in my work and paper. And, I shoot my mouth off to anyone who will listen to me about my ideas. The General of Medical Corp I (everything North of, and including Da Nang, which includes my hospital) was at the hospital at the time of the last push. I even had a nice half-hour conversation with him. He came into the O.R. that I was running. Nice guy. Asked him all about what other hospitals were doing and told him about some of the stuff we are doing. Nobody has died from our last big push. Although 2 patients have fat emboli, in the lungs, diagnosed by a test that I have set-up at our hospital.

Tomorrow will be a very exciting day for me. I have never left Camp Evans, since I arrived here, partly because I am so tied down to the O.R. And, partly because the only place I think worthwhile for me to go is to you Baby. But, tomorrow I'm flying to the hospital ship "The Repose" with the Chief of Professional Services (Sam Clark). He invited me to come with him and I thought it would do me good to get out of here for a day. He is a nice guy and is a General Surgeon.

The hospital ship has a well-stocked PX and I may buy something for you or me. I started to buy you a watch a number of times, but I keep thinking you would prefer to pick it out yourself in Japan. What should I do? Would you rather I just surprise you with what I think is nice? I may, also, get an electric shaver.

How is school, the car, your weight, pictures you are sending, recorder, etc?

As the Vietnamese would say "Mamasan Sherrie is number 1." "Bae Si Benumof has beaucoup (much) dau (pain) and is number 10 without his number 1 Sherrie."

I love you so much Honey, keep a stiff upper lip, ok?

Jonny

Dearest Sherrie,

I hate this stinking place: no wife, it was 120 degrees today, we've run out of water, no shower, I don't want to work. There is never ever anything to do except run, study, study, run and work always rearing its head. There, it's off my chest.

I got 3 letters, today, one of which you forgot to put the APO on. I'm glad you are studying well, keep it up. I'll be very anxious to see the pictures and get the pastrami. Please send more hot dogs.

I was very pleased that my call made you so happy. I'll probably call you again, when I get my leave orders for Japan, so you can make the necessary arrangements as far in advance as possible.

I do not mind that you bought the contact lenses, but I thought the curvature of your cornea was not suitable for contact lenses. Also, why didn't you tell me before? Again, I don't mind because I think you are pretty good about money and try hard. I think many women are much more materialistic than you. I, also, don't mind you taking guitar lessons, but I hope that it is not just a passing fancy. I hope that you will really stick with it because I love to hear you sing. I hope you won't chicken out when it comes time for you to send a tape with your singing on it. Will a tape really be coming soon?

I think we will go to the Hilton, that sounds best to me. I've talked to guys who have been in Tokyo already. We should get R&R rates of $13 per day. Make sure, when you *make the reservations, that you get that price.*

Take it easy my love. Stop watching TV and maybe you'll feel better. You must look so cute bawling (crying) in front of the TV.

All my love Darling,

Jonny

Dearest Wife,

Got a terrific package, from you, today. Really great cookies and stuff. Only one teeny-weeny suggestion: please make the hot dogs Hebrew National. They taste so much better.

I'll have to send you a package soon. I have 2 gifts sitting on my desk, for you, right now. One is the pearl earrings I told you about. I think they are really nice. And, the second is a picture which I think you may find very meaningful. It's a hand-embroidered cloth (Vietnamese made), 2 feet by 1 foot, depicting a soldier looking very lonesome and melancholy at a jungle river. He is sitting against a tree. Above him is the face of a girl (who vaguely resembles you) of whom he is thinking. I identified with the picture so much that I wanted it without even asking the price. It was $9. It is really nice and I think it will help you to know how much I miss you.

I got something from PACEX, today, which entitles me to a $10 refund on the projector and watch. Did you get the projector yet? They said they mailed it on March 18. The *buys are fantastic! For $60 I got the projector and watch. Why don't you check out these items, in a store, and tell me what they are selling for in the States? I bet they cost over $100. I'd be very interested in knowing.*

If I get angry at you, for anything, it is about your failure to reply or acknowledge my questions. Now I consider sending you $200, by money order, a significant occurrence. I don't believe that you once mentioned receiving it and I have asked you several times. I think you should have gotten it around April 7th or 8th. Did you get it? It is frustrating to send off large sums of money and have it sort of disappear into the unknown. I think, if the situation were reversed, you could appreciate my consternation. Please pay attention to these details, Honey. I think you are very good about money.

Incidentally, I think the projector comes with 6 slide trays, so you don't have to buy any.

I'm sure you did a great job on your dress. And, I'm equally sure that you do justice to the dress by making it look even better when it is on you.

I, too, have been thinking about New York. I think we will have a lot of fun exploring the city and doing things.

We'll talk about what we are going to do, when I get home, when we are in Tokyo. I find it hard to think about the real world over here. Can't focus my mind. I really never let myself think, about the real world, except in a very abstract way.

As always with love, devotion and feeling,

Jonny

Dearest Sherrie,

Tonight, I played football and now I'm all broken up. I have a pulled leg muscle, scratches, fat lip, etc. Woe is me. No mail, today, either. You know how well I take pain.

Still plowing through the pastrami. For some reason, it is not as good this time. So, I'm going to hold off requesting anymore for a while. I would like some of those Hebrew National hot dogs, though. Maybe 2 packages, ok?

Today, I did a spinal for an appendectomy on a Doctor. It was a mess. It really wasn't bad. But, whenever you try and take care of your own people, nothing goes smoothly. It ended up well, though.

Have you seen Ann Stevens in Los Angeles?

Not much else is new. It is becoming harder and harder to keep from thinking about leave. Some days are tough now to get through. Maybe I'm slowing up. Got to get busier with projects. Lately, I end up sitting at my desk playing hundreds of games of solitaire. I have become well liked here and enjoy the company of several of the Docs now. Friendship takes time, I guess. We kid around a lot. I may go to a beach, in the near future. It is supposed to be well protected, but when you get down to it there is no place I want to go except home. I could probably transfer out of here if I wanted to, but what for? It's not going to make me feel better about being in Vietnam. It might be safer, but I'm set up here already. And, I am used to whatever little I have and is my lot. My only real treasure is you and nothing is going to take the place of you.

All my love Bug, Jonny

Dearest Darling Sherrie,

Tonight, I received your package with the birthday cake and your pictures. We will have a little party, later, to celebrate mine and a Major's birthday. I have a nerve block to do, in a few minutes, which I have never done before. I was completely broken up, shattered, demoralized, torn and anguished with longing for you when I saw the pictures. I miss you so much, Sherrie. I'm crying as I write to you. You looked so alive, so pretty, so real, so happy, so beautiful. The pain of my isolation is so intense. I'm so miserable.

As you know, I try to bury and lose myself in my work and activities to keep myself from realizing where I am and how hard life is here and how lonely. Tonight, before I got your letters, I was informed my services were needed for a case. It presents an opportunity, for me, to attempt a difficult nerve block. At the same time, I was told that "skin flicks" were being shown tonight. I didn't care, and now I minus care, at not being able to see them. I'd rather work, learn and shut my mind to everything, but getting back to you. I'm only telling you this to try and explain, to you, to what lengths I have to go to keep an even keel. I think you can see now what the pictures you sent mean to me and how little I need dirty movies to remind me of you. Thank God, I love my work. The void left in my life, by your absence, is filled just a little bit. If I hang on real tight to that, a little bit, I can make it. Honey, you are everything to me. Please love me. I need you very much. I'm sure you know that I'm not one for much dramatics or histrionics, but I sincerely mean it when

I say that I could not find much meaning or happiness in life without you. I have to constantly deny myself the chance to go on leave, right now. I'm eligible now. I miss you so much.

The pictures of Rachel were adorable. I'm glad you got a hold of my parents. They said they were sending a poster-sized picture, of you, for my birthday. I think that is the finest gift I could ever receive. I'm happy you will be able to see them this summer.

Also, very happy you saw Greg and Madeleine. Great. I will look forward to seeing them when I get back.

The harmonica is coming along. Will be fun to play together, won't it?

I loved your bell-bottoms. Bring them to Japan. I loved what was in them even more.

With a crying, aching, but loving heart,

Jonny

Dearest Darling Sherrie,

I was a bit concerned about your health tonight. Your letter described you as not feeling so hot. I think you did a wise thing by having your LFTs drawn. If they are within normal limits, and you still feel pooped out, please consult Dr. Ben Rosen or Dr. Barbour. Repeat tests, a week later, can be positive. Remember, I want to know the results.

Today, I went to the beach on a gunship helicopter. Had fun, sort of, if anything here could be fun. I went to Coco Beach, an in-country R&R Center. Really, all it is, is a well-

guarded strip of beach. It was nice to get into the ocean. Today, it hit 120 degrees. I forgot my camera, so I missed getting some great shots. But, on coming back to the hospital, I got a few of myself in uniform to show you how ridiculous I look in the uniform. Those helicopter rides are something else.

I still haven't sent you your pearl earrings and pictures, but I will soon. The electric shaver, I bought on the hospital ship "The Repose", is no good. I have to go back out there, in the next few days, to return it. I, also, have yet to collect my $10 refund on the projector and the watch. Did you get the projector? Did you get my last money order ($200, I think)? Payday is in another 10 days, fortunately. I only have $4 left ($14 with the refund). That is enough, however.

I must look at your pictures every hour on the hour. Sigh, sigh, what I'm missing. Those bell bottoms are great. Don't I have good taste? Didn't I encourage you to get them? At the price of a few tears, if I remember correctly. Remember those horrible things you brought home 1 day before I left? The bell bottoms you have on, in the pictures, are perfect. I bet you are attracting a lot of looks from men. I don't blame them.

I think love is partly saying to yourself "I'm going to make it with you, I'm committed to you, so let's make it good." I don't mean being stuck with someone by saying committed. In our case, I truly believe the commitment was made in love. All I'm saying is that, from the time the commitment is made, one should build and strengthen it. And, that is what I'm going to try to do. What do you think?

I think you know that I think about you all the time and love you a great deal. At least, I hope you feel that way.

Jonny

Dearest Sherrie,

It is getting tough to get through a day now. It is so unremittingly hot, no respite anywhere. Just ooze sweat, get dirty, work, ooze sweat, breathe dirt, work until maybe the shower bucket gets filled and then you just sweat some more, etc. I'm getting depressed more easily and more frequently now. I'm thinking of moving my leave up to July now. I'm not sure I can make it to August. Today, we did 3 long hard cases and now we are down to 2 anesthesia people (me and Dan). If it weren't for your letters and 2 Docs (Woody and Normy), with whom I spend a lot of time joking around with, I'd go crazy. I think of mail call as my daily resuscitation. I find myself telling myself, almost every 10 minutes, it is 10 more minutes gone by. If I'm lucky, maybe I won't notice a half hour slip by. Back in the world, you get used to thinking "oh I'll do this or that now" if you've got nothing to do. Here, what is there to do? You can't cool off, you can't walk away from cases. And, running and reading all the time has become routine. Everything is routine and that is just it. There is nothing you can do out of the ordinary.

And, even if I could, I'm not sure I would because you've just got to come back to the same old bullshit.

I'm pleased with the way the Lakers are going. I have a $2 bet they win the championship against Boston. I lost $10 the last time I played poker. Oh well, can't win them all. I figure I'm about even, maybe a little bit ahead. I've got to go check on a patient now.

I think of you all the time, Darling.
I love you very much, Jonny

Dearest Sherrie,

Well, the past 2 days were something. I did a 16 hour case (axillary artery, sucking chest wound, amputation of hand, laparotomy for perforations of bowel, multiple debridements, etc), all on the same guy. Post-op, I put him on a respirator and then slept next to him on the ward. Then, I went out to the hospital ship because I had to know his blood gases and chemistries. Had a special helicopter all to myself. I think we'll pull him through. While on the ship, I returned the electric shaver, I bought, since it didn't work. I think I'm definitely going to wait, until Japan, before I buy anything else. Here you don't have much of a selection. And no time to look at it, compare it or see it demonstrated. It is too much of a hassle.

I'm a little bit concerned about your moving for several reasons. (1) I still don't know if you got my last money order. (2) Please make sure you get the projector. (3) If you are moving on the 25th, you won't get mail for several days since I'm going to continue to write you at the San Pablo address until I get notice from you to do otherwise. This will probably arrive, at the San Pablo address, on the 27th or 28th of April and you probably will have moved.

I got a nice long letter from Dr. Papper today. He said I can start when I want. I think I'll tell him September 1st, 1970. That will give us a chance to move, set-up in New York and maybe go to Florida or Puerto Rico for a week.

I'm glad your LFTs were normal. Be careful.

Today, while I ran around the air strip, a gunship came in smoking like crazy. It was shot in action. And, it was a bumpy landing, but nobody was hurt. Real drama. I was so excited I forgot to take pictures. I ran over to the chopper and pulled out the pilots, but they were ok. While on the ship, earlier today, I met another pilot who had been shot down this morning. His medic died on the ship. I've got to go to sleep, Darling. I have an elective case tomorrow morning, of all things.

I love you dearly, Precious Sherrie,

Jonny

Dearest Adorable Sherrie,

Man, it's hot. Really hot. Have been kept busy by the patient on the ventilator. He is doing well. He is going to make it.

I got some fruit from you today. About half of it was smashed up, but I'll enjoy what's left. I, also, got a letter from the Meyers, a letter from a mutual friend of mine and Ben Ezra's and a letter from Aunt Norma.

I suffered 2 great disappointments today. One was that I didn't get a letter from you. And, the second was that the poster-sized picture of you (that my parents sent me) came, but it was completely ruined. If it had come intact, it would have been the finest gift I ever received. I'm going to ask them to try again. I was looking forward to getting it so much.

Let's see, what else is new? Not much else, except I'm managing to keep busy. I like my work and like the people

I'm working with. Guess I'm not too depressed today. Mainly, I think because my patient is doing so well. The surgeons have put me completely in charge of him. I had the patient off the ventilator, most of the day, with no problems. Tomorrow, I think I'll be able to pull his nasoendotracheal tube out.

Love you with all my heart, Darling. You are never more than a thought away from my heart.

Jonny

Dearest Wife,

Today, was a hard grinding day in the O.R. No air conditioning. It went up to 105 degrees in there and we went all day with cases. But the day was saved by 2 glorious letters, from you, bouncy and love-filled. In addition, I got a package of food from the synagogue that my parents attend in New York and a letter from Nat. She is really wild about you and so am I.

Before I forget, there is something important that I want you to do. Please write for the following book. Or, go to the USC Medical School bookstore or call the UCLA Medical School bookstore to see if they have it or will order it for you. I must have it as soon as possible. It is:

Name: Post-traumatic Pulmonary Insufficiency

Author: F. Moore, Et Al.

Publisher: W.B. Saunders Company, West Washington Square, Philadelphia, Pennsylvania 19105.

If the publisher sends it to me, have them bill you, but send the book directly to me. If you send it to me, please send *it carefully. I want it very badly. It costs $12.75- Thank you, Honey.*

I'm so glad the projector came. Have you used it? You may certainly get more slide trays. What is happening with the tape recorder?

I'm holding off on sending you the earrings, and picture, until you have started receiving mail at your new address. I don't want them to get lost in the shuffle.

I enjoyed hearing about your visit with Greg and Madeleine. Almost felt like I was there. I'm glad you had a good time. I hope you have more enjoyable evenings like that. I think of you sitting home alone so often. I worry about you. Fun is important to keep your spirits up. I'm glad you have girlfriends, you enjoy your work and you go to school.

I honestly don't know where I get the energy to do the cases for these big pushes. Mainly, I guess, it is because I am a Doctor and I have professional pride in my work. And because, well I guess, I am a soldier of sorts and I'm in a war. You can't turn your back on somebody who has his guts hanging out who might be somebody's husband or brother you know and who got hurt just possibly protecting you or me. Maybe he didn't know it, but maybe in reality that is just what he was doing. I'm good at doctoring, I can do it in my sleep. Incidentally, the Chief of Surgery asked me to write a little paper for Military Medicine (a medical bulletin for the Docs in Vietnam) describing what types of anesthesia we are giving here and why. He thinks our anesthesia here is better than the anesthesia in other hospitals he has visited. Naturally, I'm bursting with pride. Dan and I are going to do it together. I figure I'll have it done in a month.

I'm giving my talk next week. I'm not sure what I'll do with the paper after that. I think basically it is not ready for publication, but it will be once I can get some data during my residency research time.

I'm pretty sure we'll be able to get silverware in Japan. I was pleased to hear Scotty is doing so well in track. If you write them, please give him my encouragement and tell him about my running. Tell him I'm ready for him.

Well, Honey, another day closer to you.

I love you so much,

Jonny

Dearest Sweet Sherrie,

Today passed as usual, but I am very anxious right now. A battalion of troops moved out this morning, to the Ashau Valley, and a big fight is going on. I know of at least 4 helicopters that were shot down. I just finished doing general anesthesia on a Major who was flying one of the choppers. They can't seem to secure the area yet to lift out the other pilots by helicopter. I'm afraid we'll have to work through the night tonight. I hate waiting for them to come. When they come, it's hard and heavy.

I went to the Post Office, today, and mailed your 2 gifts to the San Pablo Street address. As is typical of me, I am 4+ hyper about you getting them. Please watch carefully for them (picture and earrings). They could get lost between you changing apartments.

I read with interest about your hard day of work on Sunday. I certainly wouldn't mind you taking care of me. You really are a good nurse. I have always been impressed by your cooperative, pleasant, efficient way of dealing with patients and Doctors alike. Such a good girl.

I'm glad you had such a good time with Ann. She wrote me that she was going to call you when she was in Los Angeles. Good luck with the Dentist! My empathetic sympathies. I'm too tense to write anymore.

I love you, Darling. I'll talk to you tomorrow. Have you used the projector yet? Why not?

Love and a million kisses,

Jonny

Dearest Sherrie,

Not too much has happened since I wrote you last night. Patients have been coming in sporadically. It seems when you are alerted for a big push, it never comes. But, when you least expect it, all hell breaks loose. Unfortunately no letter from you, today, but I got one from my Mom and my Grandma and 2 packages from my Mom-in-Law. Tell her "Muchas Gracias." Those freeze-dried packages are not so tasty, but they are easy to make. You know what would be good for you to send? Please send an intact Hebrew National Salami (not cut up). The synagogue, my parents go to, sent me one and it was real good. I had a salami sandwich, for supper, the last 2 nights in a row. Please send one. I'm glad you sent that second (and larger) bottle of mustard some time ago. It came in real handy with the salami.

I don't know if I told you, or not, but I took a whole roll of color prints of myself. That's so you would have some ready-made shots available (rather than to have to convert the slides). I had this roll of prints and I didn't know what to do with it. So, I thought you'd like to have some prints of me.

I haven't been playing my harmonica very much lately. I'll have to begin again. I constantly find myself forcing myself to do things. I think it is because there is no escape from them. If you don't do the same things over and over again, then you do nothing. Doing nothing (in 120 degree heat) is worse than doing something because, when you do nothing, you are left with the heat and that is tough to take at times.

Lately, I have been playing a lot of solitaire (card game) with myself. I must have played 200 games of solitaire this past week. Probably reflects how I feel. Like in solitary confinement or I'm cracking up.

My patient is doing real well. He's off the ventilator, for 2 days now, and is holding his own.

Gee, Sherrie, I miss you so much. You have so much character, personality, charm, kindness, warmth, etc, etc. I miss you so much, because I miss so much not being with you.

As always, with much thought and love for you,

Jonny

Dearest Sherrie,

Well, we got hit today and hard. I've been in the O.R. for ages it seems like. Out of 20 gunships parked outside my hooch, 8 ships (helicopters) have failed to return. I know most of the pilots, and so far, 3 have been hoisted out of the Viet Cong infested area (Ashau Valley) where they were shot down. It is only 4 miles from us. I pray so hard that all will come back. I don't think they will. The Viet Cong are bunkered in and it takes time to get them out. It makes it so easy to work hard for these courageous young men, and boys, when you think of what they are doing. And, very possibly, for no reason at all.

I got 2 letters from you today, one from my Mom and one from the Reillys. Des should hear, soon, if he is going to come over to Vietnam. Maybe, he will get a reprieve because of the baby. I hope so. I bet we bump into them back East, too.

I heard on the radio, today, that the Lakers are 2-0 over the Boston Celtics. I'm delighted. I've got money on them ($2, big deal) to win the whole thing.

I'm very glad you didn't move to Cornwall Street. I feel relieved of another worry. I don't think $165 per month is too excessive since we are both making money.

I'm also delighted by your progress with the guitar, exercising and advancing smoothly through the school term. I am very confident you will do well on your midterms. Just try hard and the result doesn't matter.

Giving your best is what counts. The results will come. You are not dumb.

I'm glad to know you got the money. It's just about time for another allotment to be on the way. I don't know how much money I will send home, by money order, this time. I don't know how much I'll get.

I love you very much, Darling.

Jonny

Dearest Sherrie,

Well today is my Birthday and, predictably enough, I didn't get any mail. It is raining hard and I have been working hard. Oh well, you can't win them all.

I'm so far behind in writing to other people. Maybe I'll catch up some tonight. I know how much you like to celebrate holidays, birthdays (etc). Sorry to deprive you of this day. I realize how much you want me to be happy and just knowing that makes me happy. I hope you understand that you never need to feel compelled to buy things, gifts (etc) to show that you love me.

Wednesday, I'm going to give my talk. I've been reading over my paper 1-2 times per day in hopes of speaking well. Fortunately, I'm amongst friends which makes it easier.

Last night, I saw "Mission Impossible" on TV. It wasn't too bad, but I certainly have lost 90% of my interest in TV.

I wonder what the salary will be at Columbia. I hope I remember to ask when I write to Dr. Papper again. If we live in Manhattan, I bet the minimum rent we will have to pay will be $250-$300. We're not going to be rich, that is for sure.

As you know, I still fully expect to have $10,000 in the bank when we go to New York, if not more. I would like to know what you have managed to save, out of your earnings, so far.

Have you spoken to or heard from anybody (family, friend, etc)? Gee, I feel so far away. I miss you so much. Today, when everybody was congratulating me on my birthday and commenting on how much I have achieved, I replied that I have achieved or attained only one thing that is special and unique to and for me and that is you and your love. I meant it. That is my only real accomplishment. You are happiness in the bank for me. I feel that I have nothing without you. Well, that is it from your "old man."

I weighed 143 pounds today.

I love you, Darling.

Jonny

Dearest Darling Sherrie,

I am very, very tired. I had another whopper of a case which we just finished. I got 2 letters, from you, which picks me up a great deal. Forgive me, if I'm brief, but I'm dying to gobble down some beef stew your Mom sent me today and then make another headlong dive into bed.

Again, I'm very happy that you're not moving. I, also, don't object to you working private duty to help defer the cost of your rent. But, I hope you don't sacrifice the time you would have spent in preparing for your courses at school. I think you will get far more satisfaction out of getting A's and B's in school, rather than making money. And, so would I.

One of the articles, from "Medical World News", was indeed interesting (the one about epidural needles). Thanks. I showed everybody what a smart wife I have and told them that you are the secret to my success, which in truth you are. You are my only real success.

I think you should wait to have your wisdom teeth pulled for free, in the Army, rather than pay for it now. If it's a small fee (say less than $15), then do it now, of course. But, if it's more, why give the money away? Why don't you call that Army base, in Long Beach, and see if they do it or if the Army as a whole does it? Then, you won't have to wonder if it would be worthwhile to wait, ok?

The stew is ready, so I'll sign off now.

I love you with all my heart, Sherrie. Always remember that.

Jonny

Dearest Darling Sherrie,

Well, I did it. I gave my paper tonight. There were about 30 Doctors there. About 12 were from the 18th Surgical Hospital and the rest were from elsewhere. As best as I can judge, it went ok. Good, but I don't think great. A few (about 4 or 5) came over and said they enjoyed hearing it. And, 1 or 2 asked for copies. In spite of the heat in the room, the generally apathetic attitude of the Doctors here to academic considerations and my inexperience, I think I did alright. I'm satisfied. Part of my problem was that I was talking to 2 distinct groups: one was Board Eligible or Certified Doctors (about half) and the others were General Medical Officers.

I'm not sure the General Medical Officers had enough background to understand everything. Oh well, at least I know what I'm talking about.

Today was payday and I got $384 which is what I'll get, every month, from now on. Tomorrow, I'm going to send you $200 of that and maybe another $75 in a couple of weeks. Watch for the money. When I can get to the finance office, which is in Phu Bai (20 miles South of here), I am going to increase my allotment to you (to $800 or $850 per month). I don't know if I'll be able to get down there until I'm traveling to meet you for leave.

Please thank your Mom for all her letters and packages.

I'm glad to hear that you are hurting from your exercises. That shows you are doing something. In Tokyo, I hope one day I can run for you to show you how much I have gotten out of running. Today for instance, I ran 5 miles and felt like the wind, strong and full of power. Yes, I did say I had read "The Man" and "The Magus." I especially recommend "The Man" by Irving Wallace. I think it is the best book I have read in a great while. The packages that you send take 6-7 days to arrive. Often, they come 1-2 days ahead of the letter that you wrote that day (if it's a small package). Oh, how important your letters are!

I'm looking forward to getting the tape. I'm hopeful you'll be sending pictures of yourself, too. It means so much to see you and to hear you. Much as I would like to hear you play the guitar, in Japan, I don't think you should bring it for 2 reasons: (1) We will be doing a lot of other things. (2) It will be burdensome for you to take it.

I think Dan got a letter from Veronica. Drove him wild as usual.

All my love, Darling.

Jonny

Dearest Beloved Wife,

Today was sort of humdrum. I got up early, went to the Post Office and got money orders for $200 (which is included). I, also, got a haircut and bought a few things at the PX. I got a Mother's Day card for your Mom and mine. They happened to have a big sign up to remind us of it, so I got them. I got a nice package, from you, with the hot dogs. I'll eat them for supper over the next few days. I think you had better stop sending cookies. It is too hot to eat them, ok? Don't be hurt, but they seem to lie around for a long time even though we all consider them delicious.

I've started reading "Topaz" and I know I'll enjoy it. Good cops and robbers stuff. Yeah!

About 3 Doctors came over to me today and asked for copies, of my paper, which made me feel good. I'm pretty sure it was well received.

I heard from the Kapels today.

I wish so hard July would come. It seems like time just passes by ever so slowly. It is so painful to want anything because you can't have anything, most of all freedom. Yes, that is it. Freedom, freedom to take a shower, eat when and what I want, freedom to go somewhere, freedom to do or see something, freedom from dirt, dust, guns, wounds, cases and on and on. But most of all, freedom to be with my wife. That is how I feel, that is how I miss you.
It tears my heart to be denied of you.

Jonny

Dearest Precious Sherrie,

Today was a pretty nice day. I was busy in the O.R. most of the day, ran 2 times, studied my "Goodman and Gilman" book that you sent and just finished a most enjoyable supper. The supper was the highlight of the day because I had 2 Hebrew National hot dogs while reading a letter you sent and a long letter from Des. Boy I love sitting at my own desk, reading my mail and eating.

The Colonel just came in the hooch to announce that a group of girls, from the Philippines, is putting on a singing show over by the 101st Airborne guys. I'm not going to go which depresses me. I'm depressed that I'm not going because I'm depressed that I don't even want to go. I don't want to go because I only want you. I want you and I can't have you. That is depressing. I am depressed. Dan tried to go, and just came back, having missed the show by minutes. He is depressed, also.

Des writes that he is coming to Vietnam on September 15th. Too bad. Their baby is due in August. Before he goes, however, he is taking Madeline and the kids back to New York. He is going to apply for a junior staff position at Columbia. Perhaps he will be teaching me again (or vice versa). I would enjoy working with him again. He says his golf game is improving. His drive now goes as far as his #9 iron which is 50 yards.

I was delighted to hear you took photos at the beach. I hope you get the remaining 7 photos taken pretty soon. The book "Topaz" is pretty good. I like that cops and robbers stuff.

I felt so sorry, for you, when I read your letter that you didn't get any mail that day (which was on a Saturday). Poor Baby, that means you won't get any mail on Sunday either. That makes 2 days in a row, for you, without mail. I'm sure the letter that you'll write to me, on the next day (Sunday), will be a depressed one. I write you every day, so you will probably get 3 or 4 on Monday.

Take care Darling, I love you.

Jonny

Dearest Sherrie,

Tonight, I had a most enjoyable supper of two Hebrew National hot dogs while reading 2 of your letters. Otherwise, the day was spent exactly as all the others.

I'm sorry to hear you are somewhat dissatisfied with your job. I don't know what to say except that I know you are sensible, a good worker and pleasant and cooperative on the job. I hope very much that you won't compromise these qualities because you are embroiled or enmeshed in what might be trivial things. Even if the things that disturb you are not trivial, I'll rescue you soon. So, hang on and continue to be your wonderful self on the job. I suppose it is too late to switch to something else (Pediatrics, private office). But, you can always look into it. I'm sure, however, you would not want to jeopardize your "on call" status to Japan. At least, I hope so. I assume that the way things are now, you can leave on short notice (say 2 weeks) at any time in your present job and this may not be so with a new job.

I wish I could be helping you with your paper on the baby. Sounds like fun. You are going to be a very wonderful Mother. You know I always thought you were good with babies, etc. I was telling Dan, last night, that part of loving you is wanting to have children with you. I want that very much.

Could you send me more Hebrew National hot dogs? Please?

All I want to say about leave, now, is that I am seriously considering applying for it for July. Take it easy, Honey. Just remember, I want to see you as much as you want to see me. I should be getting 12 prints, I took of myself, for you soon. What is happening with the recorder?

All my love, Darling. Jonny

Dearest Darling Wife,

I'm going to make this short. I got back 40 more slides, today, and will begin sending them. No letter today, from you, since I got 2 yesterday. It ruined eating my hot dogs.

I weighed 139 pounds today. Boy, what a living doll I am. Very tan, too. Now don't get all emotional, I'm only kidding. I did weigh 139 pounds and I am pretty dark, but it is unavoidable here. The last thing I want to do is lay out in the sun. Today was 120 degrees. It's really torrid and there is no wind.

I continue to get compliments on my paper. I naturally eat that up. I'm going through my "Goodman and Gilman" pharmacology book now. Sort of tedious. The book "Topaz" is very enjoyable reading. I have 100 pages to go. You have great taste, Honey.

I love you, I love you, I love you, I love you, I love you, I love you.

Jonny

Dearest Sherrie,

Tonight's supper of 2 hot dogs was terrific. I got the book, 2 love-filled letters from you, a card from my Mom and a letter from Nat.

We have been fairly busy, but we have not had an all-night affair for some time.

In reply to your questions about how long we will have together in Japan, I'm very sorry and sad to tell you it will be a maximum of 7-8 days (and most likely 6-7 days). That is all. Nobody gets more than that. I hope you are not too depressed by this. I thought you knew that we would only have a week. I don't know where I will fly from, in Vietnam, to Japan. Maybe Da Nang. Then, a week in Hawaii in September or October.

I'm glad your new kidney transplant patient is doing so well. I'm sure you have helped him with good nursing care and your kindly way with people.

I hope you have been able to prepare for your exams as well as you wanted to. Good luck!

What I will do with the paper, for now, is nothing. During residency, I should be able to get some data I need. Right now, it is basically a good review of a topic which

Doctors are now beginning to recognize as the major cause of death in seemingly salvageable patients. It is pulmonary insufficiency, post-trauma. I think Dr. Papper will be leaving Columbia Presbyterian Hospital about the time I get there. Somebody else, who will be good, will take his place.

What group of snapshots did you get of me? I don't remember sending any snapshots.

As far as your moving goes, fine. Always happy to save $15 per month.

Sweet Sherrie, I'm not upset about your school plans. I think your ideas are sensible. And, the fact that you are taking guitar lessons is very important. It may be the most rewarding thing you are doing.

I just came back from doing a case in which I did a technically perfect spinal. But, the Tetracaine was no good. This has happened to us a number of times this past month. It is happening in many parts of Vietnam. Apparently, the heat ruins the Tetracaine. This is particularly frustrating and depressing and I feel miserable right now. I think, for the first time, I am feeling the load on my shoulders. I am the only On the-Job Trainee, in this country, in charge of a department and I am responsible for all the anesthesia here. I think I am giving as good, if not better, anesthesia than most hospitals in Vietnam. In fact my second paper, which the Chief of Professional Services suggested I write, is on what I am doing here and why I am doing it. And, because he thinks it is good. When I say "I", I mean me and my nurses. The Surgeons here feel we are doing things well and other places would be so much better off if they knew about it. But, it is a strain and tonight I feel it. I feel tired. I'm tired of a steady continual pressure to do everything perfectly and tired of thinking and improving things. People introduce me as "The Anesthesiologist" here as though I was fully trained. And, I don't even have a minute of residency under my belt. Oh well, maybe things will look different in the morning.

I miss you so much, Sherrie. I wish so much I could share my feelings, doubts, insecurities, confidences and growth with you. I wish so much I were with you. You would make everything seem insignificant next to our love, children, home and the business of enjoying life. Now, that is the kind of job I want.

Jonny

5/06/69
Letter 105

Dearest Darling Sherrie,

Today was ok, but something just happened which has upset me a great deal. Perhaps, I'm too sensitive. I avoided telling you, last night, because I hoped the situation would resolve. The Major (Nurse Anesthetist) is leaving in 2 weeks and his replacement (a Captain who is a Nurse Anesthetist) has arrived. The Major is a typical career Nurse Anesthetist, in the Army, and a good technician. When I came here, I did things differently, changed a lot of things, was assertive and enthusiastic. And most important of all, I was and am successful. I took over the department completely and ever since then the Major has been trying to put me down behind my back. And now, he's trying to indoctrinate the new Captain who comes to us already with fixed opinions and poorly informed. Dan tells me this.

No letters today, so the last supper of my hot dogs was not much fun. I'm kind of down in the dumps right now,

Pumpkin. So, forgive me if I end without much additional comment on how much I miss you and how much I love you. Both are constant and perhaps why I would shrug off what is bothering me if you were with me.

All my love, Jonny

Dearest Darling Sherrie,

No mail again today. It's the only thing that I look forward to. Probably will get 3 or 4 letters, from you, tomorrow.

Nothing new, in so far as developments, where the new Nurse Anesthetist is concerned. I'll wait until he gives me a good cause and then I'll let him have it.

I'm enjoying the book that you sent. I've read so much here (4 texts, part of "Goodman and Gilman", 2 journals, 14 novels). And, of course, your letters.

Well, July is getting nearer. I try not to think about it, but it is becoming increasingly more difficult not to.

Naturally, I'm interested in knowing if you got the money you were supposed to receive ($200 in money orders and $650 in allotment)? Also, is the tape recorder fixed? Did you finish your roll of film? Did you do well on your school exam? Are you working private duty anymore and if so, how much? What is the total in our checking and savings accounts? Is the car running ok? Are you doing your exercises? Is there anything you want to know from me or is there anything you want me to send to you? Can you send me 2-3 packages of Hebrew National hot dogs, some

American cheese and some Hebrew National salami? Did you get the earrings and picture? Why haven't you told me if you've used the projector and if you like it? I spent $40 buying something, primarily for you to use, and all you've told me is that you got it. That was weeks ago. Do the slides project well?

Boy Sherrie, you don't know how I dream about you all the time. Oh Sherrie, I've got to hang on. If you let yourself slip into depression, you can't work. And, you can't do anything to fight back.

I love you very much, Jonny

Dearest Sherrie,

Today, I got a letter from you dated May 3rd. From what you said, in it, I'm sure at least one of your letters has been lost. It's probably the one written on May 2nd because you talked about a rash, you had, as though you had told me about it before. This is the first I have heard about it. I'm, of course, sorry to hear it. But, it doesn't sound like it's too bad and I hope it goes away soon. I bet they gave you Triamcinolone cream (steroid cream) to put on it. Where is it other than on your forearms?

Here is another fact and figure report from your leader (that is me in case you were wondering). I get $150 per month from the government/Army each month of my residency or future training. I think I mentioned this to you before. Over 3 years that will amount to $4500. I'm getting a pay raise, in July, that will amount to $120 per month. I will *get that for a full year, so that will be an additional $1440. The $120 per month is, in part, a raise for everybody in the Army. And, in part, it is special to me since I will move from 5 years of experience to the 6 years of experience category. With the raise, I will be making $1120 per month starting in July. That is at the rate of $12,000 per year. Between the 2 of us, we should make nearly $20,000 this year. I'll die of frustration if we don't have over $10,000, in the bank, when I start in New York. Then, we can have babies, a nice home (etc) with that windfall plus the $150 per month to help pay the rent.*

I'm sure your patients were very happy with the gifts you brought them. It was very nice of you to do and I know they appreciate it. It is this kind of thing that I appreciate about you. You are even more lovely inside than outside.

Oh yes, I also never heard about the desk chair before and you sounded like I had. I guess I missed a letter or two.

I haven't written Dr. Papper yet, but I am sure we will have to find an apartment on our own.

I am very, very lonely. I miss you terribly. I get so exasperated, at times, trying to find ways to numb my mind to my situation (read, run, play solitaire, read, read, run, run, cases). But, it is hard to mix them up enough. I am learning so much, have lost so much weight (today I was 140 pounds) and I am in such good condition. If I add it all up, it comes to nothing, a big zero. A big zero next to what I would have if I just could be with my Darling Sherrie.

I probably will send you $400 by money order next month (in $200 slices or parts). This will be in addition to the $650 allotment. We're rich like crazy, but I'm so unhappy. Love is certainly priceless.

I love you very much, Jonny

Dearest Precious Sherrie,

I have no choice but to forgive you for missing a day of writing because I, too, am guilty of the same. Last night, we got in a Vietnamese soldier who we lost on the table. This was after giving him 47 units of blood and getting him through 3 cardiac arrests. I came back to my hooch too tired and too depressed to write. I had gotten 2 letters from you, yesterday, which contained 3 pictures. You looked simply beautiful, very lovely. You looked just beautiful. I hope it is for me.

I certainly hope your rash clears up soon. The steroid cream you are using usually takes care of most things. But, I would be much happier knowing it has actually gone away.

I'm pleased you are doing so well in your guitar lessons. Will be most anxious to hear you play and sing. My own little Joan Baez! I love you so much!

You said work was just busy enough to keep you out of mischief. Now, what sort of mischief are you referring to? I'm glad you liked the earrings and picture. Enclosed are 2 slides of "Sad Sack Jon" looking at the picture.

As far as the dog goes, I hope you are not disappointed too much. But, I just simply don't think I want one of those. I don't want to think about it or discuss it now, so please let it drop for now. Ok? I have enough problems without thinking about dropping $500 on a dog and breeding, selling and raising dogs.

I don't know when we will be going to Japan, but I think I will apply for mid or late July. That is all I can tell you now. I don't know anything else.

When you find time, could you send me some more tobacco, some small cans of peaches and fruit cocktail, hot dogs, salami and American cheese? Thanks!

Naturally, I'm very anxious to hear the tape. I'll make one for you, soon, after getting yours. What was done to the recorder? What parts had to be added? What did it cost?

Sherrie Honey, I miss you terribly. I am sighing at least once every 30 seconds. I miss you in every way. I'm lonely and companionless. Oh, just everything. The time never goes by quickly. I know every second that passes by and each one is unhappy. Time doesn't move along, it grinds along.

I love you very much. You are constantly in my heart, thoughts and in every desire.

Jonny

Dearest Sherrie,

I forgot to tell you, yesterday, that a big squeeze play is going on in the Ashau Valley (a circle is being formed around the Viet Cong) today and tonight. As a consequence, I have been in the O.R. since early this morning to midnight (which is now). So, I am going to make this short.

I got a very wonderful letter, today, from you. I can't tell you how much I need you, how much your letters mean to me (I literally live for mail call) and how much I love you. You are very dear and precious to me, Honey.

I hope your rash has gone and you are well. Poor Baby, all alone and sick. Please don't scratch your rash, it will only make it worse! I'm very glad you felt you did well on your exams. I'm sure you did. Such a smart girl.

Two other hotels, in Tokyo, to check out: "The New Otani" and "The Sanno." They are supposed to be good, also. I can see the fighting from here (rockets and machine guns). Boy, what a fight. I think we will be busy. I should close my eyes until the casualties come.

I love you, Darling. Jonny

5/12/69
Letter 110

Dearest Adorable, Lovable Sherrie,

Well, now I know what "The Star Spangled Banner" is all about. Man, were we ever hit and hit hard last night. Just after writing you, last night (about midnight), all hell broke loose. We took 20 rockets in rapid succession (over half an hour). I was in the bunker before the crash of the first one had ended. Now, dig this. Right in the middle of the rockets, I was asked to come to the O.R. So, I ran my ass off with helmet, gun and flak jacket to the O.R. On the way, I saw a sight that most people never ever see and I hope I never see again. With the crash of the landing rounds (shells) and the blinding of the flash as they hit, I saw Viet Cong out in the fields to the North and East of us (coming at us). Our machine guns were tearing the hell out of them. The sky was completely studded with helicopter gunships pouring rockets in on them. Flares were all over the sky. It was like daytime. Sirens were screaming out a red alert constantly. As you may well imagine, I spent the whole night (and most of today) in the O.R. In the last 3 days, I have done 32 cases personally and I helped the nurses with an additional 10 or so cases (spinals, etc). Please don't be frightened by what I'm telling you, Honey, please. I'm only relating this to you because I think you are sensible and will put this in the proper perspective. I'm not afraid and I really wasn't afraid last night (or not excessively so). I don't feel afraid of dying. I think the worst part of dying is the fear of dying. I don't fear death. I don't know why, but I just don't. Maybe it's because it is inconceivable to me and I don't think it will happen. Sherrie, you know that it is fear that makes any situation painful. If I was worried or filled with anxiety then you could be reasonably, also. But, I'm not so you shouldn't be. I don't think Camp Evans could ever be over-run by Viet Cong. I really mean it. If a rocket falls on my head, I can't do anything about it. And, neither can you or any General. It could happen at any time and any place here. That is the only way I could get it. There is nothing anybody can do about it, so don't worry. Things to worry about are things like getting killed on the freeway. That is something you can do something about. Drive more carefully, take a different route, etc, etc. Ok? You understand me? I would like you to keep this letter separate, from the others, so I can re-read my impressions of this night when I get home. Everything is quiet and normal now.

One of the nurses, who is leaving, gave me a great deal of information about Japan which I will go through in the next few days. If one hotel looks good, I may ask you to get reservations at that one. Some of them cost only $8.00 per night compared to "The Okura" which is $18.00 per night. They look really nice. We'll see. I do feel that being together is the most important thing, so why spend a hundred bucks more for a hotel room.

I think you sending flowers, to our parents, is a great idea.

I anxiously await your tape, pictures, salami, hot dogs, report of our bank accounts and to know if you have used the projector I sent.

I'm glad your rash stopped spreading and your LFTs were normal. Now, let's see if the rash recedes.

I love you with all my heart and soul, Darling. You mean just everything to me.

Jonny

5/13/69
Letter 111

Dearest Sherrie,

I'm very tired, Honey, really pooped out. We had over 20 cases today. They may be closing in on the Viet Cong, but they sure are getting a beating doing it. We must have done over 80 cases in the last 3 days.

I can't think of anything new, to tell you, except that I'm just so much more fed up with everything here. The work, the damn heat (it was 120 degrees in the O.R.- the air conditioner never works), living conditions, just everything. No letter from you today either and what is worse is that I expected it (not to get a letter).

I got a letter from John Stevens and my Dad today. John says you told Ann that Bob Fields was killed here. Is that true? I hope not.

I'm going to go to sleep. I miss you very, very much. I'll be the happiest guy in the world when I can go home to you. I love you with all my heart.

Jonny

Dearest Precious Wife,

Well if nothing else happened today, at least it passed into history. I told somebody today "If I had 246 days left in Vietnam, I'd shoot myself." He said, "Well how many days do you have left to go?" I replied "245". Get it? Corny, but true. If I had to live just one day over, I don't know if I could do it. On the positive side, I did some nice nerve blocks, ran 2 times (and ran well) and got a chance to get some rest. I think the fighting died down in the Ashau Valley.

I'm glad you are finding work now more interesting with the new kidney transplants and that your rash has stopped spreading. You are so sweet and lovely.

I'm sort of sorry I asked you to send "The Journal of Trauma" since I have read it thoroughly 2 times and we have one copy here. I mainly wanted it for a reference, so I may send it back whenever I get enough stuff to make up a worthwhile package. Thanks for getting it. Yes, my paper is on that subject and many of my references came from that journal.

I'm getting pretty dark. It is 110 to 120 degrees almost every day now, but I'm getting used to it. I would like to ask a favor of you, Darling. It seems that you must write many of your letters some time (several hours) after you have read a letter from me.

And, it is written without you making reference to or re-reading my letter. I say this because in many of your letters, answers to my questions or replies to something I've talked about seem to be tacked onto the end of your letter as after thoughts. You don't seem to remember some of the things I asked about or mentioned. I'll admit that it is very possible that I am impatient and that I probably forget that it takes close to 2 weeks to get a reply (a week coming and a week going). But, that is the impression I have. I do want you to know that the love you communicate, through your letters, is the most important thing in the world to me. I would always want to read and bask in your love first rather than to read a business-like answer to a question of mine. You do communicate your love, and believe me, I am happy with the idea that you do love me. I frequently hope you feel my love.

Dan would like to ask you a favor. He is on a weight kick. Could you call "York Barbell Company" (3236- N. Figueroa Street, Los Angeles, California) and ask them if they have "Bob Hoffman's High Protein Cookies"? They come in a box. He wants several boxes. I know what you are thinking (that I want them). You're wrong, he does. If they do have them, please get some boxes for him. Or better yet, have Judy do it.

Simply or plainly stated, but I know with much depth and strength, I love you.

Jonny

Dearest Darling,

Well tonight finds me again in the O.R. and I'm afraid I'll be too tired to write later. I got a nice letter from you, today, and I'm full of love for you. I'm 141 pounds and full of expectations of Hebrew National products to eat. And, I want to hear the greatest new singing hit "The Blonde Bombshell" by Mrs. Benumof singing and speaking to me. I've got the recorder already warmed up and ready to go. Oh, I hope it and the pictures of you come soon.

We've been so busy. I think, in the last week, we did some 150 cases. The cases are going nearly around the clock and I'm sleeping some pretty odd hours.

Sherrie, I miss you so very much. I think of you all the time, constantly. And, I yearn and long for you more than I can tell you with words. I'll just have to show you in the future by actions and deeds. I've made so many resolutions, to myself, to improve myself as a husband. I don't think I'll do too badly, for you, even if I just carry out a few of them.

I'm going to say good-night. I love you with as much tenderness, warmth and sincerity as you are able to receive.

Jonny

Sweet Precious Sherrie,

I'm just overwhelmed. I just came back from an all day, grinding, hot, 12 hour session in the O.R. to find two letters from you, one from my Mom, one from Ruby and Abe and your package with your wonderful tape. I've just finished listening to it and everybody says I've gone nuts with joy. Sherrie, it was terrific just to hear your voice. You know, on the envelope, you said you hoped I would enjoy the tape because you sang on it. Honey, the singing was the least part of it. If you just breathed into the microphone, I would have been happy. Your singing was really good. You've got the old voice back again and nobody could ever tell you had just begun to learn the guitar. Poor Baby, you did sound a little depressed and I know it must be very difficult to make a tape. But, you did good. I've only listened to one side of the tape because the $10 tape player I bought broke down. So, I don't know if there is anything on the other side. I hope you realize that you can tape on both sides. I hope to make or start making one tomorrow. I've been so busy with 20 hour days in the O.R. all week. You know you don't have to make the tape all in one sitting, as I suspect you did.

I can only remember one question, something about Hawaii. Not a chance of getting it, Honey, not a chance. It would be like before I came into the Army putting down where I would like to go (Hawaii, Los Angeles, New York, etc). We both painfully know where I ended up.

The fighting is something fierce. We're slaving away in the O.R. with the guns going and coming. It is unreal. I hope the fighting breaks for a while. I'm just about done in.

I'm glad your rash is going down and I'm hoping you did well on your exams.

On my tape, I'll play the harmonica for you. Don't be surprised if you hear planes, guns (etc) in the background. I wouldn't even be surprised if a rocket comes in which makes a really big noise. I don't suppose I'll be any good either at making tapes. I just recorded a couple of sentences and boy do I sound funny. My recorder here is a lot smaller than the one I sent you. And, it produces a lot more distortion. I don't think I'll tape it all at one session. I'll just tape whenever something pops into my mind or when I have time. These days, I hardly ever get back to the hooch. I hope you have fun listening.

I'm glad you got the snapshots of me. The gun wasn't loaded, Darling. Ok? I think my Mom will love those poems that you sent.

Sherrie Honey, thanks for taking pictures for me and the tape. I know how self-conscious you are and that doing these things may not be easy for you. But, I hope that showering you with love, affection and acceptance (which I sincerely feel very deeply) will make it easier for you.

I think you'll do a fine job on the furniture you bought. I'm very proud of you. Maybe the rocking chair could be the chair I sit in to play with our baby or when you feed the baby.

Necessity dictates that I catch some sleep, so I'll talk to you tomorrow my Darling. We'll get casualties tonight.

Sherrie Dear, don't hesitate to make another tape anytime that you feel like it (even if you haven't got one back from me).

All my love, soul and desires.

Jon

(1st letter)

Dearest Darling Precious One,

I'm so sorry to have missed writing you yesterday, but we developed a 12 hour backlog of cases. They were coming so fast that it took us until the wee hours of the morning to get them done. I'm so harassed and so tired of cases. I wish so much we could have a few quiet days. The thought of a case to do right now is infinitely repulsive to me. Guess what, I heard that another litter just came in. Ugh!

I have such a warm glow knowing that I have your voice stored away, in a little box, on my desk. I don't know when I'll get a few hours to sit down, by myself, for a few hours to record for you. But, I'll do it just as soon as I am able.

How is your rash? How did you do on your exams? I bet you are the brightest, prettiest student on campus. I'm very glad you are swimming. It is very good exercise. It is second only to running. But, they are very close to one another in terms of energy expenditure. The more you put into it, the more you get out of it.

Honey, please forgive me for making this so short, but I've got to lie down for a while. I'm looking forward to getting your pictures, although I always have a few very bad moments when I get pictures of you. That is because I am more acutely aware of how much I miss you and how much I am missing.

All my love, Darling. You are the most cherished thing in life to me.

Jonny

(2nd Letter)
Dearest Loved One,

The fighting goes on. They are trying to take one stinking hill and are getting killed doing it. It is unbelievable the steady stream of casualties for 6 days and 7 nights now. The longest rest that I've had was 4 hours, at one time, 2 nights ago. Otherwise, I've slept an hour here and an hour there.

I loved your pictures. You are just indescribably lovely. The dress you fixed up is terrific.

I've got to go. I got another case, damn it. I really mean it. I have just about enough time to scribble these few lines to you.

Oh yes, try to kick 4-6 times per stroke of your right arm. And breathe once each time your right arm comes back, to your right hip, by turning your head to the right.

Congratulations on your "B". Terrific exam you wrote. I haven't read it yet, but I will. "B" is a good grade.

I love you with all my heart, Sherrie. I miss you more than you could possibly know or realize.

Jonny

Dearest Darling,

I'm doing something unusual right now. That is writing you at this hour, nearly 4 PM (before mail call which is about 6

PM). Today was our first free interval from cases, for a long while (like 8 hours), but it won't last long. Today they are going to try and take that hill, in the Ashau Valley, with a real big push. The hill is only 2 to 2.5 miles from here and is the place where the rockets that hit Camp Evans, 2 nights ago, came from. Supposedly we got a platoon to the top of the hill, last night, but they were pushed off by the morning.

Today was very hot (120 degrees or more). I got a little sick (dizzy) a while ago from it, but I think it is because I ran 2 miles in the morning and then played some basketball.

Well, the action is starting. The choppers are coming in, so I had better get going. If there is nothing really pressing to answer, in your letters, I'm going to leave this as is. I think we may be in the O.R. for a long while.

You know, I have a real nice collection of your pictures and I look at them every day now.

I love you very dearly, Darling. Jonny

Dearest Sherrie,

Well, fortunately, today was quiet so far. So, I relaxed a bit in the sun, etc. I wondered how you liked my tape. I almost considered making another one tonight, in lieu of this letter, but there is no way of knowing how much time I would have to make it.

Today was really hot. It was 122 degrees in the shade. It's very difficult to do anything, in the heat, and that includes fighting. I believe we have the hill which was originally supposed to have based 500-600 North Vietnamese Army regulars (not Viet Cong). We did surgery on a 13 year old North Vietnamese Army soldier, last night, for a gunshot wound of the abdomen. He told the Military Police a lot of information. The top of the hill is supposed to contain a 4-story tunnel-cave network with a hospital, etc. Anyway, they traded holding the hill three times during the night last night.

Sherrie Dear, according to my figuring, so far you have not been able to save any money from your own earnings. I figured I have sent you very close to $850 per month (3 times) plus $400 when I first came in country. Plus, I left you with $600. The total is $3550 which is about $200 more than what you told me we had in the bank a couple of weeks ago. What is the story on this? How much do you take home per month? Why haven't you saved anything, out of your earnings, if I have figured things correctly? In the 4 months I have been gone, I would imagine that you have taken home $2000. As far as I can see, there is nothing to show you have saved any of it. Please set me straight. This kind of thing bothers me, a lot, as you know.

I think there is one thing, you should do, before you leave for Japan. That is, contact the people with whom we have household insurance and increase it to say $5000. This is because we will be sending home merchandise worth about $2000 (in Japan) and probably worth $3500 in the USA. As far as asking you about our savings, please don't take the above as personal criticism of you. I simply want an explanation. I know you try hard, and have taken on working private duty on your own, but somehow our bank account does not seem to reflect the progress we should be making.

I love you very much, Darling. Jonny

(1st Letter)

Dearest Sherrie,

I'm miserable. It's at least 120 degrees and I have a hangover. Last night, for some strange reason, everybody just sat around and got drunk (me included). This was following a basketball game in which I and another Doc played 2 of the enlisted men for $5 a man per game. We won 2 games in a row. Then, after the game, we went on a nerve gas alert. At all times, you must carry your gas mask with you. Plus, you must have some injectable medicine with you as well. Then we got drunk, probably to celebrate our basketball victory and to forget the idea of nerve gas.

I read over your examination paper, yesterday, and thought your answers to the first 2 essay-type questions were excellent. I have such a smart wife!

I hadn't really drunk any alcohol until last night. And boy, I'm not sure I want to do that again. Sherrie, I feel so sick. Ugh!

I will probably let you know, in the middle or latter part of June, when we will meet in Tokyo.

I was talking to one of the nurses, yesterday, and I came to the unhappy realization that you will probably need almost a whole new wardrobe for New York. Well, I've got to keep the little wife looking sharp. Most of your clothes are summery and with flowers and daisies, etc. They are not exactly cut out for New York. This time, though, I'll go shopping with you. Ok? I'm going to finish now so I can get this in the mail before it leaves the compound.

All my love, Darling. Jonny

(2nd Letter)

Dearest Sherrie,

Today, I received 2 wonderful letters from you, but was disturbed to know that you did not receive any mail from me for at least 3 days in a row. Your last letter, written on Sunday (May 18th), naturally expressed the hope that you would get mail on Monday and I certainly echo those feelings. I think I missed writing only one day during our big push. By the time this gets to you, the tape should have arrived.

I've recovered somewhat from this morning's hangover, but the day was rough. I almost died when I ran today. The heat is torrid. Everyday it's over 120 degrees and it's somewhat difficult to sleep at night. It's a major catastrophe, when we run out of water, which happens at least once a week. The guys coming back from Hawaii say 90 degrees is chilly.

Now that your skin problems have abated, I might as well tell you about mine. Most of the guys here have Tinea. On the feet, it is "Athlete's Foot", in the groin it is "Jock Itch" and on the body, it is "Ring Worm". Well, for about a month, I have had all 3 infections. I've made good progress in clearing up the "Ring Worm", but I still have a fairly active case on my arms, back and chest. It is impossible to get clear here. Everything is covered with dirt and dust and you never stop sweating. It is very easy to get these infections, but I think I'm making good progress. Incidentally, I hit 135 pounds a few days ago. I think I'm up to 139 pounds now.

I caught up on my letters, just a little, having written my parents and Nat. But, I owe at least 20 letters. I'll answer them, but not nearly as quick as I did the first time. Because the reply comes back quicker and then I just have another letter to write.

The only question I have, today, is did you answer my previous questions? Incidentally, I think it is a good thing that you are keeping so busy. But, don't knock yourself out or make yourself ill.

I will probably send home $350 in money orders this month. I love you very much, Sherrie.

Jonny

5/24/69

Letter 121

Dearest Sherrie,

As you can see, today's little letter has 2 added attractions. Namely, $90 and 2 pictures of me by the open-side of a helicopter. I think the pictures were taken when I went to the beach. Today, I went to the PX. I walked about a mile and hitched about 2 miles going there. And, I got a ride all the way back. I got a haircut, some small odds and ends and the $90 money order. I got the money order, now, before payday because you can't send out more than $200 at any one time. When payday comes, I'll send $200 and then see what's left. Then, maybe I'll send $50-$100 more.

The allotment should come as usual, of course, to the bank.

Things are slow now that "Hamburger Hill" is taken. The North Vietnamese Army is still in the area, but it is scattered and broken. The 101st Airborne will probably leave the hill, in a few weeks, and then will have to fight for it all over again next year.

In your letter, today, you reported you had gotten 4 letters in one day. Congratulations, a new record!

Glad to hear you are soliciting help in making a reservation for Tokyo. I do not want to go to Kyoto. I don't want to travel around. I've got 6 days, so let's not get too original. Tokyo it will be, pure and simple. Absolutely no discussion on this.

Without going into detail, I'm sorry to hear about Bob Fields. I'll be making you another tape soon, Honey. I think there is an "Operation Entertainment" show coming on TV, so I think I'm going to go see it now.

All my love and thoughts, Jonny

(1st Letter)
Dearest Sherrie,

This is going to have to be a quick note telling you that I love you very much and miss you a tremendous amount. I think of you all the time and long and ache for your presence and being all the time. I got into a big bull session, last night, with the guys which lasted until 3 AM and now it's 11:30 AM. I am racing to get this into the mailbox before the mail goes out at 11:45 AM.

I am the same, namely bordering on a psychotic depression. I was thinking to myself, last night, that I am lucky in one respect that you are not. That is that I have friends who can understand my dejection, frustration and loneliness at being here because they feel the same things I feel and experience the same things. I suppose your girlfriends and parents can't quite appreciate your life as well as the guys here in Vietnam can understand mine.

Well, if you are going to get today's message of love, I'd better get up to the mailbox.

I love you very much, Darling. You mean everything to me.

Jonny

(2nd Letter)

Dearest Sherrie,

Today was just like all the others, shitty. Had a very unusual patient, today, that I was called to see. It was a snake bite. The guy was partially paralyzed by the time he came in. I was able to successfully intubate him (nasotracheal) and after 8 hours or so of intensive treatment (anti-toxin, controlled ventilation, anti-convulsive medication, incision of the bite, tourniquets, etc), he is looking real good. I think he'll make it. I didn't think so when I first saw him and intubated him.

Included are 2 slides that I forgot were taken, at the beach, by another guy who apparently left them on my desk today. In one of them, I'm standing with my hands on my hips. The girl (about the only one in Corp I) is a nurse. She is married to a Marine who is out in the boonies fighting. He is a career enlisted man. Don't I look skinny in the other picture?

Please tell my parents that I received a tape, from them,

that was completely garbled up. I was so surprised that they sent a tape. Did you tell them we were now sending tapes? Ask them if they checked to see if the tape came out ok before they sent it.

I should get a bunch of slides back in a week.

I love you very much, Darling.

Jonny

5/27/69
Letter 124

Dearest Sherrie Darling,

I got your package, today, and a very lovely letter from you. Thank you for both. I've got plenty of hot dogs now and I don't think you should send any more for about 3 weeks from today. But, please send some more at that time. Hot dogs are all I eat for supper and, sometimes, the only thing I eat all day.

I'm very concerned about your rash and nervousness, Sherrie. Please take it easy, keep your chin up and grit your teeth. Don't lose your cool. You'll make it. Time is your worst adversary and you have got the patience and the willpower to beat time. Don't worry, Honey, everything will be alright. As I wrote you a few days ago, I suspected that you didn't have too many people to talk to. I understand that you have pent-up feelings that you need to ventilate. All I can say is that August 1st is not too far off now (8 weeks). Until then, steel yourself to grind the time out. Keep busy. It will be only a short time until I let you know what hotel and date to plan for. Then, both of us will have something to fixate on. To have a definite date, to think about, will help a lot.

I made one side of a tape, for you, last night. I'll make the other side tonight or tomorrow night. I wonder how you liked the first tape I sent? I figured out what made my reels open too fast, in spots, when I made the first tape. If the tape is wound slightly loosely, then it will run fast. If you cinch-up (pull) on the end of the tape, until it stops coiling off the reel and rewind the part that unraveled, the parts that sound high pitched and nasal may sound more normal. Try it.

I love you very much, Sherrie. Please try to draw some strength from that. Please don't cause yourself any unnecessary, or silly grief (and me, too), by worrying too much. We'll be alright, I know it. And, your Captain (me) is ordering you to know it, too.

Jonny

Dearest Sherrie,

We were pretty busy today. A fire base (small camp) got over-run by Viet Cong and they got hit really hard. I don't know if this had anything to do with us not getting any mail today. Naturally, I was very disappointed.

It seems as if it is getting harder to write a decent letter every day. Most of the guys, who have been in-country longer than I have, tell me that it gets much harder to write every day (and to write long letters). I guess many things, I told you about earlier, seem routine now and not worth mentioning. Maybe not much is really happening that I can report. I hope you understand if my letters are shorter. It is not any reflection of my love or feelings for you. I miss you more each day. Maybe my letters are shorter because of the accentuation of the frustration I feel in trying to be near you somehow (pictures, letters, voice, etc). I want the real thing, you! I think your letters have been shorter, also. I take it to mean that you, also, are finding it difficult to write constantly long letters.

I love you very much, Darling. Don't ever forget.

Jonny

Dearest Darling Wife,

Today passed pretty uneventfully. Although, we were very busy until 4 AM last night. I hope tonight is quiet. I would like to complete the other side of the tape I have already begun for you. I got 2 nice letters from you, today, and a bunch of magazines and comics (sent in January from you). The reason it took so long, to get to me, was because of the wrong APO on the address.

I think that was a very good idea of you to go out to get some Japanese food. Certainly, I would like to try some! How many times am I going to be in Japan? If you get some experience, in Japanese food, then you can help me order. Incidentally, I would like to take a side trip to Kyoto for a day and walk around, shop, etc. I loved those mandarin oranges you sent. I ate them for my lunch today. Please send 4 or 5 cans when you get the chance. The dinner, you had, sounded good. I think I would like that.

Yes, I know about the Reillys. Too bad. I'll write them when I get some time. I'm way behind in letters. Have you written John Stevens? If not, write him a short note. I'm sure he'd be happy to hear from you.

I'm going to use the time, while I have it, to try and complete the other side of the tape. I hope, naturally, that you will be making another tape for me and are continuing to shoot pictures.

With much tender love, passion and desire for you.

Jonny

5/30/69
Letter 127

Dearest Darling Sherrie,

Poor Sherrie, you certainly sound more distressed lately. Your letter of May 25th (Sunday), that I received today, confirmed that suspicion for me. In case you don't remember, you were crying that day. Well, I suppose it does some good to let yourself go at times. But, I sure wish you had more people to talk to. I hate to say it, for fear of you finding it an antagonistic or repulsive or stupid suggestion, but you might try calling my folks when you are really down. My Mom is a good listener and a pretty understanding person. You might find it rewarding, to talk to them, when you are feeling bad. My folks (especially my Dad) are smart and really do have some wisdom that comes with age. And, they like you. Perhaps they would have something to say that would help you more than just for this moment. As for myself, telling you my feelings really can't help you because it is my feeling for you that is partly responsible for your misery. What I mean is that when you are loved by one it is certainly easier to love back. You know I love you, miss you, live for you. I think it would be very helpful, to you, to talk to someone outside of our love and my folks might be as good as anybody. Ok? If nobody else does, I sympathize with you and very much so. I'm your #1 sympathizer. I think in this respect, I have it easier than you. I have a lot more people, than you do, to ventilate my feelings to (as I told you before).

I am almost done with both sides of my second tape. I'll be sending it off to you soon.

Although it may compound your misery, I must tell you again (as I always will), that my love for you is deep and strong.

Jonny

May 31, 1969 through July 1, 1969

Jon did not write any letters to Sherrie, during this time frame, because he flew home on emergency leave due to Sherrie being diagnosed with Hepatitis B. She was a Registered Nurse and got Hepatitis B as a result of working in a hospital Kidney Dialysis Unit (where the risk of exposure to the blood of patients was very high). Sherrie's physician contacted the American Red Cross with her diagnosis (and requested that Jon be allowed to come home) using the necessary words: "Serviceman's presence deemed necessary." The American Red Cross then notified Jon's Army Commander, with the physician's message, that Jon's presence was urgently needed at home. The Army Commander granted Jon an emergency leave, of 1 month, so that he could be with Sherrie in her recovery in Los Angeles. At month's end, Jon had to return to Vietnam.

(Inflight between Anchorage, Alaska and Yokota Air Base, Japan)

Dearest Darling Lovely Sherrie,

As you must realize, by now, we got off on schedule this time and I'm longing for you very much. I thought that we achieved an unusual and complete harmony between us. A harmony that allows for growth and maturation for each of us as individuals. I feel, and felt, very close to you all month. In the future, I know we can look forward to the most complete fulfillment a marriage can offer. I love you very much, my Darling. I experience and see you as very much a part of me.

I was able to reach Dick Anderson, in Anchorage, after a little difficulty finding his phone number. But, we had a very excited talk (5 minutes). It was nice to talk to him. He sends his best.

Coming into Anchorage, I saw such a mass collection of snow and mountains. Some mountains were completely covered by snow and there were so many mountains. Kind of pretty. Worth seeing.

Aside from getting about 100 pages read (in my book), and playing some cards with 2 young enlisted men next to me, the trip is very boring and taxing. So far, I was able to dose off to sleep for about 4 of the 12 hours we have been flying. We are due, in Japan, in another half-hour or so.

Well, so long for now. You know how deeply I love you. I hope it is matched by an equivalent amount of happiness in you.

Jonny

Dearest Darling Sherrie,

I honestly did not feel that I would be unduly depressed when I returned to the 18th Surgical Hospital. But, alas, I am. Very much so. It's been very quiet here (so they tell me), for the last 2 weeks, which really makes the time drag. I have been back here for a few hours. It is very hot, but I think I can get used to it again soon. I received a very warm welcome, from everybody, but naturally that won't last forever. Pretty soon, I think things will be the way they were before. The most talked about thing at the hospital, right now, is my eyeglasses. They all inquired about your health. Practically everybody is "short" now (having under 100 days left in Vietnam). I think my last 100 days will be difficult ones. I flew by chopper all the way from Da Nang to Camp Evans. Nice ride. I was lucky to get it. I knew the pilot.

I can't tell you how much I miss you. We had such a wonderful 30 days together and have so much to look forward to.

I had letters from the Ezras, Kapels and Mayers waiting for me. I don't have too much enthusiasm for returning the Mayers' letter. The Ezras had a baby.

Sherrie Darling, I'm going to close for now because I'm very tired from traveling. I didn't sleep last night.

You are, to me, the most cherished, beautiful, wonderful vision, memory and image imaginable. I love you so very much.

Jonny

Dearest Darling Sherrie,

I'm writing, to you, at a bad time. I just did a spinal that didn't work. That depresses me. Well, can't win them all.

I spent my first full-day here and boy it was hot. I should get used to it soon. Everybody is pretty friendly and that makes coming back much nicer.

A call just came in asking me to go to the hospital ship for 2 weeks. Their Anesthesiologist is in the hospital. At the moment, I don't know if I will go. But, there is a good chance that I will. I may go in the morning. If I do, I will send you a short note to let you know. Keep sending my mail to the 18th Surgical Hospital. I think the worst part about going will be not getting mail, every day, from you. But I think, overall, I will go because I can get a different type of anesthesia experience there (neuro-surgery, pediatrics, etc). Also, prices in the ship's PX are good. The prices are better than in Hong Kong. The hospital ship is "The Sanctuary", not "The Repose". Right now, I have $400 and I think I'll spend it on a tape deck and speakers, etc. I'll send it to you, so you can expect to receive things if I do go. I think I will go, also, because I know I will be tired of this place soon. So, the variety of a change will just delay that happening.

I miss you very much and spend a fair amount of time mooning over your pictures. I love you very dearly, Darling. You mean everything to me. We will go on R&R in October, ok? I will continue to write to you, every day, from the ship.

Goodnight, my Darling. I love you with all my heart and soul. And, I always will. Oh Sherrie, I love you, I love you.

Jonny

Dearest Darling, Darling Sherrie,

Well, I am on the ship now. I arrived at 4 PM, so I haven't done any case yet. But, I have a big one to do in the morning. The ship is just like a stateside hospital. It has 30 Docs. And, I am under a board eligible Anesthesiologist who I think will be able to teach me something in these 2 weeks. The elective cases they have here are great and each anesthesia person averages 8 hours of work per day. So, they are pretty busy. At the 18th Surgical Hospital, we have had only 3 cases all month (July) so far. I think these 2 weeks will be very informative and stimulating for me. I should go back to the 18th Surgical Hospital rejuvenated. I know for sure, I will learn 2 more types of blocks from the Doc here and that should make a big difference when I go back. However, I will miss running a great deal. And, I hope and pray fervently that your letters get to me pretty regularly. I asked a number of guys to make sure the pilots bring my mail out to me. I know I will be extremely lonely here because, for 2 weeks, I don't really expect to be accepted. But, I think it is just the thing I need to get interested in my work again. I felt stagnant and I wasn't learning anything new, at all, for a long time. To add to my loneliness here, I feel somewhat more out of touch with you and isolated because I won't be getting your mail regularly. But, for 2 weeks I can take it and I will get a lot out of it. The Anesthesiologist, I'm replacing, hurt his back. Everything is very clean here (except me) and air conditioned. All in all, the change in environment will be helpful in itself. It is late now. And, I am tired, so I'm going to bed.

Don't send any packages until I let you know when I'm going back to the 18th Surgical Hospital.

Sherrie, I'm so lucky and happy to be loved by you and to love you. I'm so happy to be able to feel love. It's so wonderful, so wonderful to feel love for you.

Jonny

Dearest Darling Mrs. B.

Funny you should mention it, but I spent $180 today.

I bought a tape deck for $115 (Sony), 2 speakers (Panasonic) for $39, some blank tapes which Woody is going to tape for me (Glen Campbell, Jose Feliciano, etc) and a pair of navy pants. Naturally, it hurts to no end to spend the money. Also, I wanted to share the shopping part of it with you. But, the buys are just too good (prices on the ship are even lower than in Hong Kong). Tomorrow, I am going to get a $50 camera (probably worth over $100), binoculars and maybe a movie projector. So, get set for an influx of packages and boxes, in a week or two. I will start sending the stuff the day after tomorrow. Tomorrow, I am first call. Today, I'm second call. The day after tomorrow, I'm third call, so I will have time. This morning, I did a neck case which went smoothly. It is only 5 PM, now, so I may work tonight yet.

I was thinking, today, what great buys I was getting.

And then, I thought of you and I wish to hell I never had

the chance to get the stuff because it means nothing to me. I'm so lonely. Well, when I get back on shore, it will be the end of July. That will mean I will have been almost 2 months away from the 18th Surgical Hospital.

Every night there is a movie, so I suppose I will go pretty often if we are not doing cases. But, I hate everything I have to do (or do socially or do for recreation) without you. It is hard to enjoy anything without you. I hope so much to get some mail from you soon. I ran around the deck of the ship, today, with one of the other Docs: not bad, not good.

Sherrie Sweetheart, I love you very much, always and forever.

Jonny

Dearest Most Beloved Mrs. B.

Hi Sweetie-Pie. Are you running? I am just about to. I figure if I run every other day at least, while I'm on the ship, I'll be ok. Whew! I ran 2 miles.

Today, I did 3 cases until 2 PM, laid outside in the sun for an hour, mailed our tape deck off to you and now I'm running, then supper, then work or a movie. Learned a great new anesthetic technique this morning. Today, I got the package that you sent me. That means I should start to get your letters pretty soon.

Now, it is after supper and I'm going to play in a game of poker. Wish me luck. I'll let you know what happened tomorrow.

I love you very much, my Darling. I think of you all the

time. I wonder what you are doing, how you feel, etc, etc. I must get going, so please forgive me if this is short. But, I will miss the poker game if I don't go now. All my love and thoughts.

Jonny

7/10/69
Letter 134

Dearest Darling Sherrie,

Today was great because I got 3 letters from you. One of the guys, from the 18th Surgical Hospital, came out and brought my mail. I'm going to run now and then eat. I have a craniotomy to do. Today, I bought a $50 camera and $25 binoculars. I'm sending the speakers, and binoculars, off to you tomorrow. I already sent the tape deck to you. I, also, was able to find an enlisted man on the ship who will make about 12 tapes (3 hours each) for me. I have people who will make tapes for me, on shore, so I should have plenty by the time I get home. I'll send off a bunch, to you, every so often. Now, this is important! You don't have to pay customs. If they should charge you, don't pay. Write them at the following address and tell them I have been in-country (Vietnam) for more than 140 days. Save this address: Customs House, 555-Battery Street, San Francisco, Ca. 94111.

Only pay if they won't give you the goods. Then proceed, as above, to get your money back. Ok?

Your letters were beautiful ones, today, and made me miss you so much more. I'm quite lonely on the ship and have no real companionship, as I do on shore. But, learning as I am and being physically comfortable makes it worthwhile.

Tomorrow, a typhoon is supposed to come. I hope so, I would like to see it.

I hope you are feeling well. And that work and life, although possibly hum-drum, are going smoothly. What grade did you get, in your course, at school?

Sherrie, my one and only, I love you very much.

Jonny

Dearest Lovable, Loved Sherrie,

I've had a very busy 24 hours, since I last wrote you. At midnight (last night), a 10 hour case came in and we got him off the table alive. But, he died at about 3 PM today, after 60 units of blood. That, in itself, is not so unusual except that all of it took place while the ship was in a storm. Boy, it was an experience! Everything was sliding around the O.R. I'm a little seasick myself, but a lot of other people are much worse off. I slept a good part of the day and I dreamt, at one time, that I was drunk. Since I've been on the air-conditioned ship (my room is, too), I have enjoyed sleeping immensely. I just snuggle up, under the blankets, while it is 120 degrees outside.

Last night, they showed the movie "Anatomy of a Murder". Pretty good flick. But, I had to leave to do my pre-ops before the end. After supper tonight, I'm going to go to the music library and pick out some tapes to be taped. That is, if I can't get a game of chess. Then I'll watch a movie, then study a bit and then sleep. I just came back, from the music library, and I picked out these 4 albums (instrumentals of the Beatles' hits, The Seekers, Neil Diamond, Aretha Franklin). I'll try and get 4 albums taped per day or every other day.

I'm excited about tomorrow. There's a new technique I'm going to learn. Then, I can go back to the 18th Surgical Hospital and do it all the time. Man, I'm telling you my residency should be a breeze. We'll have so much time together and a baby!

Well Sweetheart, so ends another day. I want you to smile because I want you to think about, and remember, that we are one. And, that I love you very, very, very much.

Jonny

Dearest Adorable, One Year Wife,

I guess I forgot to wish you a Happy Anniversary. Apparently, I'm destined to become an absent-minded old Doctor. But, I do love you and I love you more on this anniversary than on our wedding day. I expect it will grow, and grow, both in us and in our children. Your card was very nice. I got it today.

Time is passing more quickly, on the ship, than on shore. I'm much busier because there is elective surgery every morning. Today, already, I have done 6 cases. Three of the cases were done with a new technique (for me). It is interesting because I'm learning. It will be a well spent month (maybe only 2-3 weeks).

I've managed to run 4 out of the 7 days that I've been on the ship. Not bad. I think I've gained a few pounds, since coming aboard, because every meal is served like a banquet (with waiters, multi-courses, etc). Too hard to resist. I now have 2 people making tapes, for me, so I should easily have at least 6 tapes (equals 18 hours) by the time I leave the ship. These are additional tapes that I'm getting taped (Righteous Brothers, Peter, Paul and Mary, Tijuana Brass, Baja Marimba Band, the Beatles, Dionne Warwick, Nancy Wilson, Aretha Franklin, etc). All for free! Most of the songs we like are in these. Any requests? Now, think hard. You might not get another chance.

I'm buying out the PX here. All the guys on shore are asking me to get stuff for them.

I'm first call tonight, so I'd better get some rest. The fellow we did, all night (a couple of nights ago), unfortunately died. It's always sad, but particularly so, after working so hard.

I'm glad you are running and doing so well. I'm sure you must turn a lot of heads when they see such a pretty girl running around (literally, I meant).

Don't be depressed, keep busy with constructive things. And, remember how happy we were and will be. I love you so much and am very content, though longing, because of the love I feel for you.

Jonny

Dearest Darling,

Today was a very good day for me. I did 2 anesthesia blocks. They are the type I specifically came out, to the ship, to learn. And, I got all the materials I need to do these blocks at the 18th Surgical Hospital (plus drugs and equipment to do different kinds of general anesthesia that I learned). Plus, my replacement came from the states (Marv Levenson) and he took an anesthesia residency at Los Angeles County General Hospital, so I know him. I'll be going back to the 18th Surgical Hospital tomorrow morning. I'm sorry to go because I had so many things going good for me here (learning, being physically comfortable, getting guys to make tapes for me, getting good buys, making new friends, seeing movies) and, most importantly, the time just flew by. Hopefully, with the new things I learned, time will move a little quicker at the 18th Surgical Hospital.

Tomorrow (if I have time), I'm sending the speakers I bought, the binoculars and the tapes that were made for me. I'm keeping the camera. I'll probably send home the instamatic.

Honey, I'm sorry this is so short. But, I have to pay a courtesy call to the Commanding Officer (of the hospital ship) now. But, remember, I'm long on love for you, thinking of you, longing for you. Honest Sherrie, I was telling my roommate, today, that to me my time seems to be short in only 2 ways: (1) One is doing things, anything, to take my mind off wishing I was with you. And, that includes the O.R. work, running, etc. (2) The other way is when I can't do those things and I just end up longing for you and missing you.

All my love, Jonny

Dearest Sherrie,

It is very late and I'm very tired. But, I must tell you how much I love you, that I cherish you and that you mean everything to me. Today, I came back to the 18th Surgical Hospital and proceeded to do 5 cases. I did 3 of them, with new techniques, which made a big splash. What broke my heart today, however, was that while I was coming back to the 18th Surgical Hospital 5 letters were going out to the ship for me. They stand a good chance of getting lost. I'm sure most of them were from you. Tomorrow, one of the guys is going out to the ship and he's going to try and trace them down for me. I'm really hurting for mail since I have only gotten mail 2 times since coming back to Vietnam.

I shot a whole roll of film on the trip, by helicopter, back to the 18th Surgical Hospital. I hope they come back ok. This was done on my new camera.

I was really beginning to like the ship. Everybody asked me to come back including the Commanding Officer of the ship. That made me feel good. I worked hard, but I enjoyed myself.

Darling, I love you more than words can say or words that I can find to say. Maybe it's because I never thought, really deep down, that I would come to love and appreciate someone like I do you. Perhaps, in time, I'll be able to express myself adequately. But, for the time being, I'll content myself with showing you that I love you when I get home.

Oh yes, please send Hebrew National hot dogs and salami.

All my love and thoughts, Sherrie. Jonny

7/15/69
Letter 139

Dearest Adorable Wife,

Today, I got 2 letters from you and was delighted to see the pictures. You looked lovable, precious and pretty, as you always do. I've tried to get those 5 missing letters back, but I'm afraid they are lost. From what you said, in today's letters, I gather that you have been putting pictures in the letters for several days. I'm sure some of the pictures are in the missing letters, unfortunately.

I'm sitting here writing you while listening to the tapes I made at home. I'm very glad I made them. And, I'm enjoying it. I don't know if I told you, but we did a big case yesterday (18 hours, 60 units of blood) with the new drug "Innovar." I learned to use it on the ship and brought some back to the 18th Surgical Hospital. Well, he died today. This kind of thing is getting to me. I wish we could pull more of these kids through. I think we feel that we are doing all that we can and it just isn't enough. I've done 2 new blocks since coming back, both were successful.

I'm very sorry my mail has come sporadically, but I'm sure I've written every day. I think it's terrific you ran a mile. Very good, keep it up. Yes, the heat has affected my running, but I believe I'll get used to it in a couple of weeks. Today, I weighed 136 pounds. I was quite surprised since I thought I ate well on the ship. Send salami, hot dogs and bread. I hope you were able to work at Central Recovery. Got to get some money out of you.

Everybody is very happy that I'm back. Today, Doug left for R&R. He needs it badly. He was getting stone drunk every day and night. I don't think Dan is going to ask Judy to meet him for R&R. He would rather meet her under less demanding circumstances.

Our R&R will either be in the middle of October or early November. I think we will stay at the New Otani Hotel. Why don't you get a brochure? When I let you know the date, you can make the reservations.

Darling, I miss you immensely. I will only be truly happy when I am with you, again, for good. I love you, Sherrie.

Jonny

Dearest Sherrie,

Right now, I'm just waiting for the mail to come. That is all, just waiting. I've done nothing, today, and have nothing to do. There are no cases. It is hard to kill 15 hours here. Tomorrow, perhaps we'll be busy. I got those 5 letters, luckily, and 3 were from you. One had 3 pictures of you. One was from Nat and one was from my Mom. God, I don't feel like writing anybody except you. I'm really going to have to force myself to write Dr. Papper one of these days. It's really hot. I'm buying a fan, soon, from a guy who is leaving. I'll sell it when I go. I'm sorry to report that I broke the camera, I just bought, after taking only one roll of film. It will be very easy to repair. It's just the spring, that is connected to the lever, that moves the film ahead. So, I'm going to send the camera to you soon. You can get the spring repaired, take some rolls of yourself for me, bring the camera to Tokyo and I'll take it back to Vietnam. Why don't you start a list of things you might want to buy in Tokyo? Put a stop watch on it.

Tonight, I'm going to try very hard to study some. I just can't seem to find anything to do that I want to do. I know I'm very depressed. I'm just wondering what is going to happen when I realize it.

Well, I got no mail. But, I did study for an hour and I did run. I guess I'll just take comfort in looking forward to getting your pictures and letter tomorrow. I'll start a tape for you tonight or tomorrow. Please do the same.

I love you very much and I hope you know and feel that.

Jonny

7/17/69

Letter 141

Dearest Darling Wife,

Today, I got a bubbling letter from you and a package which makes me bubble. Today was better. I had 3 cases and the day went faster. Just a little while ago, I heard a tape with Glen Campbell singing a bunch of great songs including "Reason to Believe". It's a fantastic tape. I'll have it taped for me. Woody Haser is going to run off about 6 tapes (3 hours each), for me, in about a month. By the time I go home, we should have a real good collection of music.

I'm glad you enjoyed working at Central Receiving. Yes, action and being busy on the job makes the time fly. I just had a nice talk with Steve Lipson. Oh yes, I think I lost my address book on the ship. How about making me out a short list of addresses of the people I write to on a semi-regular basis (Des, Greg, etc). I was pleased to read about your accomplishments in track and in fixing up the old furniture.

We will have a beautiful home and I will have a beautiful charming wife in that home. I just ate a can of beef stew, pretty good. I've got plenty of food. It is sort of late right now, so I don't think I'll tape for you today. But, I'm third call tomorrow and certainly will be able to do it then.

I miss you immensely, Honey. I think and feel nothing other than looking forward to being with you.

All my love, Jonny

7/18/69
Letter 142

Dearest, Dearest Sherrie,

Poor little baby, you were so sad in your letter today (written on a Sunday). Apparently, you didn't work that day in Central Receiving. Things around here are extremely slow, not a case all day. Enemy contact is light and most everything is just shelling at a long range. Today, our guns were plastering a mountain top nearby. It was kind of pretty, in a way, because you could see the shells land and explode. Some of the shells are airbursts which means they explode about 10 feet off the ground. Looked like a real 4th of July.

Your mail has been coming pretty regularly or just the same as before I left. Yesterday, for example, nobody got mail. It didn't come through from the South.

Right now, I'm eating 2 hot dogs that are delicious! One of the packages of hot dogs you sent came spoiled, incidentally, so please send more. No peas or corn (canned), please.

I just had 2 cases which killed 2 hours (both were blocks). Tonight, I'm going to type out a letter to Dr. Papper and get some information on the residency (wages, program, etc). Also, today, I made up the package containing the camera. I'll let you know when I send it (probably within a week). I'll get a haircut at the same time I go to the Post Office. In the package, with the camera, is some newspaper stuffing. But, also, there is the handbook for the use of the camera and a pair of prescription sunglasses. Please put both away carefully. Also, there are 2 rolls of film. One is in a little aluminum container because I took it out of the box it came in before I discovered I had messed up the camera. Again, in the box are these things: camera handbook, sunglasses and 2 rolls of film.

Sherrie, I love you soooo much, I really do. I'm so very happy and lucky that you are my wife.

Jonny

Dearest Sweetheart,

Today was very depressing. There were no cases again, nothing to do. Tomorrow morning should be better in that I have one elective case to do. It is suitable to do a new block. The only question is the air conditioning. It is off again, right now, and we try not to do elective cases without air conditioning.

I made you a tape, today, on one of my hoochmates' recorder since mine is on the blink again. Doug, who sold it to me, is on R&R. Also, tomorrow, I have arranged for one of the O.R. techs to tape me 4 tapes. Otherwise, the future looks bleak.

I'm first call, tomorrow, so maybe I will get additional cases. On the tapes I made, today, I only made one side because I have so little to tell you. But, I did ask you 2 important questions on the tape (the wattage input of the speakers I sent home and the zip code of upper Manhattan). Oh, I do not need the zip code of upper Manhattan because the letters from Columbia were returned to me by my roommate on the ship. And, he has my address book which I will get the next time that I go out to the ship.

As of today, I have spent 186 days in Vietnam and have 178 to go. I know my tape sounds a little lackluster, but I was feeling kind of down today. I hope you are shooting pictures and making me a tape.

Tonight, our one fan will be turned towards the opposite side of the hooch from me (we switch every night). I don't know how I'll ever be able to fall asleep. Well, on that note, goodnight my love. I'll think of you all night. I dreamt about you last night.

I love you with all my heart, Darling.

Jonny

Dearest Darling, Precious Wife,

Today was better. I got up at 8 AM, ran 2 miles and then had 2 cases from 10 AM to 2 PM. One of the cases was a successful new block. Then, I took a nap, started reading "Georgia Boy" by Erskine Caldwell, ran another 2 miles and then got a real bubbly, bouncy and happy 5 page letter from you. It was full of news and love. In addition, one of the O.R. techs (Michael Brenner, same address as mine) made me 3 tapes (3 hours each) today. Listen to the great stuff I got in these 9 hours of music: Gary Puckett and the Union Gap (2 albums- Young Girl and Lady Willpower), Simon and Garfunkel (2 albums- The Graduate soundtrack and Parsley, Sage, Rosemary and Thyme), Bobby Vinton, Dionne Warwick, Platters, Modern Ink Spots, Peter, Paul and Mary (Gypsy Woman and Lemon Tree), Glen Campbell, Tom Jones, Jose Feliciano, Righteous Brothers (Old Man River), The Lettermen. He taped me 19 albums for free! Plus, we have the 5 tapes (3 hours each) that I already sent home. And, I'll probably get 10-15 more tapes before I come home. Fantastic! Don't you think the music I got is good? Why don't you send Michael Brenner a package of cookies and stuff. Please do, as he worked all day for me. Now, all I need is a short case tonight and I'll be so happy.

Now, let me answer your letter. I am glad my folks liked your cookies. They really are good. I'm glad you got Nat a gift. You know you are a very thoughtful, considerate person! You really are. I'm glad you are getting a lot of benefit from running. Keep it up. Yes, buy Tim Hardin's new song. We will be taping our records, onto tapes, because they will keep much better. Honey, I just spent half an hour telling Dan how great you are. I miss you very much and I love you very much. I'll be so happy when I am back with you again. I don't even care where they send me, when I get back from Vietnam, just as long as I am with you.

All my love, Jonny

Dearest Darling Sherrie,

Today was a typical dull, dull day except for a few moments ago. I was called to the Emergency Room to intubate a little Vietnamese girl who was having seizures. It was difficult, but I did it. Oh yes, one other thing. The Division Surgeon (a Colonel), who is new in-country, came to visit us and we had a discussion of our problems at the 18th Surgical Hospital. Well, the Commanding Officer of our hospital (also, a Colonel) came over to me later. He told me that the Division Surgeon told him he wanted to make sure that he knew and remembered my name. No big thing, but I felt really good.

I think the weather may be cooling off just a little. It is a little more apparent at night. I'm sleeping better. I'm getting pretty dark now, with the lull in fighting, and a chance to get outside for longer periods of time. I guess by now, you must have gotten my tape. I certainly hope you have made one. Don't feel self-conscious, please. It would mean so much to me.

You know, of course, that you would have found a gift for Nat (in 5 minutes) had I gone with you. Remember, it is the thought that counts. I'm glad you are running. That shows a lot of spunk. Say hello to Matt Bernstein for me.

I love you very much, Sweetie. I'm ready and willing for a lot of loving.

All my love, Darling, all of it.

Jonny

Dearest Sunshine,

Hello Love, I miss you. It seems as though you are not enjoying the night shift very much. How much longer do you have on it? How many times were you able to work at Central Receiving? Have you gotten my packages yet? Remember to tell me the wattage input of our speakers.

Today, I listened to the Gary Puckett tapes and they are of very good quality. I probably will keep some of the tapes, here, to listen to for a while. I had only one case, today, using my new block. So, today, like all the others went slowly. I got back 20 slides. Four of them are included in this letter. They were taken before I left on my leave. Today, it rained all day. But, I got out to run anyway. So, I got wet. I don't need any ice trays. I hope you didn't send them, but it is no big deal. I haven't sent the camera yet. I haven't been to the Post Office. I may wait until payday when I have to go to the Post Office, anyway, to get money orders.

Time is really dragging. I hate to sound listless, but I am. I'm melancholy with love for you. I miss you a great deal. You are my only playmate and true life-long friend. I wish so much to be with you. Well, someday.

I'm growing a moustache. It is a custom here to grow one, for a while, when you get under 6 months left in-country. Include more mustard in your next package.

All my love, Honey.

Jon

Dearest Darling Sherrie,

No mail, again, tonight. Apparently, the lights went out at the Post Office and they couldn't sort the mail. Anyway, I suppose you would be happy to know that I'm halfway through the tape. I feel pretty relaxed talking to you, in bits here and there, not pressured into trying to think of something to say.

Hey Sherrie, guess what? I just saw a TV show with Glen Campbell, Pat Paulson, Gary Puckett and Buffy St. Marie. The reception was terrible, but I enjoyed it.

I went to the Post Office, today, and mailed the camera to you. I think my prescription sunglasses were in there, also, so put them away carefully. They are worth $30.

I haven't gotten mail, for 2 days now, and many guys haven't gotten any for 3 days. I'm hoping, tomorrow, I get something from you.

Woody invited me over for some canned Chow Mein. Since I haven't eaten since 12 noon (it's 11 PM now), today, I want to get my ass over there and eat. I'm starving.

Sherrie Honey, my heart really aches with longing, hunger and passion for you. And, it's bursting with love, tenderness, affection and aching for you. Darling, you are my whole world.

I live for you. Honest, I mean it.

Jonny

Dearest, Dearest Sherrie,

Well, we got mail today. I got 2 letters, from you, both full of news and excitement about the moon flight. I, too, think it is a wonderful accomplishment. We had been aware of developments, but approximately one day late. We had very little TV coverage of the flight, but the news broadcasts were pretty good. As I said, before, everyone here is mildly interested. But, I think we all feel too far removed from the real world to generate more interest than that.

Tonight, we had a bit of excitement and tragedy. A grenade accidentally went off about 200 yards from us. The bunkers started in with machine guns which hit an ammo dump. The ammo dump exploded and killed 5 of our people. We couldn't save any of the 5. They were all infantry soldiers. Very sad thing. When it all happened, every gun ship and dust-off ship was in the air. The ammo dump was firing things in every direction. Everybody was flat on their stomachs. We thought we were being overrun. It's an hour later now, and aside from the poor guys who were killed instantly when the ammo dump went off, nobody else was hurt.

Included in the envelope, obviously, is an advertisement. Why don't you look into it? Maybe you could get cheaper round-trip tickets.

In your next package, could you please include some Chow Mein (canned) and noodles? Right now, I'm out of food, but Woody has been feeding me the last few nights. I think it is great if you could get the tennis class and part II of your other course.

Honey, I miss you a great deal. I'm very tired right now. Today was just torrid. It is 9 PM and I'm still sweating so much. Stinky and dirty as I am, I'm filled with love for you and longing for you.

Jon

Hi Dearest Sweetheart,

Today, I got a letter from you which makes the day tolerable at least. I have a lot to tell you. First off, I really got blasted (drunk) last night and have been sick to my stomach all day. I can't look a beer in the face tonight. I did run, but I almost died. I had only one O.R. case today.

I haven't told you yet, but I might as well now. Once a week I'm going to a leper colony, in Hue, to do anesthesia there. I am at no risk or danger. I find this to be a very rare chance to see, firsthand, a very fascinating facet of life. I am honored to have been asked since the Surgeons who did so respect my abilities. The disease is very interesting and there is a great deal that I can do to help out. I will start in about 3 weeks.

I'm glad you got the speakers. But, I'm also worried about the tape deck and binoculars since they were sent 3-4 days before the speakers.

Enclosed are 4 slides from the roll of film that I took with the Minolta camera. They are excellent. There is no comparison of the slides taken with our new camera and the instamatic. Wait until you see them on a screen or through a viewer. Fantastic detail.

I'm still halfway through my tape, but I'll get on with it.

I'm proud you are doing such a good job of running. You have good willpower. The same goes for you making dresses, the cabinet bookcases, etc. You are terrific and I'm proud of you.

I love you very much, Sweetheart, always and deeply.

Jonny

7/30/69

Letter 150

(1st Letter)

Dearest, Dearest Sherrie,

Forgive me for this briefest "Hello". I love you, Darling, but I've got to run. I just finished a 10 hour case (laparotomy, craniectomy, multiple debridements) and I'm quite tired. Nothing else is new, except that the dust storm we were having turned out to be a hurricane. I wonder if you read anything about it? It was really an experience. The front wall, of our hooch, almost blew down before we could barricade it up. I was ready to put all of my stuff in my suitcase, and trunk, for fear the front wall would go down.

I'm working on the second side of the tape now. I'll tell you about the case, on the tape, in the morning. I got all those magazines and much of it looks interesting. Thanks for sending them.

Darling, be happy, rejoice in our love, our future and our children. Won't it be great just to always have one another? Not just a companion, but somebody you especially like, somebody who evokes love in you? I do.

That's how I feel about you. Jon

(2nd letter)

Dearest Wonderful Wife,

Got a real happy letter, from you, today. I'm glad that you got an "A" in your course. You did the vast majority of the work, but I'm glad to have had a chance to make at least a small contribution. I'm, also, glad you got the tape. You have never mentioned making me one, but I hope one is on the way. I'm about three-fourths of the way through with the 2-sided 40 minute tape I'm making now. Also, you know how happy I would be to receive some pictures.

I was very disappointed with the rated input of our speakers (4 watts). They will have to serve as a second set of speakers, say for the bedroom. For $32-$34, I can get a good set of speakers that have a watt input of 15-20 watts which would really make a hell of a lot of noise. It is hard to believe that the watt input was low. Please send me the model number or type, as soon as possible, and I will double check it. The model number or type is probably somewhere, on the speaker, near the name Panasonic.

It is very nice that Harbor General Hospital accepted me, but all it really does is make Columbia Presbyterian Hospital much harder to accept. I still think we will go to Columbia, but I sure have my misgivings.

Thank you for making a package for the O.R. tech.

The craniectomy that we did, last night, is doing really well. Nice to have a big case pull through.

I got a haircut today. As soon as my moustache is full, I'll send you a polaroid shot of me. Tomorrow is payday. I'll be sending you lots of money soon.

Sherrie, what has happened? I've been back 2 weeks, from the ship, and no food has come. Help, I'm starving!

Think of you all the time, Honey. I love you very deeply. I hope you know that.

Jonny

My Dearest Darling,

Today, I hit the lowest point I've ever been at since being in Vietnam. I'm very depressed and it is because I have nothing to do. There's no work to do. Day in and day out, since the lull in the fighting, we have nothing to do. So, I've decided to transfer out of here and try to get into a place where they are doing elective cases. Tomorrow, I'm going to Da Nang to talk to Group Command about the possibility of going to an evacuation hospital in either Chu Lai or Da Nang. Of course, I'll let you know what happens. I may not be able to get a flight, to Da Nang, tomorrow. But, I've made up my mind to get out of here.

I'm glad you got the binoculars and tapes. Also, that you feel you are getting something out of running. I run twice a day here and I'm running really well right now. Please, please, please, Sherrie send pictures and a tape.

Tonight, I finished reading Erskine Caldwell's novel "Georgia Boy". It was ok.

I love you very much, Sherrie. Please don't worry about me. I'm pretty depressed, right now, but I'm sure I'll rationalize my way out of this depression. Just as I always do.

All my love, Darling. Jonny

Dearest Most Precious Sherrie,

Today, I got your "care" package (I put it in quotes because it is one of the few ways that you can take care of me). Now, don't forget pictures and a tape. The package was a really good one. Thanks a lot.

Today, I went to Da Nang and spoke to the people there about moving. Without going into the pros and cons, of each hospital in Vietnam, let me just say for the moment that the places I could possibly go to will be told to me on August 5th. Then, depending on whether I want to go there or not, I will accept or not. Tonight, when I came "home" (to the 18th Surgical Hospital), everybody wanted to know if I was going for good or not. It made me feel badly because the implication was that they wanted me to stay. At Da Nang, they had me listed as fully trained because of the reports coming out of here that a fully trained person was unnecessary because I was here. I corrected that, to my disadvantage, because I didn't want to operate under false pretenses. Tonight, the O.R. techs held a party (drinking) for one of the guys leaving. Since I'm popular among them, and I work so closely with them (I'm really their final authority, although I try to give as few direct orders as possible), they insisted that I come down and toast the guy who's leaving. So, I did. I got smashed.

When you make reservations, for "The New Otani Hotel", make them for the cheapest price ($13.40 per day). As long as I'm with you, I feel everything will be alright. You are all I want. I'm glad you got your wallet back. The *description of the robbery and it's recovery were in 2 letters (from you) that I received today. Honey, I love you very much. I wish you could feel the ache, for a moment, so you would know.*

Always yours, Jonny

8/02/69
Letter 154

My Very Dearest Darling,

I'm a very tired guy right now. I had 2 cases, today, but one was 10 hours. I "done good", though, so I have a sense of satisfaction. I was supposed to play pinochle, again tonight, with the Commanding Officer of the hospital (he's a really great guy). I hope I can keep my eyes open. We got no mail, tonight, because we are still in the middle of a typhoon. Man, is it ever raining hard.

Right now, I'm listening to one of our tapes. On one side is a Hootenanny and on the other side is the Serendipity Singers. The song on, right now, is on the Hootenanny side and it is "Sing Hallelujah". It's really good. We'll have so much fun listening to these tapes, especially you, since you have never heard them. And, the stereo sound is just something else. For a couple like us, who is used to monoaural records, we're doing ok.

Tomorrow, I'm third call. Unless I'm called for blocks (etc), I should have plenty of free time. I am determined to get some pictures for you.

My Darling Sweetheart, I love you so very much.

Jonny

Dearest, Dearest Sherrie,

Well, tonight, I have something to write about. That doesn't mean the letter will be longer, but at least more interesting. The day started, and continued, as all the others. It was hot, dull and frustrating. I went to the Post Office and got the $400 in money orders that are included with this letter. Then came the mail. There were 2 wonderful letters, from you, which included the information on the speakers (model number). So, I can double check the watt input. Plus, I got a letter from Dr. Papper which included the following quoted paragraph: "We do not require the signing of contracts for our positions here (that is class, first class). It is sufficient, for you, to state in the letter that you accept the residency appointment (which I have already done) that I have offered to you. The salary schedules as of now are: $10,500 for the 1st year, $11,000 for the 2nd year and $11,500 for the 3rd year. It will be good to have you in this department." Isn't the salary fantastic? With the GI bill, which gives us $175 per month (tax free), we'll be rich. Also, I got a booklet on the Anesthesia Department there which should make very interesting reading. It looks as if a tremendous amount of things are going on there.

After the mail came in, I got a case (which is unusual) and which I enjoyed. Also, today, the pharmacy guy made me 3 tapes which included: The Sounds of Motown, The Supremes, The Mamas and the Papas, Glen Campbell, The Youngbloods, Creedence Clearwater Revival and The Rascals. Tomorrow, he's making me 2 more tapes.

Honey, why haven't you made me a tape? You have the recorder. You are not that self-conscious. Please Sherrie, anything will be warmly and lovingly received. You know that I play your old one over and over.

I'm glad that your parents are running. It should do them a world of good.

Well, tomorrow, I get an answer on the possibilities of moving. The 18th Surgical Hospital is probably going to move just South of the DMZ in October.

Honey, I love you with all my soul and being.

Jonny

8/05/69
Letter 156

Dearest Beloved Sherrie,

First off, let me tell you that I love you and am tingling with anticipation over the possible arrival of your tape tomorrow. Your letter, today, said you mailed it the following morning. I hope pictures will follow soon. I'm sure your orange and white dress will be every bit as good as your light blue and white dress (which I like very much) that you made.

The Major, who was supposed to come up here to let me know what possibilities were available for a move, couldn't come today. He was sick, so I have nothing further to add to the situation except that I have reduced the number of places I would go to. There's only one place and it is Chu Lai. It has cases, better living facilities, a beach and it is not as dangerous as here.

I would very much like for you to send me the pamphlets and information that came with the speakers. I need to check out exactly what I bought. I think the 4 watt input must refer to the minimum number of watts needed to hear the speakers. I need to know the maximum number of watts the speakers can handle in order that we buy a tuner-amplifier that won't blow out our speakers. Ok? Send me the stuff, Honey.

Next, I got 3 more tapes done today. The partial list includes: The Serendipity Singers, The Supremes, Marvin Gaye, Tammi Terrell, Four Seasons, and others.

I am basically glad that you saved $5 on the customs issue. But, I am dying to know what package arrived. In the future, if the customs charge is under $10, pay it. It probably is the tape deck since it is a relatively expensive item ($115) or the camera ($50). Incidentally, when you take the camera in to be fixed, tell the repair person it is the gear or the spring on the lever (which moves the film ahead to the next frame) that is broken. Got that?

I'm glad you are happy over the coming change in your working hours. The money you make on private duty won't hurt either.

You know that I haven't written a single letter to anybody, other than you, since I have been back? I think I wrote Des once and maybe Greg. I just don't have the heart. I'm keeping a stiff upper lip, but sometimes I get scared that I'm not going to make it. Sometimes, I can't see my way to the end. I'm doing ok by taking each day, as it comes, and fighting it right there on the spot. But, it is too hard to think ahead more than a day. Because more often, than not, I can't see my way through the gap to the future. Understand? I never forget you. And, my feeling of love for you is constantly with me. I know deep down that is what will get me through. But, it is the details of getting through that is hard for me to cope with more than a day at a time.

All my love which is deep and warm and everlasting. Jonny

Dearest Darling,

Hi Starshine. I got your tape, today, and it was beautifully expressive. And, your singing was outstanding. I really enjoyed hearing it and felt your love pour from the tape. I must have played it 3 or 4 times already. I think you must have an idea how much something like the tape means to me, so I won't belabor the point. I just want to say that I mean it.

Last night, a patrol stepped into a booby trap and we ran 3 operating rooms most of the night. I enjoyed working, for once, but I hate to see these guys all busted up.

I read through the Columbia Presbyterian Hospital Anesthesia Department's pamphlet that Dr. Papper sent to me. The stuff going on there is fantastic. I really got excited about some of the work going on, and more so, since I'll be in on it. Boy, am I ever going to have credentials coming from Columbia and maybe a year at Massachusetts General (in Boston). Then, we can pick our spot on the West Coast, Honey. I'll get a good job anywhere.

Last night, our perimeter was attacked. Another 4th of July with rockets going off everywhere. Quite a show.

Honey, I've decided on what date we are going on our R&R. Or, at least what day I'm going to ask for (usually they give you within a week of what you ask for). I'm asking for November 15th. Now, take it easy, I know you are disappointed. But, let me explain. I see, around me, about 6 guys who have less than 60 days to go and it is by far the worst time for them. Everybody is emphatic about their advice to me. They say: "Take your R&R as late as possible."

And, that is what I'm going to do. I'll be coming back here on November 23rd or so. That will leave me 40 or 50 days before I then start the trip home. I can accept that. Three months is a long time to wait, but I'm trying to make the best of a very bad situation.

I miss you terribly. Honey, I want to be with you more than anything else. I'm doing better now. In fact, I've decided against moving from here. I'll stick it out here, even if we go to the DMZ. I'll be moving into the "Super Hooch" in 16 days. It has everything (a sink, big hot plates, toaster, etc).

As you must have realized, by now, my tape isn't much longer than 30 minutes. I think your gift to Rachel is just another expression, or reflection, of the beautiful person you are. It's silly to thank a person for being naturally wonderful, so I'll thank God. I do thank God for letting me have you. Sherrie, you are the most wonderful person in the whole wide world.

In your next package, please include bread, baggies, hot dogs, salami, canned beef stew, canned meatballs and mustard. If one isn't on the way, send one off soon. Mike Brenner got your package. Thanks a lot. What can I say? Honey, you're the greatest!

I love you so deeply. I'm very happy loving you.

Jonny

My Dearest Darling,

I received 2 letters, from you, today. I was delighted and desperate as always for your letters, but they certainly didn't convey the feeling that you are doing very well. I hope you have been able to resolve your depression by the time you get this letter. Perhaps the tape helped. You know that I share your feelings about our separation. Every day, I discover more fully that I love you. Honey, everything that I have is for you. I'm so sorry for the loneliness that you feel. I hope you find comfort in knowing that, when I come home, I'll always try to love and care for you and our children.

As far as going to Hue (which is 10 miles away), I haven't gone yet. There have not been enough cases lined up, on the planned O.R. day, to make it worth my while to go there yet. I suspect it may turn out to be about once every 2 months.

Honey, I just spoke to Doug. And, the idea popped into my head that maybe when you are feeling bad you can call Doug's wife. Her name is Jan Patton. Remember the card she sent you? She is in the same boat as you and you might enjoy talking over your mutual problems. I very much want the best for you.

I missed writing you, yesterday, because I did 3 big cases. I was very sorry, I meant to write you. I got back to my hooch at 4 AM. I thought I would get up in time to get a letter off, to you, before the mail went out at 10 AM. But, I overslept. All 3 cases did fine. And, I was happy to do the work.

I've started another program to study a little bit each day. I think I'll be able to stick to it. I would like you to buy a copy of the book "Aerobics" and send our old copy back to me. I have the Commanding Officer running every day and I want him to read the book.

Today, I got the last tape recorded that I wanted. I have 11 tapes here (3 hours each) and I believe that I sent 6-7 home. That is plenty. Plus, we'll have a lifetime of recording whatever records we want.

Did you get the allotment, the $400 in money orders, the tape deck, the camera and the "Goodman and Gilman" book?

Darling, I hope you realize how much I want you to be happy. And, how much I care for you because I love you very much. I do, I do, I do.

Honey, I love you. Jonny

Dearest Darling Sherrie,

Again, I must be brief, because I'm very tired. I worked all day in the O.R. (six cases). I'm not complaining, mind you. It makes the time fly, but I'm pooped out. I didn't get a letter, today, and I was really disappointed. Fortunately, several cases came in and it made me forget. I'm telling you, if those cases hadn't come in, I would have put on some kind of drunk (or something). I really need your letters.

Enclosed is a copy of an exchange of messages (first from the Commanding Officer of the ship to the Commanding Officer here and then vice versa). I feel rewarded. You might send these messages, to my parents, but please request that they return them to you. Honey, I hope you completed those pictures. Oh Sherrie, I miss you so much. So much more than I can find the words to express.

I love you very, very much. Jonny

Dearest Cherished Sherrie,

After I wrote you last night, tired as I was, I then had it really socked to me. For the rest of the night, until 12 noon, I worked steadily in the O.R. What made this second push sort of bizarre was that it was a direct result of our own hospital being hit with rockets. When they hit, I happened to be on one of the wards. I was seeing a few patients after mailing you your letter and just before I thought I would go to bed. All of a sudden it was boom, boom, boom. Something I'll never forget. I and some of the other Docs (John Flora, Doug Patton) and the O.R. techs put all of the patients on the floor. Then, the cases started coming in from all areas around the hospital. Many were from our own unit. I knew most of the people hurt. I'm telling you this, Honey, very matter of fact because honestly this is the way I feel about it. I feel no fear. I just can't seem to be scared at something I can't see. I want very much for you to accept this in the same way. Please Darling, don't worry. It's like I told you before, the only way I'm going to get it is if a rocket comes down on my head. You can die a thousand deaths if you are afraid and worry too much before anything has happened. This goes for you, too. Be brave. I felt I could tell you because you are a strong girl. And, I want very much to share my thoughts and feelings with you especially when something momentous or unusual like this happens. OK, Honey? I have a lot of trust and faith in you. And, that you will accept things as I do, so I can share everything with you. Remember, no fear, no worry. There is not much either of us can do about anything except pull together. I was really exhausted from all the cases, but I need the work to take my mind off time. August has gone by pretty quickly, so far. I've already done 50 cases this month.

I got 2 letters from you, today, which was great. I'm glad you like the day shift in the Chronic Dialysis Unit. I hope you get the tennis class. Then, you will really be good. Oh yes, I don't remember whether I told you, but I especially enjoyed your singing on the last tape. You sing really well.

I don't remember having said that "I wish you could experience for a moment the aching I have in my heart for you". But, if I did, it's true. I don't mean that you don't feel the same thing, for I know you do. I just want you to know that I, too, feel the same way about you (as you do about me). This is getting complicated.

Very simply put, I love you very, very much Darling. Jonny

Dearest, Dearest, Dearest,

Hi Honey. Today, I had a rest from cases (only one short one today) and I sunbathed and fell asleep outside. Now, I'm ready to go again tomorrow. Fortunately, I got a letter from you today which is important. On the days when I don't do anything, I usually plan everything around mail call (eating, running, napping, reading, etc).

I'll have to object to your calculation of what I'll be making, per month, as a first-year resident. The first year's salary is $10,500 (which equals $875 per month). Think about it. Plus, we'll get an additional $175 per month with the GI bill. So, our monthly total will be $1050.

I'm concerned about the delivery of the packages I sent you. There are 3, that I think are still unaccounted for, which contain the: tape deck, camera, tapes, "Goodman and Gilman" book and blood pressure cuff. If you don't hear from the Customs Office, by the time you get this letter, pay the $5 and take the package home.

Honey, I'm glad you got the $400 in money orders.

I, too, think we have a very wonderful future to look forward to. Most important is that we will be together. But, we sure have a lot of wonderful things to experience and grow through together.

I love you very much and treasure you more than anything else (much, much more).

All my love and thoughts, Jonny

Dearest Pumpkinette Tinker-Belle,

Well, today, was another slow one. I read a science fiction book (pretty good), studied, ran 2 times, sunbathed and made myself a real feast for supper (salami sandwich, vegetable soup and a coke). Last night's supper was really delicious. I made pea soup with chunks of salami in it. It was really delicious. Why don't you start making a list of things that I like to eat? Then, you won't be so distraught when you try to plan a meal. You have my permission to put down pea soup with salami or hot dog chunks, in it, made thickly. Ok? Honey, you are such a good cook! If you make me that, you'll get a kiss in the kitchen.

Next payday (August 31), I am loaning most of the money

I get (about $460) to Dan because he is going to Hong Kong on September 1st. He's going there for a week, on leave, and then to Sydney, Australia on September 11th for R&R. He needs the money. He will pay me back when we get paid on September 30th. He is going home on October 9th. And, many others (Woody, John Flora, Sam Clark, Doug Patton, and Dan) are going home by the middle of October. In a week, I'll be living in the Super Hooch with Woody. When they leave, in October, I'll then be the one who has the most time in-country (who is still here). It hurts so much to see them go. They mean so much to me. And, they are so necessary to get through the day, to have a laugh with, etc. Especially Woody and John Flora. They are my best friends and I think I will keep in contact with them for a long time. Tomorrow, I'm first call. And, I pray that I work and work hard. The time goes by, so much faster, when I do.

I'm looking for your pictures, every day, in the mail. Looks like I should get them pretty soon. Oh Sherrie, I dream about you all the time. I day dream about watching you cook, you falling asleep on my lap and holding and playing with our baby (that is one of my favorites). The pictures should feed my imagination.

Well, not much else to report except that I love you very, very much. I miss you greatly and cherish the memory of you as much as my own life.

All my love, Jonny

Dearest Sherrie,

I'm pretty depressed, right now, as I always am after I get your pictures. It reminds me of how much I'm missing. You looked very lovely in every respect. I must admit that at times, like this, I'm pretty vulnerable to little petty considerations. Like, why did you send only 14 of the 20 pictures that you shot? Were 6 of them bad? Whose pool were in 2 of them? Whose hat were you wearing? Yours? Maureen's? I like it very much. Where did you get that little cover-up for your bathing suit? I like it. Your letter, today, sounded sort of short, hurried and a little flat. I feel pretty shaky, tonight, for some reason. We are on a red emergency alert, for a ground attack, but this is nothing new. We've had such alerts before and I felt very calm. Tonight, I feel funny. Maybe it's because I feel depressed and alone. I don't know. At least, I have you to talk to. I wish I was with you. Tonight, everybody has to wear helmets, flak jackets and carry weapons. We even have to give passwords, at certain points, around the hospital and the hooches (in order to be allowed to pass). I just feel spooky. Maybe because of the pictures, I feel I have so much to lose. Maybe because I lie around all day doing nothing. Today, I had 2 short cases. Oh well, tomorrow's a new day. And, someday, I'll be able to go home. I think I have 148 days to go when I wake up in the morning. I'll make it.

I treasure your pictures and the memory of you. Just think how much I treasure and love the real you if memories and pictures can mean so much.

Jonny

Dearest Sherrie,

Now, I'm really messed up. Another day with nothing to do, it's hot, no water for a shower and now (just a few minutes ago), no mail for me. I couldn't believe it. There was a big fat pack of letters and not one was for me. Man, if I needed a letter, I needed it tonight. I've been looking at your pictures every hour on the hour since I got them. You are so beautiful. I'll just have to be a big boy and wait until tomorrow.

I started another tape today. It won't make you laugh, I'm sure, but at least I do talk on the tape for all it's worth. I've been out in the sun so much that I'm getting very dark. I try my best to read and study as much as my depression will allow. I don't do much, but every little bit helps. I'm anxious to know that all the packages, I sent home, arrived. I try to be patient, until I get word from you, but sometimes I forget that it takes close to 2 weeks to get an answer to a question I ask.

Again Sherrie, I regret that I haven't had much to say. I would suppose that, when one tells someone that they love them, it is far more meaningful if the spokesman is happy inside. Well, I'm not happy. But, I hope you'll accept and understand my love for you, is felt by me, to be deep, soulful and lasting.

Jonny

8/19/69
Letter 165

My Very Dearest Sweetheart,

Would you believe that after getting pretty well smashed last night, and going to bed at 2:30 AM, I set the alarm clock for 9 AM? I did that just so I could get up, and write you a letter, so at least you would have something for the day. I really wasn't that drunk last night. Don't worry. I'm doing much better than my last 2 letters have indicated. I've gained some understanding of why I get so depressed. Plus, I got 2 wonderful love-filled letters from you. I'm going to write you a very long letter, tonight, explaining my failure to write you at the usual time last night. No, I'll go ahead and tell you briefly now. At the time I usually write you, our Officers' Club had a meeting. I didn't get back to the hooch sober enough to write a decent letter. I have so much to tell you tonight. Believe me, wait for the next letter.

Darling, I love you with all my heart and soul.

Jonny

8/20/69
Letter 166

Dearest Darling Sherrie,

Well, I hope this letter is not a disappointment to you after my letter of last night. I simply don't have much to tell you about. Today was quiet, no cases. Although, I had one case from 2 AM to 5 AM last night which ruined a good night's sleep. I read, sunbathed, ran, looked at your pictures several times over and played your singing tape for Woody. I'm very proud of you. You know that, don't you?

I found out, today, that I originally put down New York as my home of record (for the Army). That is terrific, because no matter where we go (after the Army), the Army will transport our stuff for free to New York. If my home of record was listed as Los Angeles, then we would have to pay for the shipping to New York. They only ship, to the home of record, from the last assignment. Well, that being the case, I have decided to make out our "dream sheets" because nobody believes they even look at it. I'm, also, going to personally write the office of the Surgeon General and ask for my preferences. Also, I'm going to write our Congressman to ask him to request my preferences for me. I need you to send me the name and address (etc) of our Congressman, in Los Angeles, as soon as possible. I've decided to ask for the following: (1) Fort Ord- no explanation necessary. (2) Fort Carson in Colorado Springs, Colorado - it has skiing, beauty, weather, nice area, plus Doug and Woody will be there. (3) Fitzsimmons in Denver, Colorado - beautiful area, skiing, plus other sports. (4) Madigan in Seattle, Washington - in the Spring it's supposed to be great. All 4 are big, modern places. Ok? Now watch, we'll get sent to Louisiana or Mississippi.

I have an apology to make to you. I just had one of those big hot dogs you sent. They're delicious and very good. Send more. I'm low on food now. I would think a package every 2½ weeks would be about right.

Tomorrow, I move into the Super Hooch. No mail tonight. I looked at your pictures.

Honey, I love you very much. You are with me, in my soul, all the time. I never thank God for much, but I thank him for you. Jonny

8/21/69
Letter 167

Dearest Darling,

Today, I moved into the Super Hooch and I'm now the proud owner of a million things (toaster, broiler, pots, skillet and on and on). I have everything, except happiness. I am completely surrounded by your pictures. And, I have a beautiful desk, tape deck (Woody's) and my tapes. I have just everything, except I didn't get any mail again tonight. Well, tomorrow, I should get at least 2 letters. It took me all day to move into the Super Hooch. Without going into detail, I am 50% more comfortable than before. Tomorrow holds the promise of, at least, one case. Woody scheduled an elective case. John Flora goes home in 2 days. It hurts to see him go.

I'll be needing some food shortly. I hope something is on its way. At present, I have plenty of canned fruits, so when you get this letter stop including the canned fruits. Use the space, in the packages, for hot dogs, canned meatballs, beef stew, salami and peas. Ok, Honeybunch? Gee, I wish I had gotten a letter today.

Right now, I have 146 days to go. And, 80 days (or so) until I see you. I'll put in my application about 60 days before November 15th and I should get word late in October. Then, I'll call you to let you know the exact date and give you the go ahead on reservations, etc. Often, it is plus or minus 7 days of what you asked for.

Following John Flora's call, you will probably hear from Doug, Dan and Woody. I think you'll enjoy talking to them.

Honeybunch, I'm going to try to draft a letter to the Surgeon General now, requesting a good assignment. Wish us luck.

All my love and thoughts always and strong, Jonny

Dearest Sherrie,

I'm sorry that all I can say, today, is that I love you. We have been very busy all day, and night, today. As I sit here in the O.R. with one more case to do, I know that I won't have the energy to write when I get back to my hooch.

I got a nice letter, from you, today. I would like you to bring the dress you are making, for Maribeth's wedding, to Tokyo. I'm sure you'll look lovely as you do in everything you wear. I'll take you out for a real romantic candle-lit dinner.

John Flora left today. We had some nice words for one another. I look forward to having you meet him in the future. I respect him a great deal as a physician and person. He is not a funny guy, just sincere and has a lot of depth. Too bad you missed Rich Anderson.

I love you very much and think about you all the time. I'm obsessed with my obsession of you.

Jonny

My Dearest Beloved One,

I negotiated, fairly well, today. But, I feel a bad depression coming on. Fortunately, it's 9 PM and I'm currently writing to you which certainly serves as a windfall. I did 2 cases, today, and was doing fine until a little while ago. I sort of looked around and saw the hopelessness of the situation here (heat, dirt, attacks, Army organization and administration, loneliness). I think I have a pretty small list of things I hate (ignorance from an intelligent person and prejudice). But, you can add the Army to my list.

Sam Clark got his assignment, today, for back in the world. Would you believe that they assigned him to an administrative job as Commanding Officer of Clinics at Fort Benning in Georgia? Here is a guy who took his residency in the Army, likes and loves to do surgery, is a good surgeon and likes teaching and research. And, they put him behind a desk. He has 3 years to go. Thank God, I'll be free in August 1970. The love and happiness I will feel, when I am back with you, will make any place we go for my last 6 months bearable. I could go anywhere as long as I have you. I'm just glad I will have only 6 months.

I got the letter, today, in which you included my Grandma's letter. Thanks.

Honey, I think those Royal Canadian Air Force exercises are supposed to be good. I think many guys here do them. What do you have to do? I'm sure they are of benefit. Remember, though, you have to give a lot to anything to get a lot out of it.

Sherrie, I'm going to close now before I get morbid. I'll make out alright. I have a lot of pressure, on me, right now. We have enough cases. I'm, also, taking care of 3 GIs and 1 Vietnamese child. All of them are on ventilators. I can't seem to relax. I'd just cry, with happiness, to be with you. If I could only have you.

I do love you, understand? Jonny

8/25/69
Letter 170

My Dearest Darling,

I'm afraid this will have to be short, again. If I thought I was busy before, I'm really worked to the bone now. At 5 PM, a guy came in who I gave 40 units of blood to and resuscitated twice through cardiac arrests. This was all before the case began. We decided not to operate at all. Right now (at 12 AM), he's on the ward and he's doing pretty well. We will try to stabilize him, through the night, and do his surgery in the morning. Maybe a miracle will happen and he will live through the night, have his surgery in the morning and see some degree of happiness in the future. He probably will lose one leg. I hope he can keep the other leg. I gave him every drug in the book. I'd list them, but I don't have the energy. I am so tired.

I'm looking at 10 of your pictures with your pretty smiling face and your lovely figure. I'm literally crying, inside, with a desire and need for you. I want you so badly.

I'm sorry if I made an issue of the reception you gave the arrival of money from me. I'm an ass and I'm sorry for being so. I think you know how much I respect you. I really do. You've been terrific. Here is an example: All the guys tremble at the idea that their wives will have to take care of moving their household goods, for the family, before the guys get back home. I don't, I really don't. You're smart, efficient, beautiful and honest. I know you'll probably do a better job, with more concern, than I would. I'd trust you with anything. So, you'll have to do the forgiving, ok?

Dan will be coming, to California, for a visit. When, I don't know. Perhaps, on his 30 day leave, when he gets home in October. This wasn't so short, was it, Baby?

I LOVE YOU! Jonny

8/26/69
Letter 171

My Dearest Honeybunch,

Today, I got a very loving letter, from you, in response to a letter I must have written expressing many insecurities. What can I say, except to thank you for always being so loving and reassuring.

Today, I fought, sweat and prayed for life in my very ill patient. We got him through last night and even 5 hours of surgery today. But, tonight, he is in renal shut down (probably secondary to intravascular hemolysis). I'm taking him to the ship, in a few minutes, on a midnight helicopter ride. Kind of wild and dramatic, but necessary. The ship can do electrolytes, has a kidney machine or can even do peritoneal dialysis (for which he is a good candidate). We have none of this. Otherwise, he is in good shape (heart, lungs, etc).

Today, we were notified that we will not be going to the

DMZ for at least 6 months. This is good because I'll be gone if, and when, the hospital does move.

I got the hot dogs. Thanks. We've got a fair amount of food. Send a package about every 3 weeks.

The war seems to be picking up. I've been so busy that I've only been able to run once a day. As a matter of fact, I have to go to the ship now.

I love you very much, my Darling. I cried a tear or two when I read your letter today.

Jonny

My Very Dearest Sherrie,

Right now, I'm listening to the tape "Lots of Lettermen" that I sent home to you. Woody has the same tape and it's beautiful. They sing Righteous Brothers' songs, just great. I have a drink and I'm talking to you, loving you very much. I'm sort of happy, in a melancholy way. Melancholy because I miss you. Woody is making us a spaghetti and meatball supper, right now. I just took a shower after running. Ah yes, there are moments when I'm content, but they are few and I miss you so much.

Today, I was pretty busy. I only had one case, but I was very busy with a patient of mine. He is a 10 year old Vietnamese boy who had swallowed DDT (4 days ago). He has been in a coma, on a ventilator and had 2 arrests. I did a tracheostomy, on him, this morning. Then, I decided to take him to the ship because I can't follow him any longer with the difficulty that I have in getting blood gases and chemistries done. While I was on the ship (both last night and today), the helicopter that took me waited for me so that I didn't get stranded there. I'm a "VIP". I found out that the guy (patient) that I took out to the ship last night is doing very well. Maybe we saved him. He got 83 units of blood. He may keep both legs.

I'm sorry to report that I haven't made any progress on the tape I started several days ago. I have been so busy. But, I'll try to get with it. Please have patience. That's something that I seem to lack.

One of the reasons I have been so busy is because we are down to very few Docs. We normally should have about 12 Docs. Now, we have only 7. None are General Medical Officers or Internists. So, I'm helping out with Medicine Clinic. That takes a couple of hours in the morning. Doug (a Surgeon), the hospital Commanding Officer and the Radiologist, also, all help out. Pretty soon, we should get some help from the tremendous influx of Docs, that will come in September, from Fort Sam Houston in Texas. Remember being there? Think how happy we were there (swimming, eating out together, watching movies, being friends and of course, expressing our love).

I'm glad you like the tape deck. I agree that we will get much enjoyment from it. Let's have a good party some night listening to a real good tape, ok? Of course, we will get a turntable. The beauty, of a tape deck, is that you can record any album you want from the turntable.

I'm very happy to hear that you have an energetic, optimistic and positive attitude towards going to New York. I feel very strong with you at my side.

Well, Honey, the spaghetti is ready. So, I'm going to close. Not that the spaghetti is more important than you. I know you wouldn't want me to miss it .

I love you very much, my Darling. As I have said before,

to you, I often wondered (in the past) if I was capable of feeling love for somebody. Now that I do, you are the object of that love. I am very happy to discover that I can feel love, "true love". And, I'm simply thankful that you exist to make me feel the love.

Jonny

8/28/69
Letter 173

Sherrie Sweetheart,

I got a very loving letter, from you, today. Your letters are such bright spots in my day. Before I answer your letter, I'll tell you briefly about my day. Not that there is much to tell, but that is the usual format of my letters. Today was a quiet restful day, no cases. I laid out in the sun and read in the afternoon. In the morning, I saw a few patients in Medicine Clinic. Tomorrow, I definitely have one case to do which should be interesting. It will involve the use of a slightly different nerve block. Different than I have been doing, since coming back from the ship. Dan came back from an in-country R&R to Da Nang. And, he goes tomorrow to Hong Kong for leave. Then, he comes back for a couple of days and then goes again for R&R to Sydney, Australia. Then, he'll be back again for a few days and then he goes home. Looks like his last month is going to pass rather quickly. Woody goes on leave, to Hong Kong, in a couple of days (he has had his R&R). But, not to meet his wife. Mainly, he's going just to get out of here, shop and get clean.

I've pretty well allocated out all the equipment that came from the 22nd Surgical Hospital. Right now, I'm listening to that Lettermen tape, waiting for Woody to fix supper which will be Rice-a-Roni plus 2 of the beef stew cans you sent. Sounds great, huh? I'm reading the book "To Brooklyn With Love". It is the story of one day in the life of Albert Abrams who is 12 years old, Jewish and lives in Brooklyn, New York. You would enjoy it. My boyhood was similar, except that I was the best in athletics and street games. Whereas, Albert is the worst.

The newest rumor is that we are going to the DMZ, in 60 days. I give up! Every day it changes. I'm just going to forget, about it, until something actually happens.

I'm very sorry to hear that your Sundays are so empty. Maybe you could call on Madeleine and Greg? Private duty cases kill 2 birds with 1 stone. You can make money and keep busy. I hope very much that you aren't too unhappy. Maybe you could kill a few hours, here and there, studying about New York. Go to the AAA office and get a map of the city and its subway system. You can familiarize yourself with them. You could make up a long list of places you would like to see (etc) and then we could develop a plan to knock them off weekend by weekend. In fact, you could look up where they are and plan for 2-3 things to do in 1 day in 1 area. That would seem to be fun as well as useful and helpful.

Oh Honey, I want to make you happy very much, of course. I'll teach you to play pinochle.

I love you a great deal, Honeybunch. I'm getting "short". Sometimes I feel the birth of a little thrill, come in me, at the thought of going home. But, I kill it as soon as possible. I would go crazy if I let it grow, because I don't think I could live with the frustration of my unsatisfied desire for you.

All my love and thoughts,

Jonny

Dearest Darling Sherrie,

If nothing else, I got through today. I did one case, during the afternoon, and we had a small 4-5 hour push tonight. So, part of the day went quickly anyway. I got a letter, from you, describing your last Sunday. I was relieved to know that it passed without too much torment. Too bad you didn't get a private duty case.

There is more and more talk of us going to the DMZ (Quang Tri) in late October or early November. Guess it's true.

Honey, I'm very sorry that this is so short, but I have another case. Well, I have to go now. I'll be getting very little sleep. I'm going to send this off so at least you get something.

I love you very much, Darling. I love you more than anything else in the world.

Jonny

My Darling Sherrie,

Hi Sweetheart, I'm a day closer to you. Today was fair. I did a great nerve block (one case), today, which made the afternoon pass. Now, it's 8:30 PM. And, I have to hurry a bit. Steve Lipson is President (of the Officers' Club) and I'm Vice

President. We have designated Saturday nights (8:30 PM-11:30 PM) as Happy Hour and all drinks are 10 cents each. And, I should be there to inaugurate the Happy Hour.

Today, I met our new Nurse Anesthetist (a female Major) and I was pleased with her. She seems pleasant and I think realizes her limitations. She's willing to learn, so I think it will be alright.

Tonight, I asked one of the Nurses (who has a polaroid camera) to shoot a couple of shots of me for you. I hope she remembers to bring it to Happy Hour, if she comes. If not, I'll get some for you tomorrow.

I did write my parents about my Mom's eyesight. I guess she is getting old.

I love you with all my heart and soul, Darling. I miss you very much. I think of you all the time.

Jonny

My Precious Sherrie,

Today, wasn't too bad. I had 2 cases and never got to the point where I got depressed. Unfortunately, I didn't get any mail today. So, I'm a little hard-pressed for things to write about. Let's see, last night Happy Hour was ok. I got involved in a 3 hour pinochle game, so I didn't get around to do much drinking. I'm definitely getting to the point where I need some more pictures. Please try, ok? I didn't get any pictures taken last night. The Nurse forgot her camera. But, I'll get some in the next day or two. I would, tonight, but I just finished a case and it's 11 PM. Tomorrow, ok? I heard from John Stevens, a few days ago, as well as from the Ezras.

Honey, I've written you pretty good, haven't I? I haven't missed writing to you more than 7 days. Did you ever think I would write to you every day? Oh yes, what silverware do we have? We can buy silverware, in Tokyo, if we need it . I'm going to get you a nice winter coat, too. Also, some sort of fur piece. Boy, will you ever look classy. Married me for my money, eh?

I've decided to apply, for R&R, for November 1st. The reason is that the weather stands a good chance of being relatively warm. I was told that by the middle of November the temperature gets down to 40-50 degrees. I hope that we can get some 60 degree weather in the first week of November. That means we have 61 days to go before R&R. Not too bad.

Well Sweet-Bunchkins, I'll talk to you tomorrow. I love you very, very much. I think of you all the time.

Jonny

Love of My Life,

Sweetheart, you are a very precious wonderful girl. I love you very much and consider myself lucky to have you. I got 3 letters, from you, today. All of them were very loving. And, I got a letter from Norm (the guy who I called back home) who was here with me. I've been called for a case, just now, that will start in 20 minutes. So, I will write as much as I can in that time.

A couple of newsworthy (letter worthy) things happened today. I finally wrote to the Surgeon General (a good letter, I think) requesting the areas I told you about. I'm pretty lazy, but I finally got it done. Also, today, we had a show put on by a Korean rock group (with go-go girls, etc). It was fair. I had more fun watching the soldiers, and my friends, watch the show than I did watching the show myself.

This case coming up, now, is my second case today. Right now, we are in the midst of a good monsoon type rain. I had forgotten how hard, and long, it can rain here. Amazing.

About that slide, that I sent, it was taken when I was home. It's just a picture of some of the guys down by the sewage pool. I'm looking forward to your package, with the tape, with much anticipation.

I'm glad you are keeping track of our insurance. Outstanding! Did you increase our household insurance to $5000? I read, with interest, the information on the weather (in Japan) that you got. Pretty close to what I thought it would be. Remember, November 1st (give or take a few days). At a later date, I'll let you know about my clothes.

Sherrie, you know that you are the only true love of my life. Spiritually, I was a virgin when I met you. My love grows all the time for you. I can feel it, within myself, and it is a very beautiful feeling.

Jonny

9/03/69
Letter 178

Sherrie, My Only Love,

Hi Sweetheart, I'm very happy right now. Here's why. I got your package, today, with the tape. I have yet to listen to it because I'm waiting for some hot dogs and pea soup to cook (the combo is great). Then, I'll settle back and listen to my Darling talk to me. I thought that before I listen to your tape and eat, I'd tell you about the pictures I'm sending (I got 4 of myself today). I'm standing by my desk in the Super Hooch. Unfortunately, I'm standing directly in front of a dozen or so small pictures of you. You can see 2 of them peeking out from behind my left arm. The large one of you, on top of a mountain when we went skiing, is over my right shoulder. My wall locker is at the left of the picture which has 3 short-timer calendars on it. My tape recorder is at my right hip. If you look hard enough, long enough and in bright light, I think you can see that I'm looking for you 10,000 miles away. Now look closely, ok?

Honey, I've had a chance to listen to about 1/3 of your tape and it's just beautiful. I want to always save that first side. I'm closing, now, because we have about 8 hours of surgery to do right now. I've been in the Emergency Room for the last hour (it's 10 PM now), so I want to get this off to you. I'll be too tired later.

Darling, you express yourself beautifully. And, I'm frankly humbled by the richness and fullness of your feelings.

I love you with all my heart and soul. I really do.

Jonny

9/04/69
Letter 179

My Very Dearest Darling,

Since I wrote you, last night, I've gotten about 3 hours of sleep. We've been very, very busy and there is still a lot of fighting going on (even on our own perimeter). The big guns are pretty close, to my hooch, and they are giving me one hell of a headache. Steve Lipson, and I, lost a GI last night after we got him off the table alive (after 65 units of blood). He was so badly shot up. We got in 16 dead-on-arrival soldiers yesterday and today. Sherrie, I'm telling you, this war is bad. Things come down out of the sky, from nowhere, and blow your head off. Most of them have no chance to escape, no chance. They get it on the first rocket. The second and third rockets don't get you because you have a few seconds to hit the bunker.

I have listened to your whole tape and it is the most beautiful thing I have ever heard. I love you very much, Sherrie. I love you for what you are, who you are and for just being yourself. You're really tops, Honey, number one. I, also, got 2 very loving letters from you today. Too bad you got shut out of your psych class. I hope you get in. Are you going to take some other course? I'm very happy to hear that you got 2 cases of private duty to do ($80 can't hurt us). I hope some of it sees the bank. Did you get my August allotment?

The type of renal failure that we see is very different than what you see. It's too complicated to explain now. Our patient died after being on the ship 3 days. Very frustrating. I thought he would make it. Maybe I should have kept him, but I don't see how without any lab support. The latest word is that we are not going to the DMZ, until February, which means it won't affect me.

I got about halfway through a rather short tape for you (10 minutes per side). I hope to finish it in the next few days. I hope the photo, included, suffices for the time being. I'm not much to look at, but I do love you very much. I think I'm trying to give you the eye or something.

All my love, Jonny

9/05/69
Letter 180

Sweet Honey Pie,

Today was pretty slow. I'm on first call and had only one case, so far. But, it's getting dark now and that is when the fighting starts, rockets go off, etc. I got another very characteristically loving letter from you, today, which is very soothing and quieting to me. Guess I'm nervous. Tonight, the Officers' Club is having a meeting about our funds. I have to preside over the meeting which is in a half hour. I'm halfway through your tape that I'm making. I should be able to do some more after the meeting. I'm going to have to make this a little short, because I have to eat something before I go to the meeting (tuna fish sandwich and vegetable soup).

Today, I made out my application for R&R for November 1st and handed it in. I'll get an answer in a month. We should have no problem getting close to that date.

Honey, I'll give back every little bit of loving that you hand out on R&R. Gee, I love you so much Sherrie.

Only 56 days to R&R!

All my love, Jonny

9/06/69
Letter 181

My Precious Sherrie,

I narrowly escaped a near disaster, today, in the form of a depression. I was third call and I thought I was surely going to get depressed in the afternoon. I never have any trouble passing the mornings. I usually do the following: get up between 9-10 AM, run, shower, shave, read or study and then eat at 12-1 PM. Then, I have my problems. The whole afternoon and evening, what to do when I'm third call? Usually, when I'm first or second call, I get cases to fill in the time until 6 PM. That's when I get your letters, then run, write you, eat in the hooch (all this takes until about 10 PM), then have a couple of drinks in the Officers' Club or I'm in the O.R. all night. Well, today, I got 3 cases and they were very difficult blocks. All were successful. Boy, I'm glad they came up today. Now, it's 8 PM and I think I'll get through the day ok.

After I write you, I'm going to write letters to Dr. Papper (reaffirming my desire to come) and to Dr. Larkin (Harbor General) and Dr. Benson saying I'm not going to join their programs. Although, when I write to Dr. Larkin, I'm going to emphatically indicate that I'm interested in his hospital and would like to leave the door open for eventually joining his staff.

Last night, I was quite lonely. In my tape I described, to you, how meaningful listening to your tape for a second time was. I'll be getting my tape off to you in a day or two.

Dan just came back from Hong Kong. I spent a nice hour

with him. He sent our speakers home to you. They are real good speakers (cost=$34, watt input=32). They will really blow your mind.

I didn't get any mail, today, but I think I'll survive the disappointment (barely). My weight is 137-138 pounds and I feel better. The weather is pretty hot, again. There's lots of shooting, cases, alerts, issuing guns, etc. How I wish I were back in your arms again.

I love you very much, my Darling. Oh Sherrie, my heart leaps at the chance to make you happy in the future. You know what I was thinking today? I must get back to you.

Jonny

Precious Sweetheart,

Hi Tinkerbell, at least another day has passed if nothing else. Before I forget, I'd like to remind you of 2 things: (1) Please Honey, get some pictures of you to me. Send 2-3 in each letter, so I can get them over a period of time. (2) Remember to send your packages on a space available basis, not first class. It only takes a few more days to come that way and it's much cheaper. Ok, Sweetheart?

Doug leaves, tomorrow, and he will call you. I just read a letter from John Flora. I'm sort of disappointed because he wrote that he has been trying to call you, for days, and has not been able to reach you. Aren't you home at all? Sam Clark goes home in 4 days and he will call you, also. Woody who came back from leave, in Hong Kong, goes home in 14 days and he will call you. Dan goes home in 20 days and he'll call you, also. How I wish I could be the one calling.

I got 2 letters from you. Sounds like you're pretty involved with Maribeth's wedding. Also, sounds like you're pretty trim (107 pounds). That's pretty good. I doubt, right now, that I'll take a week to go to Hong Kong. But, I'll see how I feel after I see you in November. I'll decide after I've been back for a little while.

I love you! Sweetheart, you mean everything to me.

Jonny

Dearest Beautiful Sherrie,

Well, today, I was very sad. Doug left and I just bawled and bawled. I know it will be the same way when Woody goes. How I have depended on them. Fortunately I had a 5 hour case, with Steve Lipson, as soon as Doug left. It took my mind off his going. It was an interesting case, too. Wednesday night, Woody and I are cooking Sam Clark a goodbye spaghetti and meatball dinner. We are getting the stuff from the kitchen. Sam leaves on Thursday (in 3 days). Oh Sherrie, my heart is so torn by these people leaving. We have laughed, worked, ducked rockets, confided and helped one another (together) so many times. Oh well, I'm glad they were here. I've got you and that is worth more than anything.

Every day, I look to hear (in your letters) that you spoke to John Flora. I can't understand why he hasn't reached you unless you've been out of the apartment a great deal. Maybe you should call him or try to reach him at the address I gave you.

At present, we still are not going to move until February. That's good.

I miss you so much that I feel I need to have some contact with you. I just put myself on the list to have a call put through to you. They don't think it will get through tonight, but probably tomorrow night.

Sherrie, I miss you so badly. I need you so much. November seems so far off. I want to see you so much. I've got a feeling I'm going to be in sad shape (mentally) by November. I feel like I'm slipping more frequently and it's harder to come back each time now. Sherrie, Sherrie, my life is so empty and meaningless without you.

Jonny

Sherrie, My Darling,

The thought just occurred, to me, that I might speak to you tonight. I really am excited. I think the odds are small, however, that I will because I think you are on the day shift. The call will come to the apartment during the day. I gave them an alternate number (215-3115) for the hospital-Ward 4000, but I don't know if that is the correct number for the hospital. Today, was extremely quiet (no guns, no patients, etc). The Viet Cong and the North Vietnamese Army have declared a truce until 12 midnight tomorrow. Apparently, they are honoring it. I'm so lonely and bored. I've got to keep busy or I'll lose my mind.

I finished your tape and am sending it off to you tonight. I didn't get any mail, tonight, which just about destroyed me.

I knew I wouldn't, since yesterday I got 2 letters, but I always hope anyway.

I read the article, you sent, on Tokyo nightlife. Although I found it interesting, it doesn't sound like I'll like it. It seems so empty, meaningless, cheap and without love or any real human quality. Sort of like Las Vegas. We'll hit a few places and eat out a great deal. But, as far as I am concerned, you are going to be the feature attraction 100% of the time. I'm so anxious to talk to you. I can really only picture myself walking with you and holding your hand when we go out. When I get the R&R date, I'll call you and then you can go ahead and make reservations at the New Otani Hotel. And, get your plane tickets so that you arrive ahead of me. I will give you a time (give or take 5 hours) when I will get to the hotel myself. Make your plane reservation so that you get there 12-24 hours ahead of that time. We will meet at the hotel. You should not try to meet me at the R&R Center (which is an hour away). Ok? If any questions, just ask me.

Well, my Love, back to grinding out the time. Can you feel the ache in my heart for you? I'm hurting for you real badly.

I love you very much, Jonny

My Only Precious Sweetheart,

Today passed and that is the best thing that can be said for it. I had one case, ran twice, napped and now we're having our meatball and spaghetti farewell supper for Sam Clark. It is really a pretty good dinner. Sam goes home tomorrow.

I got a very loving letter, from you, today. And, my thirsty longing heart just literally drank up every word. I need so much more. I need you. A dozen letters and fifty pictures and tapes couldn't satisfy me. Honey, I want to be back with you very badly. In your letter, today, you described having not received a letter from me for 2 days. Boy, I'm hoping right along with you that you got a letter the next day. I was very disappointed to find no mention, in your letter, that you had spoken to John Flora. Mainly, because him being able to talk to you would bring me a little closer to you and you closer to me. But, also, I'd be a little embarrassed if my friends were unable to find you at home ever.

I'm sorry that your Unit has had some poor results with the kidney transplants. But, it will get better in the future. Progress is always being made, so have heart! Do your share. I know that you do and that you do it well.

All I want to say right now, about your going to school, is that if that is what you really want to do (go full-time) then that is most probably what you will do. I'm pretty sure we won't need you to work, but perhaps you could do private duty a couple of times per month. New York is very expensive. But then, again, we don't spend that much (not with me around). Go ahead and get all the information you need and applications, etc.

Well, dinner is ready. And, everybody is hollering for me to come. So, I'll anxiously be looking for a letter tomorrow and cursing my separation from you. Maybe my call will go through tonight?

Oh Honey, I miss you so much. All my love, Darling.

Jonny

My Dearest Lover,

Hi Sweetheart. It's another day closer to you, although it started off badly. My call got through, to the States, this morning (9:25 AM my time on September 11th, and 6:25 PM your time on September 10th), but you weren't home. And, the number I gave the operators, for the hospital, was the wrong number. Please send me the hospital number and the Ward 4000 extension number. I'll need to get in touch with you quickly when our R&R notification comes through in mid-October.

I got another beautiful letter, from you, today. Oh, how I need your letters! Unfortunately, you didn't report hearing from John Flora. Your letter was written on September 7th, so I know I won't get any mail tomorrow. It's going to be a bad day. Yes, we'll get silverware in Tokyo.

The picture that's included was taken by one of the O.R. techs. He bought a new camera, here, for $100 ($200 in the U.S.). You can see the detail so good. Our camera will produce, almost, as good a quality. This was taken 2 weeks ago.

Sam left today, much sorrow. We had a terrific dinner for him last night. Well, I've got 125 days and a wake-up left. And, it's 40 days to R&R. Honey, I've got to go. I have a case.

Sweetheart, you know I love you very much. But, I'll never get tired of telling you so.

I Love You, Jonny

Hi Sweetheart,

I'm pretty rushed, at the moment. We are in the middle of a push and I'm in the O.R. I have a nerve block on my patient, so I can at least find time to write a page. Fortunately, somebody brought their stationery paper. This morning at 2 AM (during the night), my call went through to you at the hospital. It was 11 AM your time (which made us 15 hours ahead of your time). I was sort of disappointed, with the call, because you sounded sort of cold and formal. The only reason I called was because I wanted to hear some warm loving words. Honeybunch, isn't your love a little bigger than 2 unknown, unseen operators' ears? I'm sure that the call distorted or eliminated the warmth in your voice. But, the way the conversation was going, I found myself wondering if you missed me. So, I asked foolishly, I suppose. Anyway, the whole idea of the call was to let you know how much I missed you and for you to realize I am thinking of you. Incidentally, I was in the O.R. at the time the call came through. And fortunately, I was doing a spinal so I could leave the room.

I didn't get any mail, today, as I suspected I wouldn't. I think, if I remember correctly, that you said you had spoken to John Flora. That's good. I think that, by the time you get this, you should have heard from Doug and maybe Dan.

Honey, I've got to go. Do you know how much I care for you and want you to be happy and content? Very much, Sherrie, very much. I could never be happy if you weren't. My whole life, and its meaning, lies in you. Jonny

Dearest Sherrie,

I'm sorry to report that I'm not doing so well. I'm beginning to dread each day. Today was another long, slow day. Hour after hour of nothing to do! Tonight, perhaps we'll work. Tomorrow is supposed to be the beginning of another Hamburger Hill, except this time it will be on the hill next to it called Charlie Brown Hill. They found 3 battalions of North Vietnamese Army on that hill. Tomorrow, they are going to try to take it. Everybody is running around getting ready (including me) for a big push. We'll see. Maybe we'll get nobody, maybe everybody, maybe just a few or maybe they'll bomb the hell out of us. Anyway, if we get hit hard, the days should pass quickly in the O.R. In 2 days (on Monday), a full-bird Colonel Thomas (who is the Anesthesia Consultant for Vietnam) is coming to our hospital. Our Commanding Officer (Colonel Adams), who I like and look upon as a friend, wants me to be his host for a day. Boy, I'm going to talk his ear off.

I've started playing basketball again and running only once a day. I guess I'm trying to keep from getting down, but it doesn't help.

Honey, I lost the Reillys' address in New York, so could you write Madeline and ask her to send me Des' address? Please do it soon, ok? I'm thinking of taking off, for a few days, to get a change of scene. Plus, a change should help to kill a few days. One other thing, I'm thinking of doing, is taking a trip with Steve Lipson (to Saigon) for a few days.

I'll be able to do one of these 2 things because Dan gets back September 20th. He won't leave Vietnam until October 6th, so during that time we will have 4 Anesthesia people (counting myself). So, I could take off a few days during that interval.

I replayed your last tape again, today, and it sounded just as beautiful as it did the first time. I played your singing "Softly", for the guys, and they all clapped when you finished. You know how proud I am of you. You should have my tape by now. I hope it has stimulated you to make another one for me. I got another beautiful letter, from you, today (which I very badly needed). Sherrie Pumpkin, just count the days to January 14th and make up your own short-timer's calendar. Better yet, I'll include one for you. By the time you get this, I'll be under 120 days. Yes, the fan is mine. I bought it for $18.

Honey, I hope you won't be too long in getting those pictures to me. And, please space them in your letters, so I don't get them all in one shot. And, don't make me prod you to do these things. Surprise me sometime, ok?

In your next package, include some matches and cherry blend tobacco, please. I just looked through all your pictures, again. God, how I miss you.

I love you with all my heart and soul, Sherrie. I sort of feel like I'm dying a little bit now, slowly. I really need our R&R.

Jonny

My Precious, Cherished Sherrie,

Well, here we are again, another pitiful letter. It's so little in the face of what we could have, and yet the letter means so much, doesn't it? I wonder if my letters would sound like a nightly lament, of agony, if I could sit back and read them? I'm so far gone that we took 2 incoming rockets, today, and I didn't even know it or care that we did. It seems so hard to get through a day now. How can I do it tomorrow, then the next day and then the next day and keep in balance?

Today, I had one case from 10:30 to 2:30 and then nothing. Nothing to do, nowhere to go, nobody to talk to and I couldn't sleep. I could only run and run. The climax of the day is your letter and that only lasts 10 minutes. Then, I read and then there is nothing again. Well, maybe I'll work tonight and tomorrow. I'll have to cart around that Colonel who is coming. Apparently, they could not find the North Vietnamese Army they were supposed to attack today. But, from experience, I know that sooner or later (a few weeks), they will find them and make contact. Obviously, they are around. They shot rockets at us this morning.

I got your Sunday letter today. And, you didn't sound depressed, which I was happy to note. I guess the fact that you were working was helpful. Yes, you can send me the book "The Intimate Enemy". Yes, I will stop smoking cigarettes and probably will cut down on the pipe a great deal. But, I think I would like to smoke the pipe occasionally during the day.

I received all those magazines you sent. I will look through them, I'm sure.

Honey, I wish I could tell you I feel stronger than I am. But, I just can't. I just couldn't hide the lethargy, the aimless meaningless passage of time, the loneliness and the war from my letters. If I could only have a hot shower. If I could only relax for a moment. If I could have you, then I'd have all these things. Just somebody who would care to know me, understand me and believe in me. You know that you are all these things to me. And yet, you are even more.

I love you, Sherrie. But, I feel much more than that for you. Do you know what I mean now when I say you mean everything?

Jonny

Hi Honeybunch,

I'm a little happier right now, than I have been recently, mainly because today turned out better than I expected it would. First, I was third call which usually means a very dull day. But, I did a very interesting case on a child (which is unusual in itself). I ran in the morning, did the case, ran again at 4:30 PM, ate at 5:30 PM and then met the full-bird Colonel. He is the Anesthesia Consultant in Vietnam. I had a very nice meeting, with him, for the last 2 hours. I talked so much about our accomplishments, problems, showed him around, demonstrated some things to him, etc. He said he was very impressed, with me, to our own Colonel Adams. So, at least the day went smoothly, interestingly and was a little different. Now, I fully expect to crash back into the dreariness of life here. But, at least today passed quickly. Tomorrow, I'll probably be a whipped dog again.

I'm glad you like the pictures I sent. They certainly have caused you to write a few livelier, more bouncy paragraphs than usual. Thanks for the compliments, but you are just a lonesome girl who has a distorted view of handsomeness.

Yes, I think you should tell Dr. Brooks about your Mother's history of thrombophlebitis. Be sure to find out if she was on pills at the time.

I'll be looking forward to hearing what our bank account is and receiving your package. I need the package. I hope you send it 4th class or on a space available basis. You know that, at the end of September, I will be sending you about $800 in money orders.

Honey, we just got cases. Got to go.

I love you, my Sweetheart. I love you very, very much. My heart aches for you.

Jonny

My Precious Sweet Sherrie,

Well again, it's another day gone. I sort of say this as though I didn't expect to make it through the day. I suppose there is a half-truth in that. When I get up in the morning, I never really quite see my way to the end of the day. But, of course, it always comes. I suppose part of it is due to the many different paths a day here can take. Everything is sort of unexpected (rockets, badly injured patients, many patients, no patients). Mainly, it is quiet and that is when it is most difficult. But, laziness breeds laziness. I always have to get that adrenalin flowing when cases come in. I did 2 cases today, ran twice, napped a little, made some lemonade for the hooch (send us some more please, we are out). And, now it is 8 PM again.

I got 2 wonderful letters, from you, today (written on September 10th and 11th). Your letters are so wonderful and filled with love. I need them so much. I was especially happy and delighted to read your reaction to our phone call. I'm very happy about it, too. I'm glad I made it because I can see it made you happy, which makes me very happy. I look forward to seeing you in your dress. I look forward to all the pictures you are taking.

I did write to Dr. Lorhan explaining my interest in Southern California, my regret at having heard from Columbia Presbyterian Hospital so much earlier than I did from him, my interest in respiratory care units (such as at Harbor General Hospital) and finally what training I expect to take in the next 3-4 years. I think I will hear from him again. It was a good letter.

I probably will be calling you in 2-4 weeks, from now, about our R&R. Hang on, Baby! You will have to purchase your own plane ticket. I can't do this for you. There are no reduced rates, to Tokyo, that I can get.

I wrote the Amdurs a note myself. Very sad, he was always very nice to me.

I'm very proud of you for running again. When I tell the guys that you run on your own, they all say very enviously "Gee, that's great" and it really is. We are going to be able to do many things together (run, play tennis and basketball, swim, golf, dance). Oh, how I would love to dance with you. I'll go nuts if I think about all the joys, in life, that we will have together.

I just thought of us going to movies and shows, eating out, having a party once in a while, etc. And, I just get sort of sick at being here, so it is better not to think about it at all.

I love you very, very much, my Darling. Jonny

9/17/69
Letter 192

My Dearest Darling,

I'm starting this letter much earlier (5 PM) than usual, because I'm going out of my mind with boredom. And, I'm making Woody steaks for his farewell dinner which should be pretty good. He goes tomorrow. I'll be most sorry to see him go of all people. He'll be calling you, also, about a week from now.

Today was a very dull, slow day. With Woody going, I am getting depressed. The mail should be here in about an hour. That should help some. Lately, it has been raining a great deal. I guess we're getting into winter. It's still pretty hot. But, we haven't had any 120 degree weather for a while. In fact, it has been sort of pleasant.

I did get a letter from you and one from Doug, also. He wrote, while in the air, on his way home. He had a very hard time getting out. He had to wait 2 full days, at the airport, to get a plane. Ugh!

My Darling, even though I try not to think about it, I probably end up thinking about nothing else other than R&R (43 days to go)! I have 119 days left in-country!

Woody gave me a lot of glass enclosed frames in which to put pictures. So, I'm waiting for your next bunch to put in them. It sounds as if you're going to take a whole roll of film all at once. I don't understand why you don't shoot a few all along, so I can see you at different times and places. Well, I'll be more than happy with whatever I get.

Well my Love, I love you so much. Jonny

9/19/69
Letter 193

Dearest Darling Sherrie,

Today had to be one of the worst days I have spent in Vietnam. I believe I wrote you that I had a sore throat yesterday. Well, now I have the biggest cold I have ever had. No cases today. The patient that Steve and I had (in the O.R.), 2 days ago, died.

I didn't get any mail, from you, today. It is very damp everywhere and raining like crazy (now for the 4th day in a row). Honey, please send my rubber boots back to me. Quick, I mean it! And, finally as you can see (from the enclosed letter from the Lt. Colonel of the Medical Corps Branch), we will be going to Fort Rucker (Alabama) from here. I'm so angry, I just can't say anything. I found out that I'll probably be there, by myself, with only Nurse Anesthetists. There won't be anybody there to teach me. Did you know that President Nixon called for 40,000 troops to pull-out of Vietnam? Well, that includes the Marines at Quang Tri (just below the DMZ). So, that means the 18th Surgical Hospital will be going up there for sure. And, it will probably be before I go home.

Something has happened to me, recently, that is terrific and makes me very happy. I'm going to save telling you as a surprise for our R&R.

To summarize the bad things that have happened: (1)

I'm very sick. (2) I'm bored and stuck in the hooch because I'm sick, no cases, continual rain. (3) I'm a failure because a patient died after 55 units of blood. (4) I'm angry because I got no mail from you and the Army assigned me to Fort Rucker which is one of the worst places. (5) I'm unsettled and will probably have to go North, to the DMZ, before I leave Vietnam.

Honey, I love you, but I'm not in the mood to dwell on it. Please understand. You still stand far and above all I have listed above. As long as I have you, I can take anything the Army does.

Jonny

My Very Dearest Darling,

Today passed and probably that is the best I can say for it. I'm a little better as far as my cold is concerned. I spent the day doing one short case, getting the enclosed money orders (Dan paid me back), playing solitaire and reading. Steve Lipson has moved into the Super Hooch, but I don't think it will be for long. That's because we will be moving, to Quang Tri, before the end of October. As soon as I know my new APO number, I'll send it to you. The move should not affect our R&R, but there is a very small chance it could. You'll just have to be patient and wait until you hear from me. Word of approved R&Rs, for the month of October, did not come to the 18th Surgical Hospital until September 19th. Now, if the same thing holds true in October for November R&Rs, you won't hear from me (by phone) until October 20th and by mail around October 25th. So, you might have at most

10 days to make your plane and hotel reservations. And, get travelers' checks (for $1000). Be sure to get to Tokyo 1-2 days before the time I tell you that I'm going to get there. As soon as you know your plane flight number, time of departure, time of arrival, name of the hotel and room number- send the information to me. That means that if the R&R comes through for November 1st, I'll know this information about October 25-26. Ok? I'll be bringing money, but I don't know how much.

I still don't feel like writing to anybody, but you. I managed to write my sister a half-page letter yesterday, but it was poor. I just feel so badly. I couldn't possibly face trying to write a normal letter. I hope you are finding out, for me, where Des Reilly is. Naturally, I would like to know that you received the $350 (in this letter) as soon as possible. I will be sending you $400 more in early October.

I'm rather anxious to show you my surprise, for you, on our R&R. I think you'll be pleased.

I was sorry to read that Maribeth's wedding emphasized your loneliness. Just always remember that I understand your loneliness. Perhaps you can find some comfort in my empathy and sympathy, to say nothing of the love that I feel for you, which enables me to feel these things.

Well my Love, it's another day done. Although, I'm that much the worse for wear, I'm a day closer to you. And, that is all that really matters to me. I long for you with all my heart.

I love you very deeply, Darling, very much. Jonny

Tonight, I can't seem to think of a salutation that would be appropriate to my feelings for you. The usual salutations, that I use, don't reflect the desperateness and agony I feel being away from you. Yes, you are "My Most Dearest Darling" and "Most Cherished Precious Darling" (etc), but there is more and I can't put it into words.

Today was Sunday, very slow, not one surgical case so far, nothing. I can't even remember what I did to pass 10 hours of the day, but I know I ran twice and played a game of chess. How I laid around for the other 8 hours, I don't know, but I did. And, that is what I do every day, nothing. I have taken to playing a game of chess, with Steve Lipson, every day. So far, I'm ahead 2 to 1. One of the biggest things, that I occupy some of my energy and thoughts with, is keeping my surprise for you intact when I see you on R&R.

Oh yes, before I forget, I want to let you know that I'll be sending home a lot of stuff before we move to Quang Tri. I want to be able to move as light as possible. Offhand, I'd say I'll send my books, tapes and instamatic camera.

I'm gaining on my cold. I didn't get any mail, today, which was naturally a disappointment. I sort of expected a letter, but I'll probably get 2 tomorrow.

I've played your singing "Softly" many times. You did a beautiful job with that song.

I love you very much, my Darling. I'm so desirous to start a life of total giving and commitment to you. I want so much to move through life and live life with you. I guess it's the same, for you, as it is for me. I hate life without you and nobody can take your place.

Jonny

9/22/69
Letter 196

Dearest Sweetiepie Sugarbowl Tinkerbell,

Before I forget, there are a couple of things I want to mention. First off, when I give you the date for our R&R (say November 3rd), you have to leave the U.S. a full 2 days before that date. The reason is that you lose a whole day (the international date line is crossed) going from the U.S. to Japan. In other words, if you left on November 1st (for Japan), you would arrive in Tokyo on November 2nd or November 3rd (depending on what time you left the U.S.). This would be ok, because I would be coming later in the day on November 3rd.

Don't hesitate to ask me, or the airlines, any questions about which plane flight you should take if you're not sure. Of course, you should reserve our room at The New Otani Hotel for the day beginning with your arrival in Tokyo. Secondly, it looks for certain like we are going to Quang Tri and it looks like we are going soon. An advance party is going up in 10-14 days. We are all supposed to follow from November 15th to November 20th. So, I'm pretty sure that the move will not conflict with our R&R. I should be able to get back to Camp Evans before everybody goes, so I can get the Super Hooch and the Anesthesia Department packed up. I will fight like crazy to keep our R&R early in November. But, you must face up to the small (very small) possibility that should they simply refuse to let me go, it would mean that I couldn't get to Tokyo until December or even early January. Now, don't you worry. I'll do the worrying in this case, ok? I'll know the exact date by October 15th or earlier, so you can expect me to call on or before that date.

Things are still very slow, not a case all day. We are down to 6 Docs and one is going in 10 days. When he goes, I'll have to take call in the Receiving Room and Emergency Room every day until another Doc comes. Same thing as I did a couple of times at Fort Knox, Kentucky.

I'm glad you took the opportunity to make an additional $25 by participating in Dr. Barbour's experiment. I guess it, also, gives you a little something else to keep busy with. Also, I was pleased to hear that you are taking swimming lessons. If you learn to swim, I think you will have gained a valuable and enjoyable ability. And, it's another thing we can do together.

I miss you very badly, Darling. I miss you because I love you.

Jonny

My Darling Sherrie,

Today was so-so and now, at least, most of it is gone. I had planned to go to the Dentist, today, but I got busy with a couple of cases. I had to do a spinal tap on a 10 pound baby. And, I had to see some other patients, so I didn't get around to going to the Dentist. I'll have to wait until the day after tomorrow, since I'm first call tomorrow. I'll get it done, though, I promise.

I didn't get any mail, today, which was a crushing blow since I fully expected to get some. I always get mail which was written 6 or more days ago. Tomorrow will make 8 days lapse between your writing and my receiving your letter.

I have a buyer for my tape recorder, so I'm going to sell it to him in the middle of October. I doubt I'll get any more tapes from you after that, and if I do, I can play them on somebody else's recorder.

Honey, other than the above, I've got nothing to say or add to my blah, empty, unhappy meaningless life. I miss you immensely, Sherrie. I feel love for you constantly. Please forgive the shortness of this letter. I've just got nothing to say other than I love you.

Jonny

My Sweet Sherrie,

I was thinking, today, what a fine person you are. You really are. You give a great deal of yourself with quality. I have come to appreciate you a great deal. I just thought I should let you know.

I'm starting this letter a little early today (before the mail comes at 6 PM), because at 7 PM tonight is Jim Balliker's farewell party. He's not an MD, but is sort of 2nd in command here, ever since I came. He's a nice guy and has done me many favors. He will probably call you. I'm actually sitting, here, writing in a tense mood (it's 5:45 PM) and hoping for mail in 15 minutes.

Anyway, I don't know whether I told you or not, but I want you to bring a suit, white shirt, tie and tie clip for me to Tokyo. I can buy whatever other clothes, I'll need, in Tokyo. Now, don't forget to bring a suit for me.

Tomorrow, I'm going to try really hard to get to the Dentist. I'll let you know, tomorrow, what happened.

The latest, on the move to Quang Tri, is that we might not move. The Marines and 101st Airborne people, who are moving out, don't think there will be enough security for us. So, maybe we won't move.

NO MAIL. Everybody has been missing mail for 3 days now. Honey, I'm going to sign off. I feel like all the wind was taken out of my sails.

I love you very dearly. Jonny

Sherrie, My Life's Meaning,

Tonight, as I lay on my cot waiting for the mail to come, I was in a very bad way. I had a funny feeling (maybe it was imagined, maybe not, maybe it's not possible, maybe it is), but I felt like I was going psychotic. Everything seemed flat. I couldn't tell what I liked, what I disliked, what was important, what was unimportant or even what I wanted or didn't want. I sort of felt disintegrated, lost and confused. And, of course, extremely sad. I sort of felt that I was here and would always be here. And, that the real world didn't exist. I had half decided not to write, tonight, because I could not bear to write you such a pitifully pathetic letter. Because

I know just as I need help, and strength from your letters, so do you from me. So, I felt it probably would be better not to write tonight.

Then, I got 4 letters from you, the last one dated September 20th. It contained 2 darling pictures of you. And, I got a package of hot dogs (etc) from you. Sherrie, I can't describe how important those letters were to me. A feeling and sensation of peace descended upon me. Suddenly the real world was there, a future, a bright happy future was there. My life has meaning. I have something to live for! Yes, I can love. Yes, I can give to Sherrie. Now, I feel like working again, talking to people and even laughing if I could hear something funny enough. Sherrie, my true Sweetheart, I feel at peace again. I'm not happy. And, I have very little to fall upon or support me here, but at least I feel stable and at peace. And, I feel this because I have something powerful behind me. Something is lifting me up and that something is you.

Yes, I could get several days drop in January, but I won't know it until the last moment. I could be home anywhere from January 5th to January 15th. Sherrie, I don't and can't enjoy anything without you either. I always come to that conclusion many times a day.

Although it may be selfish of me to say so, I was glad to hear you feel the same way. I read with some degree of surprise, and shock, that you went 3-par golfing with your parents. I had actually forgotten that such things exist. I'm glad you are taking the opportunity to get out, however. I would do the same, if I could. Think of how much fun it would be if we could go together. Oh yes, I had 2 cavities filled, today, and I have 6 more to go.

Don't send any more tobacco. Jim Balliker gave me plenty for the rest of the year. He's leaving tomorrow. I haven't had a cigarette in 2 weeks. You'll probably be able to reach Madeline Reilly, through that letter written to Fort Knox, and her answer to you will probably have Des' address. Good detective work, "Sherrie Holmes".

Sweetheart, I think I can't put it more simply and accurately, my feelings and thoughts about you. I love you. I love you for the person you have demonstrated yourself to be to me. I love you for the special happiness, meaning, peace and contentment you have brought into my life. I love you fully, and freely, as one who thought they could not love so much or even feel love. I love you as one who has had the deliverance of a barren soul and spirit.

Jonny

9/26/69
Letter 200

My Very Dearest Sunlight,

You know that today's salutation, to you, is exactly what I thought when I looked at your 2 pictures that I got yesterday. You were in your yellow outfit, with a big smile on your pretty face, with your blonde hair very bright and gleaming. Those pictures really lit me up. I didn't get any mail from you, today, but I anticipate with great delight opening tomorrow's letter and finding 2 more pictures of you. Today, I did get a letter from my Mom.

Today was another routine dull day and very hot (115 degrees). I did one case. Oh yeah, I spent about 2 hours (today) writing up a lecture on Respiratory Care. I'll give the lecture, to the Nurses, on Wednesday (September 30th). They asked me yesterday. I'm glad they did because I enjoy talking about this topic. It's one thing I know something about. Plus, it gives me something to do.

Good news, it looks like we will not be going to Quang Tri. The General, who runs the fighting units, says he doesn't want us to go up there even though the Medical General does. The fighting General rules over the Medical General. Boy, this argument has had so many rumors and turnabouts. I must write you something new, each day, on it.

I didn't get my teeth worked on, today, because the O.R. case came up that I had to do. I don't know if I'll be able to go there tomorrow, either, because there is another case scheduled. We'll see.

I miss you immensely, Honey, as you know. I can't be happy until I'm with you again. Whatever peace of mind I get, from your letters (etc), is so pitifully small in terms of what I feel I need and what I'm ready to give.

I love you a great deal, Sherrie. It's so frustrating to feel so much for you. And, to only be able to give you a small fraction and expression of that feeling.

Jonny

Dearest Darling,

Tonight's letter won't be exactly an inspired effort. I just don't feel too happy. I don't feel too down or anything. It's just that I'm very tired, in spirit, of being here and time goes by so slowly. It seems like forever until our R&R, although it's only 33 days or so. Within 2 weeks, I should know the exact date.

Today, I had one happy thought. The Mardi Gras festivities, in New Orleans, occur in February. We will definitely go to New Orleans on our way to Fort Rucker.

I'm glad you heard from Woody. I wonder what happened to Doug? I guess Jim Balliker will be calling you soon, too. That was very nice of Maribeth to give us that can opener. It's rather an expensive item. It certainly is a very giving and generous gesture on their part. Naturally, I anxiously look forward to getting your pictures. I have completed about a third of a tape for you.

I had 2 more cavities filled today. I have about 6-8 more to go. I hate the discomfort, but at least it is for free. The Dentist says my teeth are in pretty good shape and I should never need dentures or anything like that.

Honey, I think of you constantly. All I want in life is just to love you.

Jonny

(1st Letter)

My Precious Darling,

I just completed a brief ceremony in marking off my "short-timer" calendar. I mark if off every 5-10 days, or so, like when somebody goes home or something like that. Right now, I have 107 days and a wake-up left. And, I have 31 days (give or take a couple) to R&R. How slowly the time goes by.

Well, it was nice to work last night. I did nothing today except beat Steve in chess, got my teeth cleaned, ran twice and daydreamed about you.

I got 2 nice loving letters from you, today, which included my Uncle Abe's schedule. I think I'll hang onto it because it's possible we could be passing by a city he is playing in when we travel to Alabama (and from Alabama).

The day after tomorrow (October 1st), I'm Physician-on-Duty. I hope it helps to pass the day quickly. What I'll do is stay up on the Admitting Ward, all day and night, seeing everybody who comes to the hospital for help as needed. The reason I need to start doing this is because we are down to only 5 Docs, at the hospital, and no replacements are in sight. So, I've been recruited. I guess I'll be doing this assignment every 5-6 days.

Sweet Precious Sherrie, I miss you so much. I think about being home, with you, for hours at a time. I can't believe the deep sense of happiness, contentment and love I'll have when I'm home with you again. It will be so wonderful.

All my love and thoughts, Sweetheart.

Jonny

9/29/69
Letter 203

(2nd Letter)

My Dearest Darling,

Tonight, for the first time in a long time, I worked. It's pretty late, now, and I'm tired. So, I'm going to make this short. I just wanted to make sure that you got something anyway, even if it's just a "Hello" and "I love you".

Lately, I've been playing a lot of chess with Steve Lipson. Right now, I'm winning 4 to 1. The game he won, though, was when I was slightly sloshed. I have been sufficiently stimu-

lated by these games, however, to get a book on chess and go through it very carefully. This is something that I have never done. I am learning a great deal. I think I will be a much better chess player when I am done with it. Probably when you get down to the nitty-gritty, it's really just another way to kill time. But, it's a constructive thing to do and I'm enjoying it.

Two big questions (now, don't forget to answer): (1) Is the camera fixed? I forgot if you told me. (2) Did you get the additional household insurance? And, here is another question: (3) Did you get the $350 in money orders?

Honey, I love you with all my soul and heart. I think of you constantly and happily, for the future, and with a longing at the present.

Jonny

My Dearest Sherrie,

Once again, I'm writing you. Guess what? The letter was interrupted, for the last 3 hours, by a case in the O.R. which had a bad outcome. The patient was a Regular Army Vietnamese soldier who was losing blood from both femoral arteries, from the rectum, the radial artery, both tibias and he had blood in the belly. He had 6 arrests, on the table, and he received much blood. We couldn't save him.

Then, I came back to the hooch to find a beautiful letter from you, the pipes and 2 stunning pictures of you. You looked so beautiful. They just took my breath away. Honey, I just feel like crying out because my pain is so great and my longing is so intense. Both of your dresses are terrific. I like them very much. Please bring both to Japan.

Today, in the afternoon, I gave my lecture and I think it went pretty well. I had a crowd of about 30. I enjoyed doing it and I got experience talking to a large group of people. And, they seemed to like it. I, also, beat Steve twice in chess and I ran one time.

Of course, I forgive you for missing a day writing and especially since I didn't even know it. I hope you didn't get a bad cold. Yes, Honey, I very deeply believe in and have faith in the fact that we will be happy wherever we are, including Alabama.

Well Honey, tomorrow I'm Physician-on-Duty, so I'd better get to bed. I have to get up at 7:30 AM which is very early for me. I haven't gotten up before 9:30 AM, all year, unless it was for a case.

Sherrie, my precious love, I miss you very badly. I'm pretty excited about our R&R, too. Boy, are we going to have ourselves a time! How wonderful it will be to love, love and love. I feel so much for you.

Jonny

My Sweet Darling,

Well, today, was spent very differently than all my others. I was (and still am) Physician-on-Duty until the morning comes. I saw all kinds of problems like infected toenails, abscesses, skin rashes (etc) and did a couple of O.R. cases. I did 2 blocks in the O.R. myself. The day has passed pretty quickly. Although, the evening is going slower. The place where I have to sleep is freezing, because it is air conditioned. So, I brought over my electric blanket.

I'm very sorry to report that it looks like we are going to Quang Tri after all. Maybe it's just another rumor, but this time it looks like a certainty. The fighting guys said they can provide us with even better security than we have here at Camp Evans. So, again, we'll see. I'm past caring. I know this, however, it won't interfere with our R&R. The Commanding Officer, of the hospital, promised me that I could go even if it's right in the middle of a move.

Honey, I just got 2 more patients to see, so I might be tied up for a while. I'm going to end now. I didn't get any mail, today, but I very eagerly look forward to mail-call tomorrow and the possibility of seeing 2 more pictures of your darling beautiful face and body.

I love you very much, my only love. Jonny

10/04/69
Letter 206

My Loved Cherished Desired Sherrie,

Guess what? I just did an appendectomy myself. Steve Lipson watched me. After I had put in the spinal, Steve asked me if I wanted to do the appendectomy. So, I said yes and then went to do the appendectomy. All went smoothly (spinal and operation). It was fun doing both. I bet that was another first at the 18th Surgical Hospital.

In addition, I had 2 other cases today. So, with running once and playing chess, the day went quickly. Tomorrow, I plan to get money orders to send to you in the morning. And, maybe I'll get a trim of my hair and then get some more work done on my teeth. I'm getting excited about the possibility of hearing, soon, what the date for our R&R will be. I should know within a week. Then, I'll call you!

Today, we got a General Medical Officer who the Commanding Officer (he just came in to visit with me the last 15 minutes; we are pretty good friends and I like him immensely) tells me is going into Anesthesia when he gets out, so it looks like I have a new pupil. Right now, I'm teaching the Nurse Anesthetists spinals and nerve blocks. With the new Doc learning general anesthesia, I should have quite a program going.

I didn't get my mail, tonight, as I knew would happen. Well actually, I did get a letter from my Father and Mrs. Lillian Amdur. She apparently was quite touched by my condolence note. But, I consider that I got no mail if I don't get a letter from you.

Honeybunch, I got a call for another case, so it looks like the late evening will pass quickly, also. I'm third call tomorrow. There's nothing new on our move to Quang Tri. In 103 days, I'll be home.

Oh Honey, we'll be so happy together. I love you so much. Sherrie, I never think about anything but you. I daydream all day about the things we'll be doing in the future (loving, having a baby, going out on the town for dinner and a show, seeing friends, sailing, skiing, etc, etc). It looks beautiful and it's all because of you. You are everything.

Jonny

Dearest Sherrie,

Today it just rained, rained and rained. This makes the 6th day in a row and everything is wet, everything. It rains so long here that when it is just a fine mist and drizzling, I don't really consider it rain. No mail came in, today, for all of Camp Evans because of the rain. But, tomorrow holds new promise for mail and especially getting some pictures of you.

Today, I did very little. I saw 2 patients that I have (the one who had the appendectomy and another one who I admitted with tonsillitis) and they are both doing well. I ran in place, for 25 minutes, because of the rain. I ate in the mess hall, tonight, because they had turkey and stuffing. Boy, did I stuff myself. Otherwise, I did nothing. I couldn't go to the Post Office because of the rain. I have a tremendous lump on my head because, 2 nights ago, we took 2 incoming rockets and I banged my head hitting the floor.

I haven't got much else to tell you about, Honey. I think of literally nothing else but you. I love you very much. And, most of what I think about you concerns my dreams of transferring that love from me to you. I can't get over the beauty of the feeling I get when I think about you and I having a child. Sherrie, I want to be with you very badly.

All my thoughts and love,

Jonny

My Dearest Darling,

Tonight's letter is going to be somewhat short because I'm tired and, in addition, I have little to report. I'm tired because I've worked all day, non-stop. I'm glad I did because the day went by quickly and enjoyably. I did 3 cases (a spinal, a nerve block and a general). So, I enjoyed the volume and the variety. But, I'm tired since it took all day. Secondly, today it hasn't stopped raining for a minute, so no mail got through again. Steve Lipson corrected me on something I wrote you yesterday. I told you the Phu Bai weatherman said 22 inches of rain fell this week. Well, it was 22 inches of rain in one day. Can you imagine that? Twenty-two inches in one day! It's been very near that, today, if not more.

Otherwise, nothing is new. I want mail so badly. I guess you must get tired of hearing this every day. I keep hoping, every day, to hear about the R&R. Should be soon.

My sweet love, I need you very much. Only you can heal my sick spirit. I love you, my Darling, I love you. Pray for me that the mail will come tomorrow. It's been so long since I have been truly happy.

Jonny

My Precious Darling Sherrie,

Blessed art thou, 0 Lord Our God, who delivereth our mail. Amen. Honey, I got 2 letters today. I'm still missing several days of mail and will probably get 2 or 3 letters tomorrow. I don't understand why there are no pictures. Except that, perhaps, you took my request to space your pictures a little too strongly. Anyway, it was great to hear from you. It finally stopped raining, at about 3 PM today, and the mail helicopter was able to land. The last letter, I got, was written on October 1st. Usually, there is a 5 day lag. I got a letter from Woody, today, also.

Well let's see, I have some news. First, we are definitely moving to the DMZ. And, it will be in very early November. I'm bitterly disappointed by this turn of events. But, I guess we both have to swallow our disappointment and try to take it lightly. I promise it won't interfere with our R&R. The Commanding Officer said it would be alright. So, as for as you are concerned, nothing has changed. I will write you my new APO number, if there is going to be one, as soon as possible. The advance party is leaving in 4 days. So, in preparation, I'm sending home several packages. I want to move as light as possible. I made up one package today. Everything I'm sending home is of some value to me (and in most instances, to you also). So, please put things away carefully or you can leave the packages as they are. Today's package has an instamatic camera in it (with film), flashcubes and pre-paid processing mailers. Please use the camera and the pre-paid *mailers, since I already paid for them. Each one is the cost of developing a roll of film. Also, there are 5 blank tapes included that are worth $35 and a stapler, label maker, eyeglasses and a copy of the paper I wrote months ago.*

Last night, I got sort of smashed and was feeling very lonely. I was struck by the thought that when one loves someone else, one really places themselves in the care and protection (emotionally) of that person. So, it is with me.

I love you very deeply. Jonny

Dearest Darling Lover,

Today, I was Physician-on-Duty and I didn't know it. So, I was rooted out of bed this morning to get up to the Emergency Ward. I thought I was on duty tomorrow. Anyway, I had sort of a dramatic case come in a little while ago. The patient was a Viet Cong soldier with a sucking chest wound. I rushed him straight into the O.R. after taking one quick look, put him to sleep, tubed him and inflated his lung. He had a hole the size of a softball in his chest. Then, the Surgeon came and closed his chest. Otherwise, it hasn't been too busy.

I have some good and bad news. The good news is that we won't be going to the DMZ until November 20th. That's good because it won't interfere with our R&R in any way. The bad news is that I haven't heard anything on the R&R. It's possible that the word could come 10 days late and I wouldn't be able to call you until October 20th. You would then have to do some rushing around. I know you are very anxious to hear from me. It's been so hard for both of us, hasn't it? I'm so sorry to think of you at home alone, so unhappy. But, we'll make up for it, won't we? Oh Darling, we'll be so happy together. And, we'll heal each other quickly and then take care of one another.

I got 2 more letters, today, written on October 3rd and 4th. So, I'm missing one from October 2nd. I sure hope that wasn't one that had pictures in it. I love the dress you bought. From your description, it sounds like just the kind of thing I would have picked out for you myself. I'm glad, also, that you're going to save wearing it for me. Of course, I'll play chess with you. I'd be very happy if you showed the interest. It's a real good thinking game. Right now, I would sew dresses with you if you wanted me to.

I just heard that my new orders (for Fort Rucker, Alabama) came in today. It doesn't mean I'll be home any earlier. It is helpful in that you will be able to transport our stuff, to the Transportation Officer (at Fort Rucker), before I get home. So, it will all be there waiting for us. I'll talk to you more about that in Tokyo.

Yes, please get the camera fixed, so we can take good pictures in Japan. I thought that was understood. Well, don't worry, just try to get it done in time. Ok? Yes, I think running in place is helpful. I'm very proud of you. You know that, don't you?

You know, now, I've got only 97 days and a wake-up left before I go home. And, we have about 22 days until R&R.

Honey, I love you with all my heart and soul.

Jonny

Dearest and Only Love,

Again, today, no word on R&R. It rained and rained all day (after a one-day respite from the rain). I got your letter written on October 2nd, but no pictures. I've got to do some rationalizing, tonight, to keep from a depression. Why haven't any pictures come? You said you put them in to be developed weeks ago. Sherrie, I need as much of you as I can get.

Today was a very slow day, nothing happened. I ran twice in the rain, slept, read, etc. We (Steve, myself, the Commanding Officer and the top Sergeant) had our first meeting, to draw up the blueprints, for the move. Steve's in charge of Surgery, I'm in charge of Anesthesia and the top Sergeant's in charge of all the Enlisted Men. It's a big job. Steve and I have to get up early tomorrow. We've got to go through the hospital deciding what goes with us and what doesn't. Unfortunately, we were told today that we will have to man half of the perimeter bunker ourselves. The rest will be done by the infantry. As an Officer, I might have to make bunker rounds to be sure everybody is awake, etc. It seems ludicrous, but they say the Nurses can't go because there is not enough security. So, why the hell are they letting us (the Docs) go? It sounds a lot worse than it probably is, but still one can't help but feel that we're being sold out midstream. One good thing, for years now, is that Quang Tri has been hit much less than Camp Evans and Phu Bai. I know this is true, but the security has always been good up there (with the Marines there). But, now they are going home.

I received the book, "The Intimate Enemy", and other

goodies today. Thank you for your loving care. It really helps me. And, it helps me contribute to the hooch. Well Darling, I suppose this is it for today. Except, I want to remind you that my lovelight burns bright and strong for you and I hope it helps to brighten your day. I do care for you so very much, Sherrie. I'm sure we'll have to do a lot of loving happily to make up for the bareness of this year. I need you so much to give my love to. And, I want so much to receive your love in return. I feel so sick without you. It will take a little time for me to heal.

Jonny

My Very Loved Sherrie,

Hi Sweetheart. Today, I got sort of depressed. But, I think I feel a little better now. Especially after getting a letter from you, one from Nat and one from that guy (Normie) in Philadelphia. Actually, I had a very interesting day. But, for some reason, I felt particularly depressed about my life here. The morning was filled with meetings and planning for the move, etc. Everybody has things to do and, of course, lots of opinions. With some degree of confusion, in the planning, I'm sure the actuality will be chaos. In the afternoon, I went to the Post Office and sent the package to you that I described several letters ago. In addition, I sent $400 in money orders to you. They are the only things in the envelope. There's a new rule which says the money orders have to go out right away. So, I just had time to address the envelope and no time to include a letter with them. If I would have had the time, I *would have told you that I love you very much and that you are very dear to me. After leaving the Post Office, I went with the Chaplain (whose jeep I was being given a lift in) to a Vietnamese village about 2 miles from Camp Evans. Boy, was I scared. I think I would have shot anything that moved. When we got in the village, the first thing we saw was a Viet Cong hanging from a tree (3 days dead and being eaten by bugs). The people in this village hate the Viet Cong. They hang them to show others what will happen if they turn Viet Cong. A real cut-throat society. I saw a lot of disease which interested me. But, I sure was happy when we started home. The Chaplain goes there, one time per week, because an orphanage is there. Once is enough for me.*

Honey, I was very disappointed in not hearing about our R&R. I want to call you as much as you want to hear from me. It shouldn't be long now.

Sherrie Sweetie Pie, please continue to believe in our love as I do. Our love is everything to me. And, everything looks beautiful as long as I can see you as the center of everything.

Jonny

10/12/69
Letter 213

Dearest Darling,

Today was another slow empty day again. Every day is the same (read, run, nap, chess), so slow and painful. Also, there's rain, rain every day. Thank God, I got a letter from you today. Again, the dates for our R&R did not come up from Da Nang. And, I wanted so much to place the call through to you. It could take 2-3 days before the call gets through.

I was glad to read that you are trying to get back your deposit fee for the class you couldn't get. And, I'm more glad that you want to continue to read, on your own, via Nat's books. And, your exercise program (running in place, kicking and swimming). Wow! Tremendous, really it is. Keep it up. I'm very proud of you.

Again, I was disappointed not to find any pictures. But, you did say you put in a roll of film to be developed, so I'm thankful for that. Now, if I don't get any pictures in 3 or 4 days, I'll be upset. The only reason I want them is because I love you. Yes, I have gotten many food packages. I'm sorry if I didn't note them all in my letters. The hot dogs came destroyed, so I could use more. The cigar pipes were a great idea but, apparently, they weren't made too well. The people, to whom I gave them, said they couldn't use them very well as they wouldn't stay lit. I didn't have one since I have been smoking extremely little.

Well Honey, I'll talk to you tomorrow. I love you very, very much. I never forget you for a moment, because I carry you in my heart all the time. Jonny

My Dearest Darling Sherrie,

I'm going to repeat, to you, what I just yelled out loud, "Oh you are so beautiful". I got 2 pictures, today, and 2 letters. You were in your red dress, I guess in front of a church. Since I got 2 letters, today, I'm sure I won't get any tomorrow. But, then the day after, 2 more pictures!

After I wrote you, last night, something unusual happened. I worked all night. All day, today, I had o headache and now a toothache (since I had another cavity filled today). But, I still ran twice, napped and read. I'll probably sleep pretty good tonight. I got a nice letter from Woody, today, also.

As you know, no news on the R&R again today. I must be stopping off down in Headquarters (it's all underground) 5 times a day to see if anything came in. I'm so sorry, for you, because you are probably waiting at home a great deal. And, as you wrote, you hadn't gotten any letters from me for 2 days and no call. So, I guess it's depressing. I really feel for you.

I'm very happy that you are so enthusiastic about your swimming. Maybe we could have a race, if I give you a big head start. I doubt there is a YMCA or YWCA within a 100 mile radius of Fort Rucker. Oh yes, today, I got 6 cans of soup. Thank you. Too bad you haven't been able to get any private duty cases. We could use the money to save up for New York. Also, I was very sorry to learn Virgil was in such distress. I was surprised that his General Physician did not tell him to take frequent sitz baths. It is most important in the conservative management of hemorrhoids. Also, a prepara-

tion like "Anusol" suppositories is very soothing. I think the combination would do a great deal to relieve his discomfort until he sees the Surgeon.

My Darling, I love you very much. Yes, I agree there is much comfort in knowing we are getting on towards the end of this lousy separation. I think this year of separation, from you, was the worst thing that has ever happened to me. And, it's the most unhappy event in my life. Jonny

Hi Baby,

I now have the enjoyable privilege of writing to you about what I spoke to you about, on the phone, this morning. They got me right through to you. I found out my R&R is November 4th to November 11th. But, remember, I won't get to "The New Otani Hotel" until October 5th at approximately 6:00 AM or 7:00 AM. It was great to hear from you. And, I was so happy to have finally been able to decrease your anxiety, and frustration, by giving you a definite time.

Now, let me repeat all the essential information. I will arrive at "The New Otani Hotel" at 8:00 AM on October 5th. I will leave you at 1:30 AM on November 11th. You should leave the U.S. anytime before 12 noon on November 3rd. You will then arrive, in Japan, between 3:00 AM to 3:00 PM on November 4th (which is 15 hours later, on the next day from when you left). This will give you many hours to rest up from your loss of a night's sleep. I don't want to spend a day waiting for you to catch up in sleeping habits. Now bring $1000 in Travelers' checks and $50 in cash (which you *should change into "Yen" when you first arrive). I should get my orders in a day or two. And, if there is a serious change, in the time of my arrival, I'll call again. I guess you should make our hotel reservation from November 4th through November 11th. Your return flight will be after 1:30 AM on November 11th. Anytime is fine on November 11th. If the Minolta camera is ready, bring it. If not, bring an instamatic. You should bring some warm clothes. And, probably a rain coat and my suit. Whatever I may need, I can buy the first day (like a sweater, etc). I'll be bringing $400 with me. Well, I think that's it. I'm very excited about seeing you, but rather than tell you about it, I'll happily have the chance to show you shortly. I love you very much, my Sweetheart.*

I didn't get a letter from you, today, but I did get one from John Flora. I'm looking forward to tomorrow's mail call, especially since I may get some pictures.

Now, there is another matter I am happy (and proud) to tell you about. Remember, I told you I was up for a medal? I found out, today, that it is the "Bronze Star" for which I have been nominated. I feel proud because it's very hard to get. It's just one step below the Silver Star which is one step below the Congressional Medal of Honor. If I get it, it won't be until shortly before I go home. It's very possible it will be down-graded to the Army Commendation Award, which is nice, but not anywhere as significant as the Bronze Star. There has been only one Bronze Star given to somebody, from the 18th Surgical Hospital, and that was Sam Clark. Well, at least I've been nominated and I'm proud of that. If I get it, there will be a ceremony, a fancy medal and a glass enclosed (like a portrait) description of why I got the medal. It will be nice to show our kids.

Today was our first nice day in 2 weeks. I really enjoyed seeing the sun. I had one case this morning (from 6:00 AM to 9:30 AM), ran twice, read, etc.

Well, 20 days to go until our R&R. I love you so dearly, my love. We have so much to look forward to and you can bet that I'm looking forward to being with you in 20 days (so far, yet so near). I'll live just to see you.

Jonny

10/15/69
Letter 216

My Precious Darling,

Today, I was Physician-on-Duty again. I had a fair day, did some suturing, did some incision and drainage of abscesses, etc. I, also, had a lot of time to read "Mila 18" (which I'm nearly through reading). It's a great book! I'm a little happier inside and feel better knowing I'll be seeing you soon. Plus, that I got the chance to talk to you and give you the message about our R&R. At least, it has been settled. Now, all I've got to do is live and get to you alive.

I got 2 letters, from you, today. One contained 3 pictures of you golfing (you look very, very pretty, cute and attractive). And, one letter contained the returned tax notice (with appropriate comments on it, next to your note on the back of it).

Yes, I would love to take you to the "Adriatic" for dinner (try and remember). I'm glad Virgil is feeling better at the hospital. Don't tell him, but I think he should have epidural or spinal anesthesia for his hemorrhoidectomy. But, he'll probably be put to sleep unnecessarily. It probably depends on how young the Anesthesiologist is. I'm sure I won't get any mail, tomorrow, since I got 2 letters today. But, the fallowing day, I should get 2 pictures of you. Yes, I'm getting very tired of talking and writing about my love for you, also. I want you and nothing less. One of the O.R. techs shot the enclosed picture. I didn't know it, so I didn't take my mask off.

I love you very much, my Darling. Please, always remember that. I think I only want to live for you. I don't think anything would have much meaning without you.

Jonny

My Dearest Sweetheart,

I didn't get any mail, tonight, as expected. And, not much happened today. So, please excuse the brevity of this letter. I thought and daydreamed, all day, about our R&R, loving you, holding you, looking at you and getting to know you again. I know you are excited about going to somewhere like Tokyo (since you haven't traveled to a foreign country), but for myself I am thinking of only seeing you. I couldn't care less about Tokyo.

Today was slow, but at least we had sunshine and I laid out in the sun for a while. It felt great after all the rain and mud we have been sloshing around in. It was nice yesterday, also, but I was Physician-on-Duty and couldn't go outside.

Tonight, we are having a party for a Supply Officer who is going home. We'll have steaks and hamburgers which is a real treat. Since I weighed only 134 pounds, today, I expect to really stuff myself. I've been eating, but I seem to keep losing weight. I don't know why. Maybe I have a tapeworm or something. My skin is infected, again, with Tinea and I'm taking Griseofulvin faithfully again. Generally speaking, though, I feel pretty good.

Honey, I love you with all my heart and soul. I think about you day and night. My Darling, I love you, I love you, I love you, I love you.

Jonny

My Dearest Precious Sherrie,

Today, I got 2 very warm, open, loving letters from you (as practically all of yours are). So, I'm relatively happy. Tomorrow, of course, I won't get any mail. But, the day after, I should get some of those last remaining 4 photos.

As I told you, I finished the book "Mila 18" a few days ago, but I wanted to tell you some of my feelings about it. I am extremely proud of my heritage. A Jew is his past, his tradition, his principles, his strength and his courage. The Jewish past looks and builds for the future. We have something to strive for because of our heritage to be noble, strong, courageous and productive as were the people in the books "Mila 18", "Exodus", etc. This is what I cherish as a Jew. Out of all the religions, I would pick Judaism for what it can offer a person as to what a person should strive to be. The customs and rituals mean nothing, it is the essence of Judaism that I'm talking about. I feel if you can understand and feel what I'm saying, then we are one on religion. I don't necessarily believe in a Jewish God. I believe in just one God over all. But, I do believe in the Jew and we are Jews, Sherrie. You and I are Jews, so let's be good ones. Not through rituals, but by the lives we live. Honey, I'm so eager to hear your reaction to "Mila 18".

I started the book "The Intimate Enemy", today, but didn't get very far. It looks interesting, but very similar to the book "The Games People Play" in its theme.

I worked, again, all through the night last night. So, again today, I was sort of groggy. Between being Physician-on-Duty, and taking Anesthesia call, I have been up every night the last 5 nights. I did, however, get a chance last night to eat 2 hamburgers and 2 steaks. They were really good. Incidentally, as I'm writing to you, I'm listening to those small tapes I made while I was home. I'm fairly worried that something has gone wrong with the speakers Dan was supposed to have sent from Hong Kong. Please go to the Post Office and see if they have a package there for you. Maybe you missed the notice. Please try.

I'll try to get a note off to your Dad. Of course, I'd like to go out with Smitty and her husband. And, naturally, I'd be happy to go to a party your girlfriends would throw. Oh yes, don't forget to make sure your immunizations are up-to-date for the trip to Tokyo.

Honey, I've got to run. A bad case just came in.

I love you, Jonny

My Precious Darling,

You look beautiful in the 2 pictures I got today. I thought the dress that you made looked very nice. One of the 2 letters that I received from you, today, was your excited response to my call to you.

Sounds like you did a great job, of taking care of your

parents, just before Virgil's surgery. I suppose you know I wrote your folks. Read it, I thought it was a little amusing. Keep up the good work in swimming. Speaking of swimming, I did some myself today. I went to the beach by helicopter. Our generators broke down, so I took the opportunity to go to the beach since we couldn't do any surgery. Boy, I had a wild time and now I'm very sick because of it. I went with a bunch of Enlisted Men with whom I had 4 beers in the hot sun and on an empty stomach. When I got back to the hooch, I realized I was drunk. But, then after sleeping for 2 hours and waking up, I'm now nauseous as hell, tired and irritable. I don't think I'll be able to look at a drink tonight.

Yes, that was nice of the Sanctuary Ship staff to send my address book home. I'd like to have it back.

Well Love, I'll talk to you tomorrow. I love you so much. I want so badly to let it all out.

Jonny

Dear Flower of My Life,

Today, I got a letter from you which was a surprise. It contained 2 more pictures and some of the details concerning your reservations and plans. I was delighted that you were able to get a hotel room for $13.40 per day. Although arriving in Tokyo, on November 3rd (at 7:00 PM) is a bit early, you certainly will get a chance to rest up. You probably won't get to the hotel room until 8:00 PM-9:00 PM. So, you'll be there a total of approximately 33 hours before me. I'm very excited, also.

I'm, also, glad the speakers came. It is a relief to know it. Yes, I think you will benefit a great deal from running in place. We will probably do some together, in Tokyo, ok?

Today was slow, until 3:00 PM, when a guy came in who looked like he was dead. I kept him alive for 3 hours, but finally had to give up. Tomorrow morning, I have a case at 9:00 AM, so I hope the morning goes swiftly. The day after, I'm Physician-on-Duty again. So, with being first call tomorrow and then Physician on-Duty the next day, maybe these next 2 days will go by swiftly. Not much else to report here.

I love you my Darling. Won't be long now until we are together. Honey, your letters are so full of facts that you haven't said much else. You still love me, don't you? Nothing is wrong, is it?

I love you, Jonny

10/21/69
Letter 221

My Precious Darling Love,

Today was pretty good to me. It passed quickly. I had 2 cases. One of them was a 25 units of blood case which had a good outcome. I was in the O.R. all day, but I still found time to run twice. Then, I came back to the hooch and found 2 packages and a letter from you. The packages contained hot dogs, pickles (that was a good idea, Honey, we could really use some) and your delicious cookies. By far, the most important thing about the packages was the message you printed on the boxes. Sweetie Pie, your letters are so factual these days. I was so happy to absorb your sentiments on the boxes. I know you are happy and excited about the R&R, but

I still need to read some impassioned paragraphs from you.

In your letter, today, you scolded me for going to the village which I think is a very proper response. But, I want you to know one thing. In some respects, I'm the most conservative guy at the 18th Surgical Hospital. I don't ever go anywhere by jeep and I'm constantly asked to go to the village, Hue, Phu Bai, Quang Tri, etc. I always refuse. Just that one time, I didn't. You know there are some things I do that the others don't do. For instance, I won't leave an operating room or a ward if we are taking rockets. I have stayed in the O.R. through a number of rocket attacks, but I promise you I will never go anywhere in a vehicle. I didn't tell you yesterday, but the patient I wrote you about (who we failed to resuscitate) was killed along with 2 others by a mine on the very road I took to the village with the Chaplain. So, I promise, I won't go anywhere dangerous or by vehicle. The helicopters are very safe, especially the non-combat med-evac choppers (dust-off) that I go on. Ok?

Honey, I want you to bring this book to Tokyo for me. It is the green, hardcover Pediatric textbook written by Englishmen and I believe English publishers. I believe the only other Pediatric book I have is sort of a softcover handbook type. It might, also, be green so don't bring that one. The hardcover one I want has practically every line underlined. It looks like it has been read through many times. Please let me know if you located the one I want and feel sure of it. I don't want to load you down unnecessarily.

Well Darling, tomorrow I'm Physician-on-Duty, so at least the day will be spent differently. I'm always a little on edge, and uncomfortable, when I'm Physician-on-Duty. I know I don't write my best letters, when I'm Physician-on-Duty, so please understand. Honey, my life is meaningless without you, also. I look forward to being with you with every bit as much desire as you feel. I have a beautiful one-day trip planned, for us, where I just want to hold your hand, put my arms around you and just take a long slow walk in a beautiful country-side area and then eat a nice dinner.

All my love, Jonny

10/22/69
Letter 222

Dearest Sherrie,

As I have been expecting, for the past 3 days, I failed to get a letter today. For the past 3 days in a row, I have gotten letters that were post-dated 4 days ago. This happened only very rarely before. Tomorrow, I should get one because it will then be a 5-day post-date delay. This is how to make much ado about little things in one easy lesson.

Today, as Physician-on-Duty, I was fairly busy. It was just enough to make the day pass without too much pain.

Honeybunch, even though I'm Physician-on-Duty, I'm pretty relaxed right now. And, I can't think of a single bit of news to tell you. So, forgive me for writing such a dry short letter. Please understand. I'm just sort of dried out of things to say.

It's always easy, however, and fun to remind you that I am very much in love with you. And, that I dream and think about you all the time. I feel very strongly the purposelessness and futility of life without you. Thank God our R&R is soon. I want to be with you and love you very much.

I am yours alone,

Jonny

My Sweet Baby,

I can't believe it, but I have a grand-daddy of a cold. Can you imagine getting a cold when it is 110 degrees outside? That's what it's been since the rain stopped 5 days ago. I probably got a cold from my fan blowing directly on me all night. Well, my wishes came true. These past 3 days did go by pretty quickly. And, today, I enjoyed doing nothing. I did make up a package, however, and it is a very important package. It contains 12 recorded tapes. I'll be sending them, to you, when I get a chance to go over to the Post Office (within the next few days). I don't remember if I told you, but my flight number, to Yokota Air Force Base, is #206. It should arrive around 1:30 AM- 2:00 AM on November 5th. But, remember it will take me until about 6:00 AM- 7:00 AM to get to the hotel. The reason I'm giving you the flight number is so that you can call to find out when it landed, etc. As far as my cold goes, I'm not good, but I'm making every attempt to get over it by the time our R&R arrives.

Sweet Darling Sherrie, I love you so much. Today, I got 3 very warm loving letters from you. I just ate up all your passionate sentiments. Sweetheart, please forgive me for asking all those silly questions in my previous letters. But, you can see how needy I am for you. Your love is strong, consistent and it makes me feel that way. I'm glad to hear that Virgil is doing better.

I have a lot to do, myself, to get ready for Tokyo. I have to wash some clothes (first time), pack up my things for Quang Tri completely and partially pack up the hooch. And, per-

haps, send some more stuff home that I don't want to lug up to Quang Tri.

I'll have to admit that I, too, am pretty darn pleased about the Bronze Star nomination. I won't know if I got it, until I get it, which if I do will be shortly before I go home for good. You know you get a big plaque with a description telling how you were this and that under stress (etc, etc). Plus, I'll get the Bronze Star medal and the bar to wear on my uniform.

As far as the move goes, we are definitely going to the DMZ, sometime between November 15th- November 20th. I'll tell you all about it in Tokyo.

Oh yes, in one of your letters, you mentioned that I'll probably be tired when I arrive in Tokyo. I think I'll be too excited to sleep, but it's true. I will be up all night. I'll try to sleep during the day before I report to the R&R Center in Da Nang.

Sweetheart, I love you with all my being. Yes, it will probably be the most memorable week of my life in Tokyo. I feel so much love for you. All my thoughts and desires are of, and for, you.

Jonny

My Dearest Darling,

It's getting so hard to write you after a nothing day. I have so little to tell you about. I did nothing all day except read, pack up my things a little, ran twice, saw a couple of patients I have on the wards and laid out in the sun. My cold is under control and I should be over it in a day or two. Tomorrow, I'm first call. A case or two should go a long way towards making the day pass more quickly. Since I've wrapped up and packaged all my tapes, I've been listening to you sing a great deal. I'm very glad I have those 5 or 6 tapes with you singing. My favorites are "Yesterday", "Summertime" and "Softly". I especially like the song, I have on my little tapes, in which you sing "The Long Black Veil" along with Joan Baez. I can't tell the difference between you and her. I guess all I really did, today, was daydream about you. After I write you, I am going to make myself a couple of hot dogs and a can of chicken noodle soup. That should cure my cold, just ask my Mother. She thinks the antibiotic of choice, for all infections, is chicken soup. If the infection proves resistant, then you can add matzo balls.

My Sweet Baby, I miss you so much. We are going to be very happy together. We are lucky that we have so much to look forward to. Did you know that you are everything I used to hope for, dream about and want for a wife? You are and it's just another way in which I know for myself, and can say to you, that I sincerely love you.

Jonny

Sherrie My Love,

This is even a harder letter to write, than yesterday's letter, because absolutely nothing happened today. There were no cases, no news (etc, etc). I ran twice and packed a bit. And would you believe, I started to wash and then iron some clothes for R&R? Big day! Tomorrow, I'm doing a hernia case while Steve Lipson supervises. I'd rather do surgery than do nothing. I may then go to the beach, in the afternoon, if a chopper is going. I'm Physician-on-Duty on October 29th (which is Wednesday). No mail from you, today, but I got a card from my folks and one from friends of my folks. And, I got a letter from other friends of my folks in addition to a letter from Frank Snell (the Nurse Anesthetist who was here when I first came). Incidentally, he wrote that he got the Army Commendation Medal months after he got home. I helped to draft his nomination.

Honeybunch, I hope my letters don't bore you too much. I wish I had more exciting things to tell you about. I should get a letter, from you, tomorrow.

We all know about President Nixon's unilateral cease fire, but you can't tell anything has changed here. Everything goes on as usual. There are fights on the perimeter, howitzers shooting all night (etc, etc). The war won't be over, for any of us, until we go home.

Well, not too much to go now until R&R. Only 10 days left. It really will be a second honeymoon and I think it will be even better than the first. I love you more now than when we first married. I'm happy with feeling the love. I think you will be a happier person because the desire of my love will be to make you happy.

Jonny

My Precious, Precious Baby,

Two letters from you, today, two! They were wonderful, wonderful loving letters. One was very short and had a card in it from Lonnie. And, the other one informed me that we cannot get into "The New Otani Hotel". Let me answer your letters first. Of course, you are forgiven for writing a short letter. I'm thankful you crammed in the time to write what you did. I don't understand what the Minolta people did, because I'm sure the advance lever was broken. I hope it's not exactly the way I sent it, to you, because I'm pretty sure it was broken. Anyway, we'll see. Did you tell them that it was the advance lever? I'm sure I mentioned it to you several times. Naturally, I'm awaiting the news of our hotel reservations. But, I'm sure we'll have plenty of time. I won't be leaving Camp Evans until the morning of November 3rd. So, I'll get mail the evening of November 2nd, which means you could write as late as October 26th or 27th. I would still get the information on time. And, I could always call you on November 1st, but I'd be lucky if I got through in one day. If you think there is a chance I will not have gotten the information on time, leave a message at "The New Otani Hotel" desk for me, as well as call the R&R Center at Camp Zama where I have to go to out-process (before they let us take a bus to Tokyo). Now, to answer your questions. My R&R starts on November 4th at 7:00 PM when I report to the R&R Center at Da Nang. I have a reservation for a flight from Da Nang to Yokota Air Force Base (in Japan) at 8:00 PM on November 4th. I arrive at the Yokota Air Force Base at approximately 1:30 AM on

November 5th. Then, I go to Camp Zama and then to Tokyo and you!

I'm sure, with the effort you are putting into swimming, that you will become an accomplished swimmer. You already have a perfect form, now all you need to do is make yourself move through the water.

Sugar Pie, I've been reading the book "The Intimate Enemy", but I can't say that I'm getting very much out of it. I think most of the case illustrations of fights are very silly indeed. I don't think we have the problems that the people in the book do. I think you don't speak your mind as frequently as perhaps you should. But, I'm sure most of the time, we have addressed any issues directly rather than to argue about something when another thing is bothering us. Well, I'll read more.

Today, in the morning, I repaired an incarcerated umbilical hernia. It was an enjoyable morning because Faye Skinner (the Major Nurse Anesthetist) got some good instruction, from me, on the spinal for the case. And, also, on a supraclavicular block for a hand case that followed. She did both blocks, but I thought my comments and guidance were timely. I enjoyed it and she was so happy to be successful at both. So far, she hasn't been able to hit a supraclavicular block yet (out of about 6 times). So, I have had to do them. She has, also, missed many spinals. She is very nice (sort of like Roberta Johnson) and I enjoy working with her.

The rest of the day was like all the others, so I won't bother to go into it. I must admit, though, that I'm in sort of a groove right now. I can get through the day pretty well, when things are very slow, because I can make my mind go blank and let the time pass. Of course, knowing that R&R is coming soon, is a big help.

Tonight, I went to church (it's Sunday night) because the Chaplain is on R&R and the Colonel (Dick Adams, the Com-

manding Officer of the hospital) gave the sermon or address or whatever you call it. I had promised him I would come and listen. We are pretty good friends and I have spent many evenings shooting the breeze with him. Also, the Sergeant (in charge of the O.R. techs) was doing the singing, so all in all I saw people I see every day in a different way. It's funny how different people look upon God. And, the different approaches or attitudes they use when asking God for things.

Well my Love, my spine is doing some fancy footwork when I think about being with you soon. I love you very much, My Precious Wife. And, my heart is so open to loving you with the tremendous love it feels. Oh Sherrie, it will be so great!

Jonny

Dearest Darling Sweetheart,

Today, it rained all day. But, the ending of the day was considerably brightened by receipt of a letter (from you) that was full of love and warmth. I read some more of "The Intimate Enemy", but I find it only interesting from the point of view that other people have so much trouble communicating. I wonder often what you thought you got out of the book and what you thought I might get out of it. I'd be very interested in knowing. A thought did occur to me today, however, and I want to tell you about it so you know how I feel. And, I can set the record straight so there are no questions or misunderstandings. I may not have told you frequently or emphatically enough (in the past) how proud I am of you. I am very proud of you and I often boast to other people how you go ahead and do so many things on your own. And, you put a good deal of effort into becoming accomplished in these areas. I'm referring to your swimming, running, tennis, golfing, college classes, conversion to Judaism (in the year before we married), guitar, working private duty, sewing beautiful dresses, working full-time in the Dialysis Unit and writing to everybody. And, all while being a very wonderful and attentive wife who spends so much time and effort on me. I couldn't be anything but blissfully happy, which I am, when it concerns you. So, I hope I have made myself clear. I have a great deal of respect and pride in your ambition, drive and accomplishments. Now, that I have tallied such an impressive list of activities and accomplishments that you have achieved, I probably will feel inferior and insecure next to or being married to such an impressive and dynamic person.

Today, with the rain, I did even less than usual. I ran in place in the hooch (in my combat boots) for 30 minutes and then took the coldest shower imaginable. When I hit that water, my heart stopped, I'm sure. I turned blue and I froze in place. I would have died had somebody not turned off the water. Only kidding you. Seriously, it was cold. Ugh! We, also, played Monopoly and I slept and read, etc. I did hear about the riots in Tokyo, but I'm sure they won't affect us.

Sugar Pie, if you haven't got the message by now, let me spell it out for you. I LOVE YOU. It will be so wonderful to get to know you again. I want so much to always learn more about you, share ourselves with one another and always grow closer together.

Jonny

10/28/69
Letter 228

My Precious Darling,

It rained again, all day today, so today passed much the same way. Oops, I spoke too soon. A call just came in for Steve (who is first up on Surgery today) that 4 GIs just came in with fragment wounds. Since I'm first up (for Anesthesia), I think I'll be working tonight. Tomorrow, I'm Physician-on-Duty. So, I'm going to make this short. The only thing I wanted to tell you is that tomorrow's letter will probably be my last letter before our R&R. In case we get no mail again tomorrow, and you don't hear from me that I got the hotel reservation information, don't worry. In addition to leaving messages at "The New Otani Hotel" desk and at Fort Zama, please call Yokota Air Force Base. Tell them when I'm arriving and what our hotel reservations are and ask them to be sure to give me the message. That is the most important place (Yokota Air Force Base) to call, because I understand I can possibly get out of having to go to Fort Zama if a message is there waiting for me. So, let's try it. It could be worth an extra 3-4 hours together. So, I'll expect messages in 3 places as well as hearing from you in the next day or two. The only thing is that you will probably not know whether I will definitely know.

Honey, I've got to go. I love you so feverishly, so greatly, so intensely and so richly that I'm sure I will have no trouble communicating this to you when I am with you. Sherrie, everything looks so beautiful as long as you are in the picture.

Jonny

Sherrie Sweetheart Sunshine,

Boy, I tell you, you really wrote me 2 great letters on October 23rd and 24th. I was excited before, about seeing you, but now I'm really frothing at the mouth.

I was relieved to get the news of our hotel reservation, although you may not know this before you leave, because I have strong doubts that this will arrive on or before November 1st. In fact, I'm sure you won't. It won't go out until tomorrow, which is October 30th, so I'm sure it won't make it. So, I'm making this very short since I doubt it will be read. I was Physician-on-Duty, today, and I was very busy.

I'm glad you're bringing your running gear. I, too, would like to run if we could find a suitable spot.

Well Sweetheart, it is so hard to write believing you are not going to get this before you leave. Perhaps the best way to sign off would be to tell you that already I feel the R&R, with you, was the most wonderful week in my life. I fully expect it to be.

Jonny

My Precious Love,

Honey, I had a terrific week with you, in Tokyo. It was so pleasant, relaxing, fun and sort of a pretty week. I think you know I was happy, so I won't dwell on it now. It's late and I'm really tired. I got to the 95th Evacuation Center ok and I'm staying in my friend's room, tonight, since he is Physician-on-Duty. He's going to Hong Kong on November 26th and I may go, with him, for 4 days. I'll have to see what's what at the 18th Surgical Hospital.

I'm glad we had a quick goodbye, no tears. Did you cry? I saw you standing by the door until the plane taxied away. Listen to this, if I had missed the plane, I would have had to pay my way back myself. It would have cost me $277. Boy, we were lucky because that cab driver could have really cost us $277.

I hope you were able to work private duty. I was thinking on the plane that I will definitely moonlight, in Alabama, since I won't be able to or want to in New York. I probably will be able to moonlight in Anesthesia since the Standard-of-Practice for Alabama is perhaps lower. Of course, I would have to take out some malpractice insurance. I hope, also, that you went ahead and made photocopies of the orders I gave you. You will need them for the packages as well as for the move. I noticed tonight, in the PACEX catalog, that there is a 31% customs duty fee on movie projectors. I'm sure that they will try to hit us with that. And, in our case, it would be something like $18.

I hope you managed with your luggage ok.

Honeybunch, I've got to go to bed. I love you with all my heart, Darling. Please remember that and please feel it.

Jonny

Dearest Sweetheart,

Well, I'm back "home" again at dirty, dusty Camp Evans. It is so desolate here. Many things are torn down, the hospital shuts down in 3 days and very few people are here. It's a lonely, boring, hot place to be. I myself go to Quang Tri on November 18th. Please address all my mail, to this address, as soon as you get this: My name, my Social Security number, 18th Surgical Hospital, APO S.F. 96495.

I will not be able to go to Hong Kong in late November. I probably will try to get out in mid-December. We are supposed to be fully operational, in Quang Tri, on December 10th. But, I don't care about doing cases or anything. I just want to get out of Vietnam.

I looked at all your pretty pictures, in your pom-pom outfit, and my heart was so warmed again by your image. I got 3 letters, from you, and one from Woody. He's an Orthopedist and the Army put him in the Outpatient Clinic in Medicine. Another Army triumph over logic and reason.

Every time I think of how close we came to losing $277, by nearly missing that flight, I get sick. I am, also, anxious to learn how you managed with your baggage and taxi ride over to the International Airport (in Tokyo) and that you got home safe and sound.

Today, on the chopper flight up North, I took a roll of film.

So, I should be able to send the pictures to you in 3 weeks.

Now, I would like you to send me pictures of that cheap chinaware (pattern name: Progression) that we could use as a second set of dishes. I could pick out the one I like best, out of the pictures you send, and buy the set in Hong Kong. Also, send pictures or requests for anything else you think we might really need now or in the future. Tonight, I'm cooking, so I've got to get busy. I'm making the last of our hamburger meat with an egg (to keep it together), garlic salt and pepper. Well, I made the hamburgers. Not bad, if I say so myself.

Sweetie Pie, I love you very much. Did you feel it in Tokyo? I hope so. I feel it. I wish or hope that I communicate it to you. Do I? I really have such a warm, wonderful, deep feeling when I think of you.

Jonny

Dearest Darling Sherrie,

Today was quiet. I had one case, ran twice, went to a meeting and napped (etc, etc). The same old things as before. I'm waiting for the depression to hit me as it has hit everyone else after they come back from R&R.

I suppose you read about the massacre, that took place up at Quang Tri, last night. I only mention it because I want you to know, that as a result of that massacre of our GI's, the 101st Airborne Division has moved a whole battalion of soldiers up there today. So, when I go up in 5 days, security should be much better and I will be extremely careful. I'm not going outside of my hooch, ever, without a gun, flak jacket and steel helmet on. I think I'll quit running, up there, if the situation doesn't improve much. Don't worry about me, I'll be looking out for "old number 1". I really felt very bad about that ambush. We took 30 dead and 70 injured. Just think, those guys were just like you or me. It was so useless, so tragic and so wasteful to lose lives like that. There isn't enough money, in the world, to pay me for what I think my life is worth. And, yet, I should risk it over this war? Oh Sherrie, I want to get out of Vietnam so badly. Only 63 more days left.

Now, this is very important. The new address (APO 96495), that I gave you yesterday, is the correct one. You should start addressing your letters to that address on November 26th. I know I told you to start right away, but that was wrong. Our mail will come to Camp Evans up until December 1st. So, the letter you write on November 26th should go to Quang Tri on December 1st or 2nd. Got it?

Everybody says I act like I'm on "Cloud 9" compared to the way I was before our R&R. See what you did for me?

Honey, I miss you as always because I love you as always, if not more. I'll soon be home and we can forget this horrible year.

All my love and thoughts, Jonny

My Precious Baby,

Honey, what can I tell you? Absolutely nothing happened today. I'm sorry if I bore you, but here are the dull events of the day as they occurred. I got up, ran, showered, shaved, went to the PX to get some film, got a haircut, came back, read, packed up some of my things for Quang Tri, read some more, ran again and showered. And, now, I'm going to a cookout that the "dust off" (med evac) pilots are having. I should go. I contributed a whole bottle of booze to the affair.

Oh yes, tomorrow, I'm going back to the PX to get a hand-painted picture of you on black velvet (2 feet by 2 feet). The artist will paint it from a composite of about 10 photos you sent me. I want to hang it in my study, someday, so I'll have something beautiful in the room.

Sweetie Pie, I love you with all my heart and I miss you so much. Life is so empty without you. Please understand the brevity of this letter, but I really don't have much to write about.

Jonny

My Precious Sweetheart,

I'm so worried about whether you got home safely or not. So, I just put a call through to you. I didn't get a letter, today, and I'm anxious to know. I worry about you.

Today, I went back to the PX and paid a Korean artist to paint a portrait of you from 3 pictures of you that I gave him. I hope it comes out ok, because I spent $17 on it. I'm concerned about the 3 photos that I gave him, because none of them are the portrait kind. And, it won't be on black velvet either. He ran out of velvet, so it will be on canvas.

Today was slow. Steve and I packed up a lot of stuff today and the hospital officially closed today. Tomorrow, I'm going to start packing up the Anesthesia Department. Then, I go to

Quang Tri on November 18th.

The cook-out, last night, was ok. I had some steak and chicken, but today I had a lot of trouble running. I had a pain in my epigastrium. It was there all 3 times that I tried to run today. My best effort was only a little more than half of what I usually run. I hope it passes and that, tomorrow, I'll be normal. I feel fine when I'm not running. Yesterday, I ran 2 miles in 13 minutes 15 seconds. And, that might explain it, because I may have strained myself doing it. That was just before the cookout. I finished that run with a pain in my epigastrium and I never had that before.

Oh yes, I finished the book "The Salzburg Connection". It turned out to be a pretty good book.

My Darling, I wish I had more to write to you about. But, all I can think about is getting home. I want to go home so badly, because I love and miss you so very much.

Jonny

Precious Sweetheart,

Today, I got your short note (written November 11th) telling me that you arrived safely, which I was much relieved to hear. I didn't get through to you last night. It was 10:00 AM your time and you weren't at home or at work. So, I hope you got a private duty case. But, I'm going to try again tonight, since you may have been told at the hospital that a call came through for you from Vietnam. I don't want you to worry as to what the call was all about.

Today, I packed up some more of the hooch and the Anes-

thesia Department. And, I'll do more of the same tomorrow. Then, we go the day after. It will have to be by jeep. But, don't worry. I, and everybody else, will be heavily armed. And, all the way, I'll have a steel helmet and flak jacket on. I'll try to go with as many people as possible. We'll have gunships in the air over us, most of the way, and a mine-sweeper in front of us. So, I really don't think you should worry. Ok, Sweetheart?

Do we need a vacuum cleaner? Please let me know. It is an expensive item in the States. I'm sure we would want one someday (maybe for New York). Should I get it? You're the housecleaning chief, so your word goes. So far, my list for Hong Kong is: (1) bicycles, (2) clothes, (3) connecting jacks for our stereo equipment, (4) vacuum cleaner, (5) cheap chinaware.

Darling, I miss you so much. Life is so empty without you. I guess that's because my life is so full of love and happiness when I'm with you. Oh, I just wish I could see my way through to the end of this. Maybe, when I get settled in Quang Tri, I'll be able to see the end better.

Jonny

Dearest Sweetheart,

Today, I got your first real letter since we had our R&R (it included the golf score) and a big postcard. It was great to read them. You must have had fun golfing. It sounded like it. I didn't get you at home or at work again, last night, so I'll try again tonight. I don't want you to worry if you were told I had tried to reach you. Since tomorrow night I'll be in Quang Tri, I don't think I'll be able to call. So, I hope I get you tonight. I hope my calls have not alarmed you.

Yes, the book "Mila 18" is quite a story. I think part of the answer, to the Jewish people, is that success lies in exercising self-discipline. I was often reminded of Rudyard Kipling's poem "If" while reading "Mila 18". Do you know it? "If you can keep your head when all about you are losing theirs" (etc, etc).

I hope you got private duty cases on those other 2 days. And, that you were able to finish that other furniture you were working on.

I'm glad you'll be sending the pictures 2 at a time, because the delivery of mail is bound to be confused for several weeks. Some letters might be lost. How I need them.

Now listen to this carefully. I would be willing to stay in Los Angeles (until January 27th) in order for you to get your vacation pay. More than willing. Now, if you have to sign something or other in order to get the money, then we will definitely stay and leave for Alabama on January 28th. I suspect it will be necessary for you to do that (sign something or get the money personally). You should check on these things. I'm definitely going to moonlight while I'm in Los Angeles and waiting to go, with you, to Alabama. Please look up Matt Bernstein and ask him to see about lining me up a job in the "drunk tank" at Los Angeles County General Hospital or something. He's in Ophthalmology. I'll, also, register with an Anesthesia agency as soon as I get back. I can make $80 a shift (8 hours) at the hospital. So, in 2-3 weeks' time, I should easily make $600 (could pay for a TV console). It won't be a waste if we have to wait a week or so longer than we thought. In fact, it may be a good thing. We don't have to be at Fort Rucker until February 19th. So, if we left January 28th, we would be able to get to Alabama by February 5th. Every day *short of February 19th, however, is leave time that could be used for a trip to the Caribbean.*

Well my Precious Love, tomorrow I go to Quang Tri and I will literally be "riding shotgun". I'll shoot anything that moves. One thing you can say about me is that I have good reflexes.

I love you very much, Darling. I hope you can feel it and it helps to sustain you. We really don't have too much more to go, do we?

All my love, Jonny

My Dearest Love,

Today was quite a day. I'm totally exhausted, but alive and well in Quang Tri. We moved, today, under extremely difficult conditions. It poured rain all day long, bridges washed away and detours had to be made. And, I lugged so many heavy things on and off trucks that my back will never be the same. Fighting is still going on up in the Dong Ha area. But, we won't be doing any cases for about 10 days until we set up everything. Steve and I have about 3 days of hard work ahead in setting up the hooch. For tonight, we just set up our beds into which I'm about to collapse. I fired my first real bullets today. I saw something moving in the brush, off the road, and I let "it" have it. I didn't stop to find out what it was.

The setup here, as far as the physical plant, is good (better than at Camp Evans) and we have hot showers! I'm going for one as soon as I finish this letter. I believe I would have been much happier spending a year here instead of at Camp

Evans. I couldn't pick up your portrait, today, but the artist lives in Quang Tri at the PX here. He commutes to Camp Evans every day. So, I'm going to make a strong effort to reach him tomorrow and get it. Not only am I very anxious to see how it turned out, I paid $17 for it.

Honeybunch, I'm so anxious for a hot shower and some sleep that I'm going to finish now. It's still raining very hard. Beginning around November 23rd, I'm going to start putting down my new APO number on the return address.

I love you with all my heart and soul and my mind's meaning.

Goodnight, my Love. Jonny

Dearest Darling Sherrie,

I was very pleasantly surprised, today, when I got a letter from you that was brought up from Camp Evans. It had 3 pictures of you. I liked all of them. It's too bad you didn't get any private duty cases, but it should be easy for me to make up for it by moonlighting when I get home.

Today, I worked on the hooch, trying to get things organized. But, my heart isn't in it. I have only 7 weeks to go. I can't share Steve's enthusiasm for fixing things up. Tomorrow, I have to take Sick Call. We aren't doing any operations, so I can't complain about it since I'm not doing anything anyway. I won't be able to get your portrait again, today, but I stand a good chance tomorrow.

Remember to use the new APO number starting on November 25th. Honey, Steve is crying for me to help him with something, so I'll finish this letter. I have 55 days and a wake-up left!

I love you with all my heart. Jonny

My Precious Baby,

I was lucky, again, today. I got a letter, from you, with 2 great photos of you (they had detail, clarity, spontaneity and beauty). And, I got your package with salami and hot dogs. Our mail is still coming up, every day, from Camp Evans.

I just had a delicious salami sandwich. Unfortunately, the mustard jar broke and ruined one loaf of bread and 2 of the packages of Rice-a-Roni. If you would, please send some mustard (like the old kind) with the spout taped shut, another salami and bread.

I was pretty busy, today, seeing patients. I had to go to the Graves Department, today, to pronounce somebody dead and I hated it. I don't mind blood, feces, vomitus or doing anything that a patient needs as long as there is a breath of life left. But, this guy was dead and I really disliked doing this. It seemed so sad to me that this guy lost his life for something he doesn't understand. I hate to see the final proof that some of what I do (being a Doctor) doesn't come out successful. I've lost plenty of patients that I've worked on, but when they die, I never go back to the body or think about the patient being dead. I only think of what I might have done when he was alive. Seeing dead people is no fun. I could never do autopsies, that's for sure. Well, enough philosophy.

Honey, I love you dearly. Every day, I count the minutes

I have until I get back home to you. Right now, I have 78,480 minutes to go. How my heart cries for you!

Jonny

Dearest Darling Sherrie,

Hi Sweetheart. I feel so frustrated, when I sit down to write you, because I have so little to tell you about. I didn't get any mail, today, so I don't even have a letter to respond to. Please understand if my letters lack any luster, so does my life. I miss you a great deal, you know that. I get irritated with myself, for stating the matter so simply, since 99% of what I feel concerns that matter.

Today, I got your portrait and it didn't come out looking like you. So, I wasted my $17. I worked around the hooch and saw a few patients. It has been raining steadily, since I left Camp Evans. Quang Tri is much lower (our old hospital was on a little rise), so it's very, very muddy everywhere. It's difficult to run, but I have managed to run once daily for the last 3 days.

My replacement arrived today. He's a Doctor who has been in-country for 7½ months. He's had 1½ years of Anesthesia Residency (according to Steve). He told me that he was turned down by Columbia Presbyterian Hospital's Anesthesia Residency Program. I'm glad he is here, because I probably will definitely be able to go to Hong Kong in December.

I miss you very much. If this last month (plus 2 weeks) would only pass quickly. But, it probably won't.

I love you with all my heart and soul. Jonny

I Love You Sweetheart,

Today was another nothing day, but at least it stopped raining and I was able to run twice. I can't say anything else of note happened, except I got 2 letters today from you (with 5 beautiful pictures of your pretty face).

Now, let me answer your letters. Do we need a toaster? Do we have one? If so, what is wrong with it? Of course, I'll look for bicycles in Hong Kong. And, I'll probably get a zoom movie camera since you were so enthusiastic about having one. This will be my only chance to get it for half price. My list for Hong Kong now is: (1) Bicycles- possibly with little attachable motors so we could take 50 mile trips, on them, from home. (2) Wires and jacks- for our electronic equipment. (3) Toaster- depending on your answers to my questions. (4) Movie camera. (5) Vacuum cleaner depending on your answer to my questions. (6) Cheap set of chinaware- depending on what style you send me. (7) Some clothes- suits, etc.

See, I do take you into consideration on everything. I only went to the expense of meeting you in Tokyo, rather than Hawaii, so you could share in the shopping.

I was very touched by the letter, you sent, by the girl with leukemia. I wasn't aware that cutbacks had been made in medical research. No Sherrie, I don't feel removed from the issue. As you know, I tend to think a little more than I talk about political issues. But, I have thought for a long time, that there was a tremendous disproportion between the amount of money spent on health, education (etc) and the amount spent on space arms, airlines (etc). You should write a letter of protest. The life of that leukemia patient is worth far more than any super-sonic jet.

Well, Darling, keep my love for you close to your heart. I do. I always think of your love for me. It is the one thing that causes me to be happy and to keep going.

You are always very close, to me, in my heart and mind.

Jonny

My Precious Sherrie,

Today was ok, so far. I always write between 6-7 PM. I took Medicine Call, today, and saw some interesting cases. So, it made at least part of the day enjoyable. I ran once, but I look forward to running twice tomorrow if it doesn't start raining again. Today was cloudy all day, but at least it didn't rain again. After I finish writing you, I'm going to finish off that delicious salami you sent.

Beginning on November 25th, I hope you start addressing your letters to APO 96495. I don't remember if I told you November 25th or the 26th. But, I can always hope it was November 25th.

I didn't get any mail, today, and I probably won't get any tomorrow. That's because they are in the process of shifting the mail delivery up here or something like that.

Sweetheart, I don't remember if I told you how proud I am of your interest in swimming. I'm sure you'll become a good swimmer. I hope you'll be able to swim a few laps without stopping, for me, when I come home.

Darling, I love you very, very much. I sort of see it crys-

tallizing in you. And, then reflecting (back to me) much warmth, concern, tenderness and beauty. Maybe that's why it's so wonderful to feel love. The reflection of love, off the loved object, is so wonderful.

Jonny

The mail delivery is still mixed up and I didn't get any mail, again, today. What happened was that the mail came up from Da Nang, to Camp Evans, and since nobody was there to receive it (for the 18th Surgical Hospital) the mail went back to Da Nang instead of coming up here to Quang Tri. It's so messed up.

Guess what? My replacement came. He's had 14 months of Anesthesia Residency. But, the Chief of Professional Services and Steve Lipson (who is Chief of Surgery) want me to remain as Chief of Anesthesia even though the new Doctor has more experience. I was pretty embarrassed, today, when he told me he thought he would run the Department. I commented that he probably wouldn't because the powers that be want me to remain as I am until I leave. I think it is fair because my Nurses have been happy, as have I, with the Department. There is no hostility between us. In fact, I like him. I'm really being passive in so far as arguing for the Department. I really don't care. And, I have so little time left. But, if they want me to remain Chief, I will. I think the Nurses, however, will be unhappy with him. He does not want to take first call. Nor does he want to let them do any regional anesthesia, at all, no less teach them. I have always taken the position that what you let the Nurses do reflects your own confidence in your own ability. Well, it will all be his headache shortly.

Today, it rained, but I managed to slip out twice to run during lulls in the rain. Otherwise, I read some of my British Journal of Anesthesiology. I've begun studying these past few days again. Also, I did some reading in a novel. I really can't report much else. We'll start emergency surgery on November 28th and elective surgery on December 10th.

Well Lover, I continue to love you as always. The only time I become afraid is when time seems to slow down. And getting home to your love, which sustains me, seems further away. Oh, these last days are so agonizing. All my love is for you, and only you, Darling.

Jonny

Dearest Lovable Darling Sherrie,

Hi Sweetheart. Guess what? At 5:00 AM, today, Steve and I did the first case at the new hospital. What fun. I really enjoyed doing it. Today, I was sort of busy having talks with people and straightening out things in the Anesthesia Department. Things worked out pretty well, as far as I'm concerned. Everybody wants me to be Chief, so I will be. We have 4 people in the Department (me, the new Doctor who has completed 14 months of Anesthesiology Residency and 2 Nurse Anesthetists). I had to make one compromise, however, and that is not to allow the Nurse Anesthetists to do blocks or spinals. One of the Nurses has been with me for 4 months, we get along well and I have taught her quite a bit. The other

Nurse is new, so I'm not going to try and start teaching him. As a result of the new Doctor having different ideas, on how to run the Department, I have to make out the Call schedule myself. I need to do that in order that I can best please everybody, most importantly myself. I made up the Call schedule for November 28th through December 6th. Out of the 9 days, I put myself on first call three times and everybody else on first call two times each. During those 9 days, I'll be Physician-on-Duty twice.

So, at least on 5 of those 9 days, I'll be busy. In addition, I'm second call on 2 of the remaining 4 days. And, the other 2 days, I'll be fourth call (essentially having those days off). But, from November 29th through December 6th, I'll be taking second Surgery Call and doing operations (in addition to my Anesthesia Calls and being the assigned Physician-on-Duty). The reason for this is that 2 out of our 3 Surgeons are taking their Board Exams, in Saigon, which leaves Steve as the only Surgeon that we'll have here. So, I'm second Surgeon. I'll most probably get to do most of the simple operations. And, I may do a major belly case if Steve is operating on a big case (and he can't leave that case) when another big case comes in. So, it looks like I'll have some varied and interesting days ahead. And, I'm very happy about it. The reason that we did a case, very early this morning, is that the weather was so bad we couldn't send the patient (a Regular Army Vietnamese soldier) anywhere. He had a gunshot wound of the abdomen. Tonight, will be the same thing. It has been raining hard all day and the choppers can't get out to the ship. So, we'll have to do any cases that come in tonight. We're not open officially until November 28th to do Emergency cases because the wards aren't set-up. But, we do have an O.R. ready to go.

Today, I received a letter from you that was dated November 20th. The previous letter that I received, from you, was dated November 16th. So, I'm missing 3 letters. I'm glad some of our packages are starting to come in. Yes, I agree I'm a "sweet, adorable, unselfish husband" and you may certainly "spend the rest of your life doing all that you can to please me". I agree. I'll do the same for you, ok?

I'm pleased to hear you feel you are making progress in your swimming class. It must help to practice if you feel you are getting ahead.

Apparently, you found a little puppy and now are giving it away. Well, since this is the first I have heard of it, I'll wait for your missing letters to fill me in.

Honeybunch, I'm getting writer's cramp, so I'm going to quit. Tomorrow should be a slow day since nothing will be going on. Maybe another case will come in tonight. I'm taking all cases until we start our Call schedule on November 28th. I'm hungry for work to do. Work makes the time go faster.

All my love, thoughts and desires are of, for and about you. I'm so happy to think about being home with you in 51 days. When I sleep, I don't usually dream.

But, when I do lately, it seems to usually be a nightmare. Oh well, win a few and lose a few. You are my big winner all the time, always. Jonny

My Precious Sweetheart,

Hi Baby, what's happening? I wish I knew. I didn't get any mail today. I was demoted today. The new Doctor complained very vigorously, to the Chief of Professional Services, that he should be Chief of the Anesthesia Department because of his superior or longer training (14 months of Anesthesia Residency). And, since there is no getting around that argument, he will be Chief. I don't really care, just as long as I do lots of cases. The Chief of Professional Services said he was sorry and that he wished I could remain as Chief. But, his hands are tied by the rules and so they are.

Again, last night, I was called for a case at 5:00 AM. I enjoyed doing it, however. I ran once, today, even though it continued to rain. But, it was miserable (cold, wet and extremely muddy). Yesterday, I didn't run at all, because of rain and mud. My boots look like a mud clay statue of real boots. I'm really roughing it.

Well, that's it. Oh no, I forgot to tell you one other thing. The hospital got in some new Bennett respirators. And, I spent a good part of the day studying the respirator on how to assemble it from scratch and use it fully. It's affording me an excellent chance to know the respirator well. It's a good thing to know, because people are always fumbling around respirators and never quite knowing what to do with them.

Thinking of you all the time, Sweetheart. My love for you burns bright, strong, true and loyal. It is a great deal of love. I miss you very much, the time just can't go fast enough.

Jonny

My Precious Adorable Baby,

What a day! Honey, I'm so bone-tired. I worked like a dog for about 15 straight hours today. I did 3 operations and did my own anesthesia for these cases (spinals and blocks). And, I resuscitated a cardiac arrest and administered 5 anesthetics for operations that Steve did. What a week this is going to be. I was rewarded, at the end of the day, by 2 letters from you written on November 17th and 18th. I'm going to answer them quickly and then hit the sack, ok?

I'm glad you liked the phone call. As far as having a baby or trying for one as soon as I get home, I have no real objection, but I do think that the best time to start trying would be around April-May. Then, you could have a good 4 months in New York without being late in a pregnancy.

Honey, what do you want to do with the dog? You know I like dogs. But, try to be practical in your decision. We do have to move to Alabama and we both are out of the house during the day. Well, tomorrow, I'm first Call for Anesthesia and second Call for Surgery again. What a day!

All my love and thoughts, my Precious Sweetheart. I long for you so much.

Jonny

11/28/69
Letter 247

My Darling Wonderful Sherrie,

Today, I was pretty busy, although I did only one nerve block. I don't know if I told you, but we also have a Pediatric ward here, and one of the infants arrested (cardiac). I was busy, the whole day, with him. Now, he's doing pretty well. I, also, was lucky today in obtaining the dates of R&R flights to Hong Kong in December. Regular Leaves, go on R&R flights, on a standby basis. But, it's not really standby, because they always leave a certain number of seats available for Leaves. And, you get them by the amount of time you have in-country. The dates available to leave are on December 5th, 6th, 11th, 18th and 20th. I will go on the 11th or 18th. I'll make up my mind in a few days.

Today, I got 4 letters from you which was great. But, since the last one was dated November 23rd, I'm sure I won't get any for the next day or two. I see you gave up the puppy, which was probably best. I think it's a lovely idea that you're burning the Hanukkah candles for us. I haven't been able to run for the past 2 days, because of the rain, mud and cold. But, the slack has been taken up by being busy at the hospital. It's pretty cold, now, much like when I first came here. I guess we are into the monsoon season. It rains all the time. The local Vietnamese say it will be like this until March.

I think of you all the time, Darling. I love you very, very much. Yes, it will be wonderful to be back with you.

Jonny

My Darling Love,

Well, I struck out tonight, as expected with no mail. I had a very quiet day, today, doing nothing but playing around with some respirators and running once. I nearly died when I ran today. I really hurt. It stopped raining, today, but it is still extremely overcast.

I put my leave request in, today, for December 11th. I should be able to get on the plane (with 11 months in-country) at that time.

Last night, a bunch of the Officers sat around singing. And, one of them (a dust-off pilot) who likes to sing soul music, sang some songs by the Righteous Brothers. He was terrific. I really enjoyed listening to him. He could do the high and low parts identical to the way the Righteous Brothers do it on their records. I found myself wishing you were there to sing "Yesterday" for everybody.

Honeybunch, I know this is a skimpy letter, but there is not much news to report. I miss you intensely and think of you all the time.

I love you so much,

Jonny

Dearest Honeybunch,

Today was so-so. I did one case, today, a spinal. And I, also, did the surgery for that case. But, I'm beginning to dislike doing both on the same case. It's too much of a strain. I worry about the anesthesia, which I can't do anything about, since I'm scrubbed up for the surgery. And, I worry about the surgery since everything is so new. Another Surgeon is coming, tomorrow, to help Steve. So, I think I'll be relieved of my surgical duties.

Apparently, the new Anesthesiologist is not very good from what I hear from Steve and the Nurses. He has done only one case, so far. But, it's reported that he did a lot wrong on the case. Maybe he was nervous and will settle down.

I got a chance to run today, again, and it felt good. And I got a long letter from you, today, profusely apologizing because you failed to write me one day. Forget it. It has happened before, and it will happen again, I'm sure. I know you are not perfect, but you come pretty close to it.

I'm extremely interested to know if Matt Bernstein was able to come up with a job, for me, or if he gave you any assurances. It could mean quite a bit of money for us. You probably should ask Bill Rader, also.

I'm glad that you're pleased with your weight loss. Yes, I'm proud of you. And, I'm proud that you swam the whole length of the pool. I would like to see that when I come home.

The guy I did the surgery on, today, cried his heart out (throughout the whole case). We failed to resuscitate his best friend and he saw the whole thing. It was so very, very sad. I could find no words to console him. What could I say? I felt the same way.

Sweetheart, I miss you very badly. We'll really have to grind out these last days. But, it will be such a wonderful and joyous occasion to come home for good. I don't think I'll ever forget the loneliness, desolation and despair of being in Vietnam.

I love you with all my heart, Jonny

Oh Baby,

Please forgive me, but tonight I need a break from writing. I'm so tired. I worked all day from 5:00 AM until 10:00 PM tonight and I've got to go to sleep. At 5:00 AM this morning, my day started with an amputation of a leg. I had to do it all by myself, including the anesthesia. Steve was tied up on a big case. My patient did well, fortunately. Then, all day as Physician-on-Duty, I had to be on the run. It was a busy day.

I didn't get any mail tonight. We got a General Medical Officer, today, and a temporary Surgeon. So, maybe the load will be eased for me.

I love you very, very much, Sweetheart. This letter is short, but my love for you is long.

Jonny

12/02/69
Letter 251

Precious Baby,

If I wrote you that things were bad up until 10:00 PM, last night, they got a lot worse after that. Around midnight, I got a comatose Vietnamese 52 year old lady, who I had to stay up with all night. I think she blew an aneurysm, in her head, secondary to a hypertensive crisis. I got everything under control now. To boot, a guy came in who shot himself in the belly. And, there were 2 guys who needed to be treated for combat fatigue. Now, I have combat fatigue. I got a few hours of sleep during the day, today, but tonight I'm really going to crash for at least 12 hours. I'm second Call in Anesthesia, so I'm praying that no more than one case comes in at a time. And, that none are blocks, etc.

The pictures of me, by the chopper, are on my way back to Camp Evans. No mail today. It rained all day and the mail didn't get through. I ran anyway. Oh Baby, I miss you and long for you very much. I love you dearly.

Jonny

12/03/69
Letter 252

My Precious Darling Honey,

Yippee, I got a letter today! It was written on November 26th and post-marked on November 28th, so I must have missed receiving a couple of letters. Anyway, it was refreshing and heartening to know that you miss me, also. I do miss you.

Today, I worked all day on the hooch. I was tiling the floor and moving things around, etc. The "Super" hooch is once again functional. We built our sink, also. The hooch doesn't look too bad. I haven't done any cases today. I'm first Call. And, I couldn't run today because of the constant rain.

Sweetheart, I love you so very much. Tonight, Steve and I had supper in the hooch (hot dogs, beans, salami sandwiches) with one of the Nurses. They asked me what I really wanted to talk about and I thought for a while and then told them this. I told them that I wish one of them knew my wife pretty well like I did. Then, we could sit back and say isn't she a terrific person in this respect and isn't she terrific in that respect and so on. Of course, it wasn't possible since neither of them knew you. But, that is all I could come up with (to talk about you).

I love you,

Jonny

12/06/69
Letter 253

(1st Letter)

Dearest Darling Sherrie,

Today, I was Physician-on-Duty and I had some interesting things to do. And, I had one dramatic case to do in the O.R. When I'm Physician-on-Duty, I don't take any Anesthesia Call, but Steve Lipson insisted. He said that I was the only one he wanted to do the case, which was very flattering. I was happy to do it, because I enjoy it, and I got out of being Physician-on Duty for 4 hours. The case was a little boy who was shot through the neck. But, he is doing quite well now and should recover fully. It's been a long day. I fell asleep, from 8-9 PM, and then had some more patients to see. I thought I wouldn't write, tonight, when I went to bed at 12:30 AM. But, I tossed and turned for 1 ½ hours and so I got up to write to you. I don't think I could kill time any better than by writing, to you, until I get exhausted enough to sleep. The place they have for the Physician-on-Duty to sleep is terrible and I can't fall asleep in there very well.

I didn't get any mail from you, today, but I did get a bunch of magazines. I did get a letter from John Flora and one from Bud (he's in Saigon).

Tomorrow morning, I have a case to do on a child. I hope I do lots of children before I go home. It's a good opportunity with the hospital, for children, being right here.

I'm getting so fed up with being here. I'm getting to the point where I don't care about anything. I don't argue much about things I don't like. The leave should be just the thing for me. The time will pass better there, than here, but I sus-

pect I'll be bored because all I plan to do is shop. I'll probably be pretty lonely. I couldn't get anybody, from here, to go with me. For most of them, it's too early in their Vietnam tours of duty. I hope there are American movies for me to see. When I come back, I should only have about 25 days left. But, even 25 days is too much.

I miss you immensely, Sweetheart. You are always in my heart and mind. I send you all my love.

Jonny

(2nd Letter)

My Precious Baby,

Life gets worse, not better. After being up all night, I then did an 8 hour case that received 40 units of blood. It was so hectic. And, the Surgeon (our Chief of Professional Services) had a mild heart attack and had to go to the hospital ship. So, now I'm left to care for this patient by myself. He had 60% of his liver taken out and he is showing signs of impending renal failure. If he gets septic, it's all over. I'm so tired that I can't see straight. I'm first Call in Anesthesia tonight, also. And, I'm Physician-on-Duty (on December 9th) the day before I go to Hong Kong. But, I'll just do the work, get as much out of it as possible and not look back. I'm sure that is better than complaining. I'm getting something out of this. I learned a lot from working with the liver patient. I got a beautiful letter, from you, today. I'm so thankful for your love. Also, I got a letter from Woody.

I love you with all my heart. Jonny

12/07/69
Letter 255

My Dearest Love,

Today, I got another beautiful letter from you. And, I share your distress at not having received letters, from me, for 3 days. They'll come. I'm sure I didn't miss any days. I, also, heard from Nat and my parents. I really appreciate what you are doing regarding Hanukkah gifts for the family. You are a perfect wife.

I finally had a relaxing day, today. I had time to think about my patient who has now received 60 units of whole blood. He's doing extremely well. He has many problems and can still die. I'm going to be first Call for Anesthesia tomorrow and then Physician-onDuty the next day. Lately, I've had to do some anesthesia when I'm not on Call, because the Surgeons keep requesting me to do the anesthesia for this special thing or that special thing. Tonight, though, I'm off and will have time to drown my loneliness and misery in booze. Nat says she's following the aerobics walking program. Isn't that great? You are even better, because you run when you can. Well Sweetheart, try and find some comfort in my love, desire and longing for you. All your feelings, of despair, I share and feel for the same reasons.

Jonny

Dearest Precious Darling Sweetheart,

I'm glad you finally got a letter from me. I got one today, also, which surprised me because for 2 days now I have gotten letters mailed only 4 days before. Your letter was very loving.

I was busy all day with the liver resection patient and he is doing remarkably well. I'm very flattered by the respect that the other Doctors are showing for my handling of this complicated problem. I'm happy about it, too. I've learned a great deal, because I've been stimulated to read a lot.

Tomorrow, I'm Physician-on-Duty. And then, the next day, I'm off to Hong Kong. I have lots of requests to buy stuff for other people. I hate going by myself, but still I'll probably enjoy just being out of here.

I read that hospital workers' bulletin and I share your feelings. A lot of people want something for nothing and don't or can't think straight. The change of the Chief of the Anesthesia Department means nothing to me. Everybody tells me, in one way or the other, that they still think I'm the Chief. But, I really don't care. I know that I know my stuff and so does everybody else.

Honey, I need to go back to the ward to check some things.

I love you dearly, Sweetheart. I hope you know and feel that. I'm getting extremely excited by the fact that soon I'll get out of here and back to you for good. I can't believe it. I think, basically, I've felt that I probably wouldn't make it. But, now I'm getting close! Maybe I will make it. Jonny

12/09/69
Letter 257

My Dearest Precious Baby,

Tonight, I was made very happy by getting a letter from you. I was hoping very much that I'd get one, today, because tomorrow morning I'm leaving for Da Nang. Then, on December 11th, I'll be on my way to Hong Kong. So, naturally, I won't receive your letters while I'm gone. I'm borrowing $100 from Steve, because I want to be sure I have enough money to buy stuff if I want it. I'll be thinking of you and will most probably get you a vacuum cleaner and a toaster. I wish you were with me, so we could shop together.

Today, I was Physician-on-Duty. And, the day passed sort of quickly. Now, it's the slow hours of the evening. My patient is doing terrific and everybody is pronouncing it the therapeutic success of the year. I'm very happy about it.

Tonight, one of the Nurses came to me to look at the results of a CBC done on her today. The results looked a little strange, so I told her to get a heterophile test done. That's a test for mononucleosis. She did the test and it came out positive. Another diagnostic triumph for me.

Well Sweetheart, I'll write you from Da Nang and Hong Kong every day. I'll give you a running report of what I'm doing. And, each day I'll send all my love devotion and longing desire for you in abundance. I've got 36 days and a wake-up left in Vietnam.

Jonny

My Precious Baby,

I'm so sorry that I didn't write you last night. But, I was so angry and frustrated to even think words, no less speak them on paper. This is what happened, to me, since December 9th. As you know, I was Physicianon-Duty on December 9th and that night, I decided to call Da Nang to make sure the R&R flight was scheduled for December 11th. Well, I got through to Da Nang, which was accompanied by the usual frustrations. But, when I did, they said that they wouldn't have a flight until December 16th. My leave orders are for December 11th to December 17th. So, I decided to go all the way to Cam Ranh Bay Air Base, on December 10th, to try to get a flight from there to Hong Kong. Their flights are supposed to be more frequent than the flights from Da Nang. Well, when I got there after travelling all day, they told me they didn't have a flight until December 15th. It was so late that I had to sleep there. Then early this morning, I got a flight back to Da Nang. Just by chance, or on second thought, I called the R&R Center (at Da Nang) and they said that they had a flight going out today. I was so angry at the guy who had told me that they had no flights. He caused me to travel, for 2 full days, for nothing. Well, I just made the flight and I'm now writing to you on it. Just think, I had already given up and I was minutes away from getting on a plane to go back (to Quang Tri) when I made that call.

Well, at least the story had a happy outcome. I have $1280, with me, of which $550 is mine (including $100 that Steve loaned me). The mood I'm in, now, makes me want to *spend every cent of it. I'll buy happiness, since I'm so angry.*

Honeybunch, I'll be thinking of you all the time. I already feel so lonely going without you. I'll miss you a tremendous amount. I already do. I hope they have good movies there. I love you with all my heart.

Jonny

Hi Darling,

I've missed you so much since being here. I really feel lonely. I sure wish I had you with me. I thought of calling you, but when I inquired as to the price, I found out that it costs $50 for the first 3 minutes.

I'm in a room for about $9 per day. But, it's just a little room. Hong Kong seems very harsh compared to Tokyo. It seems like New York City. At night, the whole city is all bright lights. I went to bed early last night, so I haven't observed anything yet. But tonight, I plan to just stroll around. There are a couple of movies showing, so I'll probably catch one tomorrow.

I spent the whole day shopping. I mainly bought stuff for the guys at the hospital. But, I did buy 3 things for myself and you: (1) Canon Zoom movie camera for $94. It's a fantastic buy. I know it costs more than $200 in the U.S. I had to mail it to myself, in Vietnam, because of the customs rules. I'll mail it to you, later, as a used camera duty-free. (2) An aluminum tennis racquet for $33. (3) Connect wires (etc) for our stereo set-up for $14. I found terrific buys on bicycles, but I couldn't find a way to get them home cheaply enough.

I looked into several shipping lines, the regular mail, other carriers (etc) to get them home, but I just couldn't figure it out. I'm sorry. We'll get some good used ones, in Alabama, as soon as possible. I think it will be great for the 2 of us to go on bicycle trips together.

Tomorrow, I'm going to get fitted for 2 suits, some slacks and a sport coat. And, I'm going to get you some "Joy" perfume. The toaster and vacuum are definitely out, because they are slightly higher priced here than in the U.S. Shopping knocks me out, so I'm going to take a nap.

Talk to you tomorrow, my Love. I miss you so badly. Everything I see to buy (dresses, carpets, etc), I can't do without your opinion. I'm just half of me here. You are the other half.

Jonny

Woe is me, My Baby,

Here I am writing to you, in a restaurant by myself, prior to going to a movie by myself. Well, such is the disadvantage of a good marriage which is me feeling lonely without you. I think, though, that the advantage of a good marriage makes the disadvantage of loneliness seem worthwhile. Nothing of great interest happened, last night, except that I wanted to see how good I was at bargaining. So, I talked a watch dealer down from $24 to $11 for a watch. Maybe I did so well, because I wasn't going to buy it anyway.

Today, I bought clothes. I bought a tailor-made suit, sports jacket and over-coat for $113. And, I bought a tailor-made shirt for $10. I, also, got 2 sweaters (for me) for $17 *and a mohair scarf for you for $3.*

Honey, I'm completely overwhelmed with the savings on prices here. And, I'm in such conflict because I don't know what to buy. You can probably imagine my distaste for spending money on something you wouldn't like, for yourself, even though it was a good buy. I have spent only $308. But, I don't know what else to get. I'll probably keep on doing what I have been doing most of the day today. Which is to keep wandering along the streets until I see some little item that I really want to buy.

I had lamb chops for supper. Not bad. Today, I passed a YMCA and tried to arrange to use the basketball court on Monday (tomorrow is Sunday). I have a 50-50 chance of being able to use it.

Well, I'm off to the movie now. I obviously miss you a great deal. I love you.

Jonny

Dearest Darling,

I was sitting here thinking about revisions to make on my paper that I wrote months ago. And, I just realized that I hadn't told you what happened to me last week. It's probably so fantastic that I simply passed over it. The head Surgeon, in Vietnam, is a full Colonel (Geiger is his name) and he's a Board-Certified Thoracic Surgeon, a fine person and a gentleman. What in the world he is doing, in the Army, I don't know. But, he may be like Colonel Moncrief (who is a well-known Surgeon). Anyway, he read my paper last week and he wants to publish the paper with me. I'd be the senior author. With him backing it, it would stand a good chance of getting into print. So, I'm working and thinking about the paper again. The liver patient, I just successfully took care of, represents a good example of what I talk about in my paper. I'm pretty excited about this. It's a real feather in my cap. It would be great, for my career, if I stay with a University and research.

Today was a little better than the others. I went for a formal fitting of my tailor-made clothes. You wouldn't believe how well the clothes look on me. It took an hour in the fitting session. Even I could tell the difference between ready-made clothes and clothes, like these, that are fitted exactly to your body. They're tapered and the whole bit.

Hong Kong is having a festival, now, and I watched many of the public shows.

I miss you so much, Baby. You know, I don't think that I really believed I was going to get home. Maybe I will now. Maybe I will. Most other guys (who are short-in-time left in Vietnam) tell me that they think the same thing. Maybe I'll make it. I love you so much.

Jonny

Dearest Sweetheart,

Today was kind of slow. I mailed off things that I bought. Today's box included, for you, a cashmere muffler, cashmere sweater and "Joy" perfume and cologne. I got so frustrated, with doing nothing, that I found a cricket field. I went to the hotel to get my shorts and sneakers and then ran around the cricket field. I enjoyed it. I don't feel quite as fat and sloppy as I did before I ran.

Tonight passed, rather pleasantly, because I went to see the movie "Gone with the Wind". It certainly was a touching and moving story. Very sad, too. The wounded soldiers reminded me of so many scenes in our hospital in Vietnam. It was a long movie, too. I think it was almost 5 hours long (including the intermission).

I'm looking forward, so much, to reading all your letters when I get back to Vietnam. I have been lonely, here, in Hong Kong. At least, in Vietnam, I had companionship. But, all in all, I think the week here is still much better than being in Vietnam.

Well, it's days now until I'll see you. I miss you a great deal. I love you with all my heart and soul.

Jonny

Hi Precious Baby,

I'm back in good old Quang Tri, again. It's a dirty, muddy mess here. During my last 2 days, in Hong Kong, I kept telling myself that I'm better off being lonely in Hong Kong rather than here. And now, I know I'm right.

One good thing, I had 8 letters from you waiting for me and I really enjoyed reading them. I, also, heard from Ben Ezra, John Flora and Woody Haser. And, I received 2 packages from you.

Sweetheart, I'll write you a much longer letter, tomorrow.

I'm very tired and I have so many things I want to ask you (and answer you), but I'm just too tired. I was up at 3:00 AM, this morning, and had a very trying day travelling. It was especially trying from Da Nang to Quang Tri. It was so difficult to do.

On my last day, in Hong Kong (December 16th), I bought a typewriter. It's a great model. It types in script and has many desirable features. It cost $48 and is $80 in the U.S. I got it since I knew I would want it, someday, so I got it now.

Honey, I'll write you a long letter tomorrow. I'm always thinking of you. And, I was so warmed by your loving letters. I miss and love you very, very, very much.

Jonny

Dearest Baby,

I just finished solving a terrific anesthesia problem. And, I'm still so excited about it. I hope I can calm down enough to write to you. One of the new Nurse Anesthetists messed up with the use of curare. And, I had a great time reversing it. It took 3 hours and it was a good experience for me.

Today, I was first Call and I did 2 cases. I'm a little embarrassed, because everybody calls me Chief to show how they feel about me no longer being Chief. But, I'm asking them to stop because I'm sure it makes the new Chief feel bad.

It just rains all the time and I can't run. I guess it's a monsoon. The movie camera came, today. I'll try to mail it to you, tomorrow, along with another package of books, etc.

I worked some on my paper. Today, I wrote the Thoracic

Surgeon a section of the paper for his approval. And the liver resection patient, that I took care of, is doing beautifully. His course of treatment will be part of the paper.

I got 3 letters from you, today, and it made me so happy. The letters that I got, in the past 2 days, are all messed up regarding time of their arrival. They range from November 29th to December 13th. Like, today, I got a letter written on December 5th. I'm sure that explains the erratic delivery of mail to you. I don't think I missed writing you, more than a day or two, in the past month.

Tomorrow morning, I'm doing another special request case on a 5-day old baby with an imperforate anus. It should be interesting.

I'm following, with great interest, the developments concerning me obtaining work for a couple of weeks when I get home. I would best like to work in the "drunk tank" since it's close to home. So, please see if you can get Dr. Clyman to commit himself as far as giving me a job. If not, I'll go to the agency.

Honey, the Commanding Officer of the hospital has nothing to do with letting me off early from Vietnam. It's "Washington" that makes that decision. And, odds are that I won't get much (if any) of a decrease in time in Vietnam. Word comes late, too. I don't know if I'll be able to let you know, but I'll try.

I'm extremely proud, and pleased, with your improvement in swimming. Atta girl. I'd like to go swimming, in that heated pool, at the YMCA. Also, I'm 4+ glad that you went ahead and started to renew my license. You're terrific!

I'm worried about the Garrard turntable. If it doesn't come, by January 1st, please put in a claim for the insurance.

Please give my best to Matt and Greg. And, thank Matt if he does anything for me. Tell him I'll run him silly when I come home.

I'm very glad you got the day shift for your last 2 weeks. I love you so very much, Baby. I have you with me, in my feelings and thoughts, all the time.

Jonny

Sweet Precious Sherrie,

Today, I got a letter from you that informed me that the 4th day in a row had passed in which you hadn't received a letter. I'm so sorry. I really haven't missed more than a day or two, this month, in writing you. I'm sure the letters will start coming in.

Today, I did a special request by the Surgeon. It was a very interesting case on a 5 day old baby who had an imperforate anus. It was a good experience.

Tomorrow, I will probably be able to send off two packages to you. One of them contains the movie camera (in a wooden crate) and the other has books, papers and journals.

Now Honey, this is most important. When you get this letter (probably on December 25th or there about), please contact the Transportation Officer at Fort MacArthur in Los Angeles. Please get the application forms for initiating a move on January 16th (the pick-up date). I'll be home to help you decide what should go and what shouldn't. If I recall correctly, when you make out the application, you have to make some sort of an estimate of what is going to be transported. But, we can make changes to that on the actual pick-up day. Arrange to have our stuff sent to the Transportation Officer at Fort Rucker. So, please Sherrie, get on this. Otherwise we will be waiting for a month or so, after we get to Fort Rucker, for our stuff to come.

Darling I love you very, very much. I can hardly believe I'll be getting out of here. I get to feeling so much joy that I can hardly bear it.

Jonny

12/20/69
Letter 266

My Precious Baby,

I'm getting "short" (not much time left in Vietnam). Time is moving along nicely, since I got back from Hong Kong. I hope it continues. Everyone has Christmas spirit, so it's nice to be among friends. Out of the clear blue sky, Steve told me that he was going to miss me a great deal. I was quite touched, because we have gotten along exceptionally well these past 3 months. And now, we are very close. The Surgeons have requested the Commanding Officer to get the new Anesthesiologist out of the Anesthesia Department. He makes bad mistakes, but I'm too "short" for this B.S. So, I'm keeping out of it. They are demanding that I be made Chief, again, at the very least. But they are, also, serious about trying to get rid of him. He is a nice guy and I like him. I feel sorry for him, but I've got to admit that he doesn't know a lot.

Today, I got the 2 packages ready for mailing tomorrow (one with the books and journals and one with the movie camera).

Last night, we had our first mass casualty situation since Hamburger Hill. We worked through the night and a good part of the day. "Super Doc" (that's my new nickname) swung into action. I did 3 operations (one was an amputation of the leg) and my own anesthesia for each. Steve, and the other General Surgeon, were doing laparotomies. What a mess the Emergency Room was in. There were 25 patients all at once. They were ambushed. I was running around putting in chest tubes, endotracheal tubes and cut-downs. Sherrie, some of the wounds were horrible. It all really made me sick. I would like to grab some of the "silent majority" and stick them close to the wounded. Then, let's hear them continue to support the war.

I got a letter from Lonnie, today. And, I got a letter from Norm who was here with me for 4 months.

I love you, Sweetheart. I missed you today. And, I'm always thinking of you. God, I get excited when I think I'm going home soon.

Jonny

My Precious Darling,

Today, we had sun. I could hardly believe it. It was the first time, I had actually seen the sun, since coming to Quang Tri. I really felt just great walking around, etc. I ran, we got up a volleyball game and I did a couple of cases. Tomorrow, I'm first Call. And, I'll probably have a lot to do. I'm no longer on the Physician-on-Duty schedule. So, I have a little more free-time. It looks as if the Commanding Officer is going to remove the new Chief of Anesthesia. I'm very sorry for him. I like him personally, but I really think he is a danger. Well, nobody likes to do this. But I think, for the patients' sake, it is necessary. I couldn't get to the Post Office, today, because just as I was going a call came in that a helicopter crashed. They (the dust-off helicopter crew) were bringing in 11 wounded soldiers. With the crash, nine of the soldiers were dead. I felt so bad. I had to go outside and just cry. It is so tragic. Lately, I'm getting very emotional when patients come in and are badly injured or dead. Their bodies are so mutilated. I put endotracheal tubes in for people who have no jaws, watched an eye fall into the palm of my hand and put IVs into the stumps of amputated legs. I'm sick of it all. I can't stand much more of this.

All my love, Darling. I'll be very happy to be back in your arms and loving you. I think I'll get drunk tonight.

Jonny

Dearest Darling Sherrie,

I only have 23 days to go! Oh Honey, I'm getting so excited. I feel like I'm going to bust. Today was a quiet day, for me, and luckily so. It was a nice day and I was outdoors a great deal. I ran once, started reading a novel " 'The Battle of the Bulge", lay out in the sun, daydreamed about you and nursed a cold that I started to come down with today. I didn't get any mail from you, tonight, but I did get a Christmas card from your relatives in Bay City, Texas.

After I finish writing you, I'm going to wrap all the surgical hats and masks that I got for the O.R. techs, the O.R. Nurses, the Surgeons and the Anesthesia staff. Their names are embroidered on each item. It cost me $20 to do it, but I *think everybody will like the idea. Honey, I haven't bought you a formal gift or anything. But, I will be your gift if that is ok with you. Happy Hanukkah, Sweetheart. I was really touched by the idea that you were lighting the candles every day. It makes me happy to know that.*

I love you very much, Darling. I think about you so much and I'm happy about spending the rest of my life with you. That really gives my life meaning, along with having children. Won't that be something for us?

Jonny

My Precious Darling,

I didn't get any mail today, from you, but I did get some magazines from you. And, I want to thank you for outlining those articles in the Hospital Tribune. Those articles were of great interest, to me, and I probably would have thrown out that paper had you not marked them off.

Today, a burn patient came in that I may possibly be able to escort to Japan, since I'm the Doc with the shortest amount of time left here at the hospital. The whole thing is up in the air because the Colonel has not given us an answer. Everything is complicated by the fact that we don't know if the new Chief of Anesthesia has been removed from Anesthesia or not. I guess we'll have to wait until the morning for the Colonel's answer. If I do go, it will be the day after tomorrow. If the new Chief of Anesthesia is out of the Anesthesia Department, then I can't go, because I'll be the only Doc in the Department. Oh, the Colonel now says nobody can go.

Tonight, there will be a little Christmas party, at the hospital. But, it doesn't look too promising. I'll put all my hats and masks (for the O.R. techs, O.R. Nurses, etc), under the tree, in the O.R. tonight.

I've been sick, the last 2 days, with a cold and GI upset. But, for some reason, I ran beautifully today. I ran farther, and faster, than I normally do.

Oh yes, if I do get to Tokyo, I'll try again to buy bicycles. That's the only reason that I would want to go.

Honeybunch, Happy Hanukkah and Merry Christmas. God, will it be great to be home with you. Right now, for the month of January, there are no reports of anyone being scheduled for reductions in their service time in Vietnam. All my love, thoughts and desires. I miss you very much. It's a lonely Christmas, isn't it?

Jonny

My Precious Baby,

Well, guess what? Tomorrow, I'm going with the burned patient to Tokyo. The Commanding Officer, finally, said it would be alright. I'm not sure I want to go, but at least it will make 4-5 days go by quickly. I'll stay in Tokyo for about 2 days, do some shopping and come back. I'll probably be back on December 31st or January 1st. So, we'll see. I hope I'm not making a mistake by going.

Today, not much has happened. I'm first Call in Anesthesia. But, so far, no cases. Although, I just heard a couple of choppers land on the pad outside the hospital.

I got 3 lovely letters, from you, today. And, yes Darling, I'm getting very excited about coming home too. I'm afraid, however, that I won't get any reduction (at all) in the time that I have to stay here in Vietnam.

I will have only a maximum of $200 to spend in Tokyo. One thing that I'll buy will be a movie screen. I'm going to go through a Sears Roebuck catalogue, tonight, and mark down everything I would want and its price. Then, I'll see what I can get it for in Tokyo. I'll get the things that I can buy for a good savings.

I think about you, all the time, Sweetheart. I just wish these last days would go by quickly. But, I know they won't. I love you, I love you, I love you.

Jonny

12/27/69
Letter 271

My Precious Sherrie,

As of tomorrow, I have 18 days left in Vietnam. Will it happen? Can it be? Is it true? It seems as if all my life can be divided into 2 stages: (1) Vietnam, (2) What comes after Vietnam. I'm almost done with the first stage.

I didn't go to Tokyo. I decided that I didn't want to spend any more money. And, that the number of days involved in travelling was far out of proportion to the number of days (2-3) I would have in Tokyo. I sure created a lot of confusion when I decided I wasn't going. New orders had to be issued, for the new Doc who will go, and schedules had to be rear-ranged. But, I think I'd rather just wait it out here. Besides, I would have had to go to Da Nang by chopper. And, it was raining today. I'm too close, to going home, to risk flying around in the rain.

I didn't get any mail today. And, I was very disappointed because I wanted to hear from you very much. In addition, I've asked you to do so many things recently (like the move and checking into what happened to our Garrard turntable) that I was anxious to hear about them.

Today, I did a few cases on special request even though I worked all night. I guess I didn't tell you, I worked through the night on Vietnamese casualties. I think I'll sleep good tonight.

Honey, I love you very much. It's such a beautiful thought of just being around the house with you. It's so comforting. Guess that is what makes love.

Jonny

Dearest Darling Sherrie,

It is getting so hard to write. I can't think of anything new to say. Nothing is happening here that is worth reporting about. I'm trying to think of what to write you and I came up with a big zero. Nothing did happen today. Last night I won $8 in poker. Honey, I can't even tell you how happy I am to be coming home soon. It's too big of a job. It's like trying to tell you that I love you and miss you. And yet, that really doesn't do any justice to my true feelings. You know that as well as I. I'm sure you have the same problem. I guess we have written so much that there doesn't seem to be much around that hasn't been said 20,000 times.

I didn't get any mail today. That makes 4 out of the last 5 days that I haven't gotten much mail. Oh well, there is always tomorrow, I guess.

So, I'll close with my usual sentiments of a great deal of love and longing for you. I know it's a lousy letter, but I hope it does the job of resuscitating you for a day.

All my love and thoughts,

Jonny

Hi Honey,

Today, I was busy. I've had 5 cases so far and the night is still ahead. I did get a chance to run today. And, I was very happy to get 2 letters from you today. One contained a letter from Des Reilly. How come you never sent me his address? One of the letters, from you, was written on December 18th and the other one was written on December 22nd. So, the delivery of the mail is still mixed up.

I'm glad to hear you have so much help in waiting out the last few days. It always helps to share your burdens. And yes, I would like you to work in Alabama very much. Not only for the money, but because I think you will be very bored and lonesome during the day if you don't. Our living conditions (house or apartment) won't be nearly as nice as the one at Fort Knox, so you won't enjoy being at home as much as before.

I doubt very much that you will be able to take any swimming lessons in Alabama. It is a very isolated post and I bet there isn't a YMCA in the whole state.

I'm very happy the clothes arrived ok, but I'm really concerned about the Garrard turntable and the other stuff that hasn't come. Remember, if it doesn't come by January 1st, institute a claim.

Yes, I was a little surprised by the letter from Des. I wonder if he's drinking a lot and if it isn't a reflection of marriage difficulties. Steve Lipson told me that Des was drinking a lot at Fort Knox.

I'm glad you got the car license renewed. I wonder if my driver's license needs be renewed, also.

Honey, I enjoyed talking to you. I love you and miss you very much. I hug my pillow every night pretending it's you.

Jonny

Dearest Darling Sherrie,

I'm not going to fight it. This will be just a "hello" letter. I've got absolutely nothing to write about. Maybe, it's because I have so little interest in things around here. Just one thing, I agree that the 12-8 shift at the Drunk Tank doesn't sound too inviting. If that is the situation, when I come home, then I'll go to one of those agencies you mentioned. Please have the names, addresses and phone numbers ready so I can contact them right away.

I've got 15 days and a wake-up left in Vietnam! Won't that be a great day, when we get together again? I got no mail today.

Sweetheart, I just want you to know that I'm thinking of you. And, that I love you a great deal. Jonny

My Precious Baby,

I've got 2 weeks to go! It seems so long. Today, I was pretty busy, so the day passed fairly quickly. I got 2 warm letters from you, today, and one from the Kapels. I was glad that you were able to do a private duty case, as $40 pays for a lot of things.

Tonight, I suppose we'll have some sort of party since it's New Year's Eve. But, I sure don't feel much in a party mood. Now, if I was going home tomorrow, then I would really celebrate! I'll probably end up doing cases anyway.

Honey, I know my letters are pitifully short. But, I really don't have much to say. Maybe, I'm tightening up my strength to finish and get out of here. But, I sure don't feel talkative. The only things I have of importance to say are: I love you very much, I miss you immensely, I want to go home. Happy New Year, Sweetheart.

Jonny

My Dearest Darling,

It's January again! Well, I spent New Year's Eve pretty much the way I thought I would. I had barely eaten a steak, at the Enlisted Men's party, when I was called to the O.R. and then spent until 5:30 AM doing cases. Then, I went to sleep, but was again called to rush to the Emergency Room where a guy was being resuscitated after being shot through the head. Nice way to usher in the New Year. It made me sick. After that, the day passed pleasantly enough doing 2 or 3 cases, lying out in the sun a little and running twice. Today was a real nice day, the first in a long time.

I wonder what you did New Year's Eve? Did you go to a party or anything? Poor Baby, were you lonely? I'll be home, soon, to take care of you. God, it's a great feeling that it's January now. Yesterday, I even washed and ironed my khaki uniform in preparation to go home. I wonder, if I do get a Bronze Star, if it will come through here or at Fort Rucker. I'd much rather get it here.

I didn't get any mail today. I'm curious to know what is happening with our move, arrival of gifts from Tokyo and Hong Kong, etc. Well, that's all for now.

I miss you very much, Sweetheart. I think of you all the time and I'm very much in love with you.

Jonny

My Dearest Darling,

I'm writing you while talking to the Colonel. Today, I did something that sort of made me feel "short" (a person with not much time left in Vietnam). I picked up my finance records, today, since the last payday for me has occurred. Picking up finance records, to me, always made a guy seem "short" since it's the first irreversible step in going home.

Today, I didn't do much. I'm reading a good book called "The Godfather". It's about the Mafia.

I got 2 loving letters from you, today, in which you wrote about your concern for the critically ill patient in the ICU. It's too bad that he died. I know how you feel. I've had approximately 20 patients die, on me, for whom I spent more than 6 hours of time working on (knowing from the beginning they wouldn't make it). They each received over 50 units of blood. For some, I worked for 24-48 hours trying to save them. Still, no luck. But, then again, I've had 3 make it who received over 50 units of blood. So, you keep trying. The same goes for you. Everything you do, and the faster and more efficient timing of the care, contributes to the good of the patient. And all the while, you are doing your best, other people are working in laboratories thinking about a better way to do things. Eventually, they are done better. But, meanwhile, you have to do your thing and do it well. So, keep your spirits up. I'm sure you did your job well.

Well, Sweetheart, another day closer to you. I'm thinking about you all the time. And, I miss and love you very much.

Jonny

Dearest Beloved Sherrie,

Well, what can I say? I'm in fairly good spirits. And, I passed the day pretty quickly doing 7 cases, running, etc. I finished a novel I was reading and now I need to find another one. I got 2 warm and loving letters from you, today, and one from my Mom. I'm getting so close to going home, I can almost taste it. I walk around saying things like: "Attention please, now announcing the immediate boarding and loading of TWA's flight #Alpha 2, Bravo 3 to Fort Lewis, Washington at Gate 1. Order of line will be all Officers, then Senior NCOs, E-6 and above and then Enlisted Men (etc, etc)." That is exactly how they say it. I've heard it at least 10 times, this year, when I have been at airports.

Incidentally, if I were you, I would stop writing to me on January 7th. That's because I'll be leaving here (between January 9th to 11th) to go to Da Nang, then Cam Rahn Bay, then Fort Lewis, San Francisco and finally Los Angeles.

I was glad to hear you got moving on the Garrard turntable and our move. It seems to me that a lot of things are still missing (the typewriter, movie camera, projector, etc).

Bye Sweetheart, I guess you won't be writing after you get this. I love you very, very much. I look forward to, and think about, being with you all the time and with much happiness.

Jonny

My Sweet Darling Sherrie,

After I wrote you, last night, I have been working straight through for the last 20 hours. Finally, we got everybody done and through their surgeries. I'm getting too "short" for this kind of stuff. Tonight, I'm third Call (except for blocks and spinals). So, maybe I'll do some serious drinking.

I don't know if I told you, but the Doc who took my place (to take the burn patient to Tokyo) was that new Anesthesiologist. Well, he's been gone for 11 days. And, everybody is very upset that he took off for so many days. He should have been back after 6 days. We haven't gotten that Major (who is a fully trained Anesthesiologist) that we were supposed to get. So, when I go, there is going to be a confusing situation. The Surgeons don't want the Doc, who is in Tokyo, to do anesthesia for any of the cases.

I got a nice letter, from you, today. You probably will get this letter only a few days before I'm home. I'll probably stop writing, to you, on January 10th. Enclosed are 2 negatives that Steve took, of me, with his camera. If you run them over to the photo shop, you probably can get them developed right away (so that you can see them before I come home).

I dreamed about you, again, last night. It was about us not being married, but we were dating. And, I decided to marry you. But, the significant thing is that I decided to marry you (knowing you the way I do now, not as I did when we got married). Need I say more?

I Love You, Jonny

Dearest Precious Baby,

I'm just going to say hello. I've just gone another 24 hours in the O.R. and I can't see straight. The war isn't over. I'm as busy as I was during Hamburger Hill. I pronounced 6 dead today. I counted that I gave 141 units of blood to 6 patients today. That's an average of about 23 units per patient. They had such bad wounds. And the injuries were to their arteries, nerves, bones, chests, hearts, livers, kidneys, bowels, just everything. I'm so sick of it.

On the cheerful side, I got 2 letters from you today. One of them was urging me to help your parents. I had already decided to do that yesterday, on my own, as I wrote you. And the other one was telling me that we had received the Garrard turntable (which delighted me greatly).

You can reassure your parents that we'll help them out. But, I think it should be on a no interest basis and with an indefinite timeline. Maybe, by the time they are able to pay it off, I'll be willing to forget it completely. I hope you see this as a way of loving you.

Well, I'm going to hit the sack. I love you very much. I've only got 8 days left, Honey. I dreamed again, last night, about you. I believe that makes 3 days in a row. It was a good dream, only I can't remember it.

All my love and thoughts, Jonny

My Dearest Darling,

Today was a quiet day for me. I was fourth Call in Anesthesia, so I just relaxed here around the hooch. The other Anesthesiologist came back, yesterday, from Tokyo. I promptly put him on Call for today. He was gone for 11 days which was way over the time he should have spent there. I'm taking first Call tomorrow and then I quit. I'm not taking any Call, at all, on January 9th and January 10th.

I got a letter from you, today, which was great. I share your excitement fully about coming home. I'm glad that you're taking care of the move. I hope very much that you'll be able to get those private duty cases. Honey, I haven't got much else to say or report about. So, forgive me for making this so short. I love you very much. I'm thinking and day-dreaming about you all the time. I'll be extremely happy, to be back with you, and to start living again.

Jonny

Precious Baby,

This being my last day of work, I naturally was hit hard. I won't have much chance to say anything other than a quick hello. I got another letter, from you, today. I noted all the news items with much interest and received your love warmly and happily.

On January 10th, the night before I leave, I'll be guest of honor at a steak dinner (me, Steve, Oscar and Wayne). Then, after that, I'll pay for free drinks for everybody. That will cost me $30 for all the Officers.

See you in a week! I love you very, very much.

Jonny

This was Jon's final letter to Sherrie from Vietnam.

One week later, January 14, 1970, Jon's tour in Vietnam ended and he returned to California – and Sherrie.

PART 3:

AUTHORS' COMMENTARY

WHAT WAS JON'S LIFE LIKE AFTER RETURNING HOME FROM VIETNAM?

To efficiently, coherently, and meaningfully summarize the next 50 years of my life, after my return home from Vietnam, my life history is going to be divided into: (A) Family Life; (B) Professional Anesthesiology Life; and (C) Alcoholism and Recovery from Alcoholism.

(A) Family Life

When I returned home from the Vietnam War, I finished the remaining 6 months of my 2-year tour of Army duty, finished my Anesthesiology training at Columbia-Presbyterian Medical Center in New York City and then went on to a 47-year Professorship in Anesthesiology at the University of California San Diego Medical Center.

Benjamin (our son) was born in 1970 while we were in New York City and Sarah (our daughter) was born in 1974 during our early years in San Diego. Both of our children did well in every aspect of their lives (education, athletics, relationships with others), married wonderful spouses (Kim, our daughter-in-law and Jeff our son-in-law) and they created and parented our 5 wonderful grandchildren (Maile, Taylor, Brooke, Kai, Mikaela). All 5 grandchildren (ages 18-12 in 2020) are doing well in life.

Sherrie has been a wonderful wife (for 52 years as of 2020) and partner in life for every possible reason one could possibly think of.

For recreation I ran long distances (10 miles/day and many marathons) for a long time (30 years) and the entire family regularly participated in all possible vacation and holiday get-togethers.

In short, family life was a very good part of my life.

(B) Professional Anesthesiology Life

In my 47 years as a clinician-teacher-scientist professor at the University of California San Diego Medical Center, I was successful far beyond my wildest earliest hopes of success. To be brief, I became one of the best-known Anesthesiologists in the world. I produced 8 best-selling books, 100s of high-quality papers, lectured to large audiences (frequently and around the world), won many prestigious awards for excellence in Anesthesia and was hotly recruited to opine in approximately 500 medical malpractice cases as an expert witness. To stay meaningfully succinct, looking back, I could not have been (nor would I have wanted to be) more successful in my professional life than I was. I was simply at the top in every respect.

(C) Alcoholism and Recovery from Alcoholism

When I came home and undertook my Anesthesiology Residency, I remember drinking alcohol every evening (after work) during my 2-year Residency in Anesthesiology at the Columbia-Presbyterian Medical Center in New York. The pattern of drinking alcohol in the evening, prior to going to bed, continued for many years. I never drank alcohol during the day. I was far too busy being a husband, father/parenting, being an

Anesthesiologist, and running long distances (typically 10 miles/day).

I tried, and occasionally succeeded for a few months (or perhaps once or twice for a few years at a time), to stop drinking alcohol in the evening. But these relatively short periods of non-drinking were pure physical abstinence, were unaccompanied by any sort of spiritual or emotional sobriety, doomed to failure, and inevitably did fail. I would always return to drinking alcohol in the evenings.

As I got older, it got harder and harder to stop drinking for any length of time even though I tried harder and harder. As the years wore on, my drinking at night became secretive (I tried to hide it from Sherrie). Finally, at age 66 (in 2008), Sherrie and others prevailed upon me to get myself evaluated for alcoholism. I went to the "Betty Ford Center (BFC) for Alcoholism and Addiction" for evaluation and the diagnosis was that I was a clear-cut alcoholic.

I underwent 3 months of in-house residential treatment for alcoholism at the BFC, came home and continued Recovery from Alcoholism by being regularly and significantly immersed in the Alcoholics Anonymous (AA) program. By doing so, the "Promises" of AA have come true for me. I have been happy, joyous and 100% free from my many years of enslavement to alcohol. Spiritually, the last 12 years of sobriety have been the best years of my life.

WHAT WAS SHERRIE'S LIFE LIKE AFTER THE YEAR 1969?

In January 1970, when Jon returned home to Los Angeles, we were both so happy and relieved that he was safe and that he had successfully completed his 1 year tour-of-duty in wartorn Vietnam. We were very anxious to get on with the next chapter of our lives and for Jon to complete the 6 months of Army service that remained for him.

From Los Angeles we headed to Fort Rucker, Alabama. There Jon worked at the Army's hospital, as an Anesthesiologist, for the next 6 months. We made the most of any weekend, that Jon had off from work, by driving to Panama City, Florida (which was only 90 miles away), and staying there at a small hotel right on the beach. These weekends made our time, in Alabama, tolerable.

While waiting for the Army to clear me to work as a Registered Nurse (RN), at the Army's hospital, I got an RN job at a small community hospital not far from the military base. I only worked there for a total of 1 day, because I couldn't tolerate the horribly racist way in which the black patients were treated. They were relegated only to the hospital rooms in the basement. I couldn't tolerate this despicable segregation and told the Nursing Director that this was why I was not going to return to work there the next day or any other day! I quit.

A few weeks later, I started working in the Army hospital's newborn nursery. Sometime in April (1970), we learned that I was pregnant. We were both ecstatic over the idea of becoming parents. Jon had frequently written in his letters from Vietnam that he was very much looking forward to the time when we would have a baby.

In July 1970, Jon completed his 2-year Army commitment and we headed to New York City for Jon to begin his 2-year Anesthesiology Residency Program. During these 2 years, we were very busy. Our time in New York City gave us the opportunity to deeply connect (as a couple) with Jon's parents, his extended family and some friends from his youth (especially Ben and Marcia, who remain our friends to this day). Because Jon's Residency required him to be on-call every other night and every other weekend, and I was pregnant, we decided that I would not seek an RN job.

On December 31, 1970, our precious son Benjamin was born. We both were so excited to be parents and we absolutely loved having this new little one in our lives. At the end of Jon's Residency Program (July 1972), we headed to San Diego, California, where he began an Anesthesiology Fellowship year at the University of California San Diego (UCSD) Medical Center. He became a full-professor in the Anesthesiology Department and retired in May 2019, after a long and very successful 47-year career.

I was fortunate to be able to be a stay-at-home mom while Jon was excelling in his medical career. Within a couple of years of being in San Diego, I started taking part-time college classes to work on obtaining my Bachelor of Science in Nursing (BSN) degree. And, at this same time, we wanted another baby and were eagerly looking forward to adding a little one to our family. In fact, during the summer of 1974, I was taking a community college statistics class while in my ninth month of pregnancy. On July 24, 1974, our precious daughter Sarah was born. We had now completed our family and we loved every minute with our adorable children.

I went on to obtain my BSN (with Public Health Nurse Certificate), in 1978, from the University of San Diego (USD) Hahn School of Nursing. I was a stay-at-home mom until 1983 when I was able to get a part-time job with the County of San Diego's Public Health Department as a Public Health Nurse (PHN). I was so fortunate that I was able to work part-time up until 1992 (which was the year that our daughter graduated from high school and our son had just completed his Junior year in college). Public Health Nursing was the best of all worlds because it allowed me to do challenging work (that I loved) and I still had a lot of time to be a wife and mother. I was able to take our children to all their extra-curricular activities, volunteer in their elementary school classrooms, be around for their friends to hang out at our home after school, and was able to be available for any other needs or interests they might have.

Over my 36-year career with the Public Health Department, I was able to work in a variety of interesting specialties of PHN Case Management: Maternal-Child Health PHN Case Manager, Tuberculosis PHN Case Manager and Public Health Nurse Consultant in the Foster Care Program. My work as a PHN brought me many friendships and feelings of accomplishment.

But, greater than this was watching our son and daughter become very fine young adults and finding the loves of their lives. They have brought so much love, enrichment, fun, laughter and joy into our lives. When Jon and I acquired the new titles of Mother-in-Law and Father-in-Law (to our son Benjamin's wife Kim and our daughter Sarah's husband Jeff), our hearts and love expanded even more as we officially welcomed them into our family. The icing on-the-cake came when, over the next few years, they brought grandchildren into our lives. Benjamin and Kim Benumof gave us two granddaughters (Maile and Mikaela) and one grandson (Kai). And, Sarah and Jeff Fischbeck gave us twin granddaughters (Taylor and Brooke).

When Jon and I both retired, in 2019, we moved from San Diego to South Orange County (CA) to be closer to our children, children-in-law and grandchildren. It was during this year (2020) when Jon and I, for the first time ever, decided to sit and read the 282 letters (together) that Jon had written to me from Vietnam. They are a testament to our deep, strong and abiding love for one another—the power that love can have to help one survive the worst of times and how that same love has helped to sustain us over the past 52 years through the ups and downs of life. We are so fortunate to have these letters. We hope that our family, friends and others will find them interesting and meaningful to read and that this book will provide insight into how we survived a year of separation, how the war affected us, and how we dealt with it.

July 7, 1968: Jon and Sherrie on their Wedding Day. Jon's year in Vietnam in 1969 showed just how strong our love was for one another. While writing this book together in 2020, we celebrated 52 years of marriage.

2019 – Our Family (left to right): Jeff Fischbeck, Kai Benumof, Brooke Fischbeck, Sarah Fischbeck, Sherrie and Jon Benumof, Taylor Fischbeck, Maile Benumof, Ben Benumof, Mikaela Benumof, Kim Benumof.

CPSIA information can be obtained
at www.ICGtesting.com
Printed in the USA
BVHW012255170521
607610BV00010B/188

9 781953 120205